FIERCE JOY

a memoir

ELLEN SCHECTER

GREENPOINT PRESS, NEW YORK, NY

This book is for my family

Jim

Alex

Anna

Peter

Doris

Stanley

You lived it with me just the way I wrote it:
day after day.

Thank you for never forsaking me.

ISBN 978-0-9832370-4-4
Greenpoint Press,
a division of New York Writers Resources
P. O. Box 2062
Lenox Hill Station
New York, NY 10021

New York Writers Resources:
www.greenpointpress.org
www.newyorkwritersworkshop.com
www.ducts.org

Designed by Noah Arlow
Cover artist: David Wander
Typeset in Galliard Roman
Display type: Big Noodle Titling
Printer: Lightning Source

Library of Congress Cataloging-in-Publication Data
Schecter, Ellen
Fierce Joy
ISBN 978-0-9832370-4-4

Printed in the United States of America on acid-free paper

FIRST EDITION

*What is to give light
must endure burning.*

Viktor E. Frankl

CONTENTS

PART 1:
THE WOMAN WITH WINGS

PART 2:
A LONG, DARK CORRIDOR

PART 3:
STAY WITHIN YOURSELF

PART 4:
A CASE OF MISSING IDENTITY

PART 5:
WRESTLING WITH GOD

PART I

The Woman with Wings

So teach us to number our days

that we may gain a heart of wisdom.

Psalm 90:12

CHAPTER 1

Something

Fair Harbor, Fire Island

1988

IT'S AUGUST. NEW YORK CITY IS BAKING AND GLITTERING IN A HEAT WAVE. My husband, Jim, and I escape with Alex, six, and Anna, three, to Fair Harbor on Fire Island, for our two-week vacation. Our house, rented sight-unseen, turns out to be a ramshackle A-frame, where the key waits under the red geranium. It's cramped, with plywood walls, touches of mildew, and a hideous nautical decor. "It'll be fine as soon as the sun comes out," we assure each other. "The kids can play on the fenced-in deck, and we'll finally have time together to talk, read, even nap nearby. It'll be heaven."

Not quite. My left foot feels like a chunk of wood and can't feel the ground. Ignore it, I tell myself. Don't think about it. And don't tell Jim; it could ruin the vacation. He still knows nothing about it.

How can I keep ignoring it? Something's been going on for more than a year. This numbness. Painful tingles in my fingers and toes. A tiny white Christmas bulb flashing in my left eye. Hot spots on my left ear and arm.

We unpack, bring out the toys, make the beds, cook a quick meal.

"Let's go look for the deer," Jim says, just before the sun goes down.

"Great idea, but let's take them in the wagon in case they get sleepy." Our cottage comes equipped with a red Radio Flyer. We dress the kids in footed pajamas and dab their PJs and our clothes with mosquito repellent.

Buttoning, zipping, unscrewing the bottle—sparks of pain jab through my fingers and shoot up to my elbows.

I do have to pay attention to this, I think. It's getting more pronounced. I've been too afraid to go to a doctor, whether to find out something's really wrong . . . or that it's all in my head. Because the symptoms are so odd, I'm not sure which scares me more: really being sick, or imagining it. I definitely don't want to find out I'm a hypochondriac like my mother.

Jim swings Alex into the rusty wagon. Anna insists on climbing in herself, then Alex slides her back and puts his arms around her in a hug.

"Take a picture of this with your eyes," I whisper to Jim. "Peace."

"Enjoy it while it lasts," he whispers back.

I tuck blankets around them—ouch—and we set off into the thickening blue twilight, the wagon squeaking softly.

It's so peculiar, walking with pins and needles jabbing the bottoms of my feet. I have a great imagination—I write children's books and television programs—but who could make this up? So it must be real. Okay, okay, I'll call the doctor when we get home.

We pass people headed for parties, rattling ice cubes in their drinks. I remember how I used to watch the families when I came here as a hopeful single, thirty-two and aching for a husband and family. I wonder how we look to them now, both of us still looking younger than our years—thirty-nine and forty-four. I watch Jim pull the wagon, chatting and laughing with the kids, pretending to be a Nascar racer. Just the look of him made my insides jump at first sight: he's tall and slim, with compelling dark eyes, wavy black hair and a short beard with one narrow strip of white. I'm more than a head shorter and fit right under his chin when we hug. Which is often. He has duck feet and bowed legs that make the kids laugh. My long copper hair is also streaked with silver, my brown eyes shadowed by circles no amount of sleep can erase. People are always flabbergasted when I tell them my age, but my days of getting carded in bars ended after my first pregnancy.

Soon we're in pine woods, alone with the fireflies, each with its tiny golden nimbus in the gathering mist. As we near the spot where the deer might come, we stop. I bend close to the children and whisper, "We may see the deer soon, so we have to be perfectly quiet. Can you do that?"

Alex nods "yes" very elaborately, and Anna pretends to zip her lips. When we turn the next corner, Jim taps each of us, and points.

Just twenty feet away stand a small doe and her tiny twin fawns. They see us, too, yet all of us stand perfectly still in the deep lavender quiet. As our eyes open wider to the night, I see them even more clearly: the fawns with their tidy little hooves, trembling; their mother's immense brown eyes, her legs slender as twigs. Her large ears skew toward us. Her head tilts toward her children, as mine does to mine.

Alex taps me. "Can I go make friends?" he whispers, his warm hands cupping my ear when I lean down.

"Yes, you and Annie," I signal back after Jim nods "yes."

Jim lifts them one at a time out of the wagon and sets them on their feet. Alex takes Anna's hand and they walk slowly, slowly toward the deer. It's like watching Hansel and Gretel without the witch.

The deer and the children study each other. One step, then another, till they are only about seven feet apart. Jim takes my hand, palm cold as snow as it always is in moments of deep feeling, good or bad. The children step closer. Another step. Another.

Then—the spell breaks. The doe and her fawns slip away into the pine brush.

They don't run, they don't show alarm—they just disappear.

Was I about to—disappear?

New York City, Riverside Park Playground
Autumn 1988

"Push my swing, Mama," calls Anna.

"Mine, too," Alex says.

Something makes me so gray with fatigue that I feel welded to the ground. Pushing my kids on the swings takes all my strength. I can't imagine how I'll walk home.

"Push me higher, Mommy, I want to fly," Alex sings out.

Damn it, I don't want to be sick.

"Look at me, Mama—my toes touch the sky," Anna sings back.

I don't have time to be sick.

"Watch me, Mommy!"

I want to push away pain and just see how beautiful our children are.

"Look at me, Mama!"

I will not be sick.

"Mommy, watch this."

I refuse to be sick.

"Mama, look at me."

Damn it: I won't let anything hurt us.

CHAPTER 2
Something Terrible

1988

AFTER NEARLY TWO YEARS OF SILENTLY ENDURING THESE MYSTERIOUS, increasingly severe symptoms, I both want—and fear—a diagnosis. No one—even Jim—knows anything about this strange pattern of pain, including my internist, whom I rarely see. In truth, I don't want to know what this physical cacophony means, yet feel a growing need for someone to name and explain the strange and frightening sensations crawling over my body. When I finally describe it all to my doctor, he packs me right off to a neurologist he describes as "brilliant, no-nonsense, and thorough."

Right, except he forgets to mention that Dr. Linda Lewis is also a very attractive, energetic Amazon of a woman—over six feet, with prematurely white hair cut short and blunt; big gray eyes behind glasses that make them even bigger; thick black lashes and brows in a strong face with wide cheekbones and a generous mouth. Her large, strong hands look capable of doing anything well, from setting broken bones to rappelling down mountains. She listens carefully to my strange conglomeration of maladies.

When I finish, she makes a sketch in red ink on one of those human-body outlines doctors often keep close at hand for recording afflictions. It mirrors my mental picture of my pain, which feels so tangible that I envision it as a network of chartreuse neon lines crisscrossing my body. Now there's my pain, in red ink, on paper: my own painful sensations—heard, understood, recorded. I feel a burden lift.

"You probably thought you were crazy, but you're not," Dr. Lewis says. I feel my shoulders drop away from my ears even more. "These sensations may seem peculiar and unrelated to you, but they draw a very clear picture for me. They follow the nerve roots all over your body."

So it's real. Here is objective confirmation. I'm not a hypochondriac. I take a deep breath for the first time in months. She understands me. And my pain. I will be eternally grateful just for that.

But a split-second later, it slams into me: corroboration is cold comfort. Something is actually wrong. While I struggle with this paradox, Dr. Lewis writes a flurry of blood test and laboratory slips, then hands them to me. "These tests are used to diagnose nerve disease. Maybe they'll make the picture clearer. Come back when I get the results, and we'll see."

I want to get the tests over with ASAP, but it takes a lot of jiggling with my schedule to do the most complicated one. Jim and I take turns dropping the kids off at the Calhoun Early Childhood Center on 81st and West End—the school that looks like a television screen—then he rushes off to court, and I race around to script conferences and production meetings for *Reading Rainbow*, the PBS children's series I write. I can't schedule anything until we button down an outline for our newest show, which grew out of *Keep The Lights Burning, Abbie*, a beautiful book about lighthouse keepers in 1856 on the rocky coast of Maine. It involves a conversation with LeVar Burton, our star, a script conference with the producers and production team, and setting deadlines for my script delivery, etc. As head writer, I'm responsible not only for my own scripts, but for the other writers' work, which means even more reading and face-to-face meetings. I also have to squeeze in as much of my writing as I can before the kids get home from school.

We have a lovely housekeeper, Mrs. Sarah Parker, who takes the kids on play dates and to the playground in Riverside Park. I try to spend as much time as I can with them, alone and together—and I hate to miss our Mommy-and-kids playgroup, which began when Alex, then Anna, were infants. And then there are my ballet classes (I'm not good, but I love the discipline), lunches or coffee grabbed with my friends Jane, Sarah, and Isabel, and . . . and . . . I literally have no time to be sick.

I finally make a late afternoon appointment at the Neurological Institute and quickly learn to loathe the electromyography, or EMG. First I ride the elevator to a suspiciously quiet floor in the Neurological Institute. When asked, I shed my clothes and identity as I don a frumpy hospital "gown." Then I wait an unconscionable length of time in a frigid cubicle until a white-coated man, whose badge identifies him as a PhD, appears. With no greeting or explanation, no apology for the delay, he orders me to lie down on a narrow examining table, grunts "Don't move," and—with absolutely no preamble—jabs long pins attached to electrodes and wires deep into the most painful parts of my muscles until they make contact with my most painful nerves. In my efforts not to scream or kick, I force myself to think about something—anything—else. Dr. Josef Mengele, the Nazi doctor who took pleasure in torturing his patients, comes immediately to mind.

"We will now begin the procedure," he announces to a spot somewhere near the overhead light fixture. He still has not looked once at my face.

Begin? I thought it was over.

"Do not move," he repeats. I wouldn't dare.

With this, he turns on electric currents that feed into the needles stuck in my legs. Then he blandly records my pain as a wavy graph on what looks like a TV screen. It now feels as if my legs are hard-wired into electrical sockets. Or, fifty times worse than the way it feels when I crack my elbow exactly the wrong way on the edge of my desk. Or, like the neurological equivalent of the electric chair. I do not die, though it crosses my mind as an attractive alternative.

I think I'm a wuss about all this, until Dr. Lewis later tells me that a well-known professional football player tore the electrified pins from his legs and ran cussing from the room because he couldn't bear the pain.

Finally, before I start to smoke, Dr. Mengele turns off the machine, removes the pins, and leaves the room without a word. As I dress with shaking hands, I remind myself that this modern medical variation on the medieval rack is designed to yield objective and presumably helpful measurements of how quickly my nerves receive and relay information to and from my muscles and spinal cord.

But even before the results are in, the test proves one thing unequivocally: I am a total coward when it comes to pain—any pain, but particularly cruel and gratuitous pain administered without compassion.

Dr. Lewis sounds undaunted when she calls to tell me the test results are equivocal. They reveal no clear pattern of nerve damage. Then she announces, in what I'm learning is her characteristically cavalier fashion, that it's time for a nerve-and-muscle biopsy. The following week, I meet with Dr. David Younger, a lively, handsome and yes, young, neurosurgeon, who explains that he will remove about a tablespoon of muscle and a smidgen of a nerve—the sural nerve—from the back of my left calf for examination under a microscope. Unfortunately, I must be fully conscious during the operation so he will know when he cuts the nerve. I'm gratified to discover that nice neurosurgeon is not an oxymoron, as he is warm and funny.

Barely a week later, I'm in an operating room, lying prone on a narrow padded table that looks more like my nana's ironing board than any Hollywood version of an OR I've ever seen. In fact, nothing's what I expected: the small white-tiled room looks like a kitchen; the nurse has a beard and tells me how much his little girl likes *Reading Rainbow;* and Dr. Younger not only has split-second comic timing but also a soul.

The biopsy turns out to be an excruciating procedure. It takes far more searching than any of us like to find that skinny skein of nerve, but while the surgeon is digging around in my left calf, we chat quietly about religion, Brahms, and this-and-that. The nurse holds my hand whenever he's not busy, and we all make awful puns about having a lotta nerve, lacking nerve, being nervous, etc. But when Dr. Younger finally finds and severs the sural nerve, there's absolutely no doubt: I shriek. Pure pain explodes in my leg, drills up my spine, and makes me puke.

Yet even in hell there are funny moments. When I croak, "How come I throw up when you cut a nerve in my leg?" Dr. Younger doesn't miss a beat: "Don't you know the leg bone's connected to the stomach bone?" Then he comes closer and says, "Local anesthesia blocks some transmission of pain to your brain. But your body always knows when it suffers an insult like this—and it rebels."

His respectful explanation makes me feel human again, not like a wide-awake corpse being dissected. He walks closer and looks kindly into my eyes over his surgical mask. "Are you really OK? I hate to hurt you. We can take a little break if you need it."

"No, I'm OK," I lie.

Then, as if rehearsed, he and I and the nurse, who's holding my hand again, launch into an off-key rendition of "Dem bones, dem bones, dem dry bones," as he finishes removing muscle and starts sewing the first of twenty-nine stitches.

I know I'll love this guy forever.

It takes two weeks to get the biopsy results. Late one Friday afternoon, Dr. Lewis's secretary, Gloria, calls and tells Jim and me to be in Dr. Lewis's office the following Monday at one. "Dr. Younger will be there, too," she says.

"Of course we'll be there, but can I just talk to her now about the biopsy results?"

"No, no, she's busy now. She'll see you Monday."

Great.

Our weekend looks normal: wall-to-wall kids, terminal exhaustion and, for me, my regular pain plus breath-snatching post-op anguish. Jim and I take turns getting up early with the kids on weekends. Instead of snuggling together in bed and getting interrupted every two minutes, one of us sacrifices pleasure so the other can tank up on lost sleep. This Saturday it's my turn, so I'm up before dawn with the kids bouncing around, smelling like fresh-baked bread still warm from the oven. We cuddle inside a quilt on our window seat overlooking 72nd Street and West End Avenue, watching the West Side wake up: first the parade of garbage trucks, then a rising tide of buses and cars, then yawning dogs walking their yawning owners.

Our high point is the Newspaper Dog across the street. Each day at six a.m., the doorman at 253 West 72nd Street opens the door for a scruffy yellow dog wearing a red bandana around its neck. It pads slowly to the corner Korean deli, fetches the *New York Times,* then returns home holding the paper in its mouth. We applaud every time we see this.

But beneath the mundane—the PB&J sandwiches, endless cups of milk and apple juice, macaroni-and-cheese lunches, spaghetti and turkey balls, and the bubble baths with my hands shooting so many electric sparks I almost expect to electrocute us—I feel as if I'm walking on a thin M&M sugar-shell reality that I'll crash through on Monday at one. What's waiting for us underneath?

Monday brings full-blast sunshine, an intensely blue autumn sky, and trees shouting with color. But I've discovered on visits there over the years that it's never sunny inside the Neurological Institute, no matter how vibrant the weather is right outside the sliding glass doors. The light is always a waxy yellow fluorescent that turns the unhealthy gray and makes even the healthy resemble the dead. The floor, waxed too many times, seems too slippery for canes and crutches, and there are never enough seats where the infirm can perch while we wait in silence for the maddeningly slow elevators. I try not to see the people with Frankenstein stitches showing through the new stubble on their scalps; or the ones with empty eyes slumped in wheelchairs; or the walking wounded who limp, shake, drool, and drag their feet—sort of the way I do today. A few poor souls get walked along like flaccid, obedient dolls on invisible leashes held by hollow-eyed relatives or blank-faced aides. Some simply stare at the ugly linoleum and cry. A few minutes in that lobby and I feel waxed to the floor—helpless, hopeless, inert.

All this, just waiting for the elevator.

This is it, the moment I've been seeking and dreading: my post-op diagnostic consultation. Which doesn't mean we don't have to wait. And wait. Jim and I sit in the over-crowded waiting room, alternating between stiff silence and loopy giggling. His hand is icy. Slippery. I try to concentrate on the new and attractive decor: purple tweed chairs. A line-up of the same Impressionist poster of trees, four or five of them, from an exhibit at the Met. Quite attractive, the repetition. Clever. I bet Dr. Lewis did that.

The action picks up when an agitated woman rushes into the room.

"Are you Ellen Schecter?" she yells. I nod, and she hands me an envelope with my name typed on it. Misspelled. "Dr. Lewis said to be sure to read this before she meets with you." She exits at a run, as if relieved to get away from me.

Jim and I move even closer together and read the letter, clutching hands.

Dear Ms. Schechter: [also misspelled]
As you know, the biopsy is abnormal . . . It indicates demyelination with

axonal changes . . . The teased muscle fibers are abnormal . . . shows
demyelination in sensory, motor, and autonomic nerves . . ."

"What the hell does this mean?" Jim asks, looking desperate.

"Not sure." My eyes speed-read, clutching at phrases. "I certainly did not know the biopsy was abnormal. Nobody had the guts to tell me. But demyelination—not good. That's the protective coating on the nerves—"

"Right," Jim squeaks, his throat constricted.

We read it again, mystified. We don't like that "demyelination." It could mean Lou Gehrig's disease or multiple sclerosis or who knows what horrible "osis" we know nothing about.

"Where the hell is Dr. Lewis?" Jim asks, getting up and pacing, which he often does when he's nervous about a legal case.

We're so nervous we get punchy again. But now Dr. Lewis appears, looking especially stately. She follows us into her office. She doesn't look happy. Or sad. She tries to watch me walk without appearing to watch me.

Neurologists have a terrible habit of doing this, something I learned when I had severe back pain and was at this very same hospital in my late twenties. Interns, residents, neurosurgeons—they all wanted to walk behind me to check out my gait. Did I limp? Drag? Stumble? Wobble? It must be a little trick they learn in medical school: Remember to observe the patient without being observed. Sneaky, though I actually prefer it to the alternative, when the neurologist commands "Walk!" and I must perform a humiliating, lopsided promenade up and down an examining room or corridor under intense scrutiny, while wearing an incredibly frumpy shmatah, gaping open in the back, that the medical community insists is a "gown."

Now I try to walk behind Dr. Lewis so she can't watch me limp. I must move slowly, leaning on the cane I just acquired. My friend, Sarah, insisted on buying it when she saw how hard it was for me to use my leg. I hate what it symbolizes, but I need it. Just for now.

I can't put my left heel down on the floor, and the merest brush of my skirt against the two biopsy incisions on my left calf is excruciating. Pulling on panty hose is a duel between determination and agony that leaves me in a cold sweat. I know Dr. Lewis knows my incisions hurt, but she can't imagine how much. I'm afraid to tell her. It will make it too real. Or brand me a coward.

She keeps trying to sidle behind me, and I keep trying to slip behind her. It's an awkward minuet, and I half-giggle.

"Nice skirt," she observes. "New?" I nod yes.

"Trying to hide your scars?"

This is her version of small talk. I don't answer, though it's true.

Kind Dr. Younger hasn't arrived by the time we file into Dr. Lewis's office. I sink gratefully into the maroon leather chair in front of her mahogany desk, which is roughly the size and heft of a coffin. I notice that the room has been redecorated since she sent me for surgery. Someone worked quite hard to re-create exactly the same perfectly dull and innocuous 1930s consulting-room style as before: same ugly no-color cretonne drapes with large maroon somethings floating on them, same old tomes with depressing titles—*Brain Tumors, Multiple Sclerosis, Diseases of the Nervous System*. Same leather chairs with brass studs, same enormous desk piled with files, same little examining room off to one side with white everything—white enamel cabinets and basins, with sharp, pointed chrome instruments displayed behind glass doors. This all-white chamber of horrors is already haunting my sweatiest nightmares.

I sit, inhaling the musty air. The place reeks of stale sunshine and despair. I wonder how many other people sat in this same massive leather chair—much grander, probably, than the ones they—and I—have at home, waiting for the watershed news that forever slices lives into Before and After.

I imagine them, like me, trying to calm down and stop shaking, trying to conjure up all the rational questions they have along with the ones I can't remember or haven't thought of yet. Like all those other people, I take deep breaths as I convince myself the news cannot be all that bad. Denial. I glance at Jim; his sweet dark eyes look even bigger than usual, frightened and a little too shiny. He still grips my hand, his knuckles white, as if he's afraid I'll float away from him.

But now something weird begins to happen. I start to discover the advantages of Denial—a psychological state that allows persistent negation of the facts in front of your nose—an evasion I'd always assumed was "bad" and "weak" and thus reserved for weenies. But I am about to discover that Denial is actually good. Very good.

Dr. Lewis wears a blouse that at first glance resembles silk but is really polyester. "Less up-keep," I muse. The blouse is crimson, which looks especially handsome with her white hair and big gray eyes, which look pretty even without make-up.

I'd love to see her wearing mascara just once, I think, drifting further into Denial. The make-up tangent, designed to keep me thinking about anything except what's happening right now, reminds me of a story I heard from Kathy, another patient, when we were both in-patients in Neuro, about eight years ago, when I had excruciating but unexplained back pain. She told me how Dr. Lewis suddenly appeared in the hospital on New Year's Eve, just before midnight, to check a dangerously ill patient; how everyone stopped breathing for a moment when all six feet of her swept into the ward in a floor-length swath of black velvet. I fall in love all over again with that image of her: the avenging Doctor-Angel guarding her patient from Father Time's scythe, robed in black, glittering with the sharp scintillation of knowledge and proficiency and diamonds—except, wouldn't she wear rhinestones? She's far too practical to spend all that money on diamonds . . . isn't she? The image dissolves and I now concentrate on the dust motes dancing haphazardly in front of the very dirty window.

Throughout my reverie, Dr. Lewis rustles papers into piles, sorts pens and pencils, puts large paper clips around letters and lab reports bulging out of my expanding chart. I watch the clips immediately slide off again. She avoids looking at me. She chatters about something very neutral and irrelevant, so I go back to the sun mote ballet, humming the *Sixth Brandenburg Concerto* in my head and waiting for the movie to begin.

Now she clears her throat, pushes her glasses back up her nose, shoots one quick look at my face, then tries fitting a large, evil-looking pincer clip around the unruly papers. It bites and holds. She clears her throat again, looks up at me, and says, "Well, you've got a disease."

CHAPTER 3

The Movie In My Mind

Diagnosis and the Dissociation Factor

1988

FADE IN.
INTERIOR: OFFICE OF DR. LINDA LEWIS

Jim and I sit dazed in front of Dr. Lewis's coffin-shaped desk holding hands—his icy, mine numb. Her office, newly renovated in 1930s consulting room style, reeks with the dusty odor of despair.

"Well, you've got a disease," she announces, fiddling with a file clip that resembles a prehistoric raptor. Her words seem to unfurl before me, emblazoned in gold on a white satin ribbon. Well, this is an Annunciation. Of sorts.

Except it feels more like a B-movie than a medieval painting. And as I watch it, I feel myself slowly shatter into parts: there's Rational Ellen, Scared Ellen, a third Wiseass and sharp-tongued, and a fourth—the Observer—all looking down from their perches near the ceiling. These are separate from me, the real Ellen, who's sitting in the maroon leather wing chair trying to look normal as the movie begins.

"Well, you've got a disease," Dr. Lewis repeats, still fiddling.

"What disease?" I ask.

"I'm not sure what to call it yet," Dr. Lewis says. "A rheumatologist would probably call it systemic lupus. I feel safer calling it a lupus-like autoimmune syndrome. But it doesn't really matter. We see it in your nerve and muscle biopsies." She starts playing with paper clips and pens, as if my query doesn't fully occupy her attention. "It's some form of peripheral neuropathy, which means it affects the nerves after they leave your spinal cord."

"You're sure it's not multiple sclerosis? Or Lou Gehrig's disease?"

"We're sure," she answers.

"Say it out loud. Please."

"You don't have MS or ALS."

Jim relaxes a bit, wiping his sweaty palms on his suit pants.

"Well, that's a relief," I say, relaxing for a nano-second. Then I bolt upright again. "Will it affect my brain?"

"No."

"How do you know? I mean, how can you be sure?"

"Myelin in the brain and spine—the central nervous system—is chemically different from peripheral myelin. They're each attacked by different antibodies."

Rational Ellen nods sagely, as if to say, *Why of course, any idiot knows that.*

Scared Ellen interrupts: *Don't be so sure. She may not be telling the-whole-truth-and-nothing-but-the-truth.*

Be quiet and let me handle this, Rational Ellen thinks. Aloud she says, "Tell us again what myelin has to do with it."

Dr. Lewis pulls out a sheet of paper and makes a rough sketch. "Myelin insulates nerves the way the outside rubber coating insulates an electric cord. It assures a smooth flow of the electrical impulses that make muscles work." Then she draws a nerve and the myelin coating around it. She pushes the sketch across the top of the coffin—er, desk. It looks like a cockeyed tree with its bark gnawed off by a plague of locusts

"Demyelination—injury to this protective coating on the nerves"— she draws big red arrows pointing to the gnawed bark—"gradually inhibits the flow of electricity and neurological stimulation, and this affects muscle tissue."

Jim leans forward and picks up the sketch, as if examining it closely will enable him to see into the future.

"So the nerves stop working properly?" he asks in his lawyer voice.

"Right," says Dr. Lewis, capping her elegant pen.

"All the nerves?" asks Scared Ellen.

"We can't predict numbers. In your case, all three kinds of peripheral nerves are affected. Sensory nerves that carry sensations from the body to the brain. Motor nerves that carry impulses from the brain to the muscles and control movement. And autonomic nerves, which are responsible for involuntary bodily functions like capillary action, breathing, digestion, temperature, heart beat, that sort of thing."

That sort of thing. Dr. Lewis continues speaking, but none of the Ellens hear what she says because the CAMERA SWINGS WILDLY around the room, unable to focus, making them seasick.

"When nerves get sufficiently demyelinated, the muscle fibers can atrophy and stop functioning. I'll show you."

Dr. Lewis's beautiful pen gets busy again as she draws tight, symmetrical rows of small, stacked circles. "These are supposed to be muscle cells," she explains. "They usually stack up nice and symmetrically, like this."

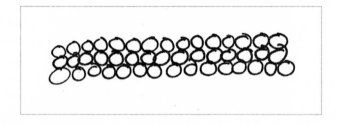

"They look just like the oranges in the Korean Superette across the street from our apartment," Rational Ellen observes, sounding like a brown-noser.

"Yup," says Dr. Lewis. She makes another doodle, this time of disorganized muscle cells.

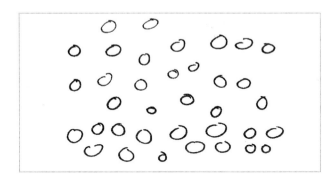

"But this is the way your muscle cells look now: disorganized and chaotic."

Rational Ellen clears her throat and tries to sound casual. "I get the picture."

Scared Ellen wants to get into the act, but the best she can do is murmur "mm" as she desperately tries to stop her lips from quivering. Despite her best efforts, the shaking spreads to her hands, then her entire body. All the Ellens are determined to prove to Dr. Lewis that they are strong, invincible, and—whenever possible—jocular. For some reason, they believe that if they act lighthearted, they may turn out to be witty. But Scared-Ellen is about to be exposed as a lily-livered scaredy-cat, who may even break down and cry, when rescue arrives in the form of a gentle knock at the door.

ENTER: DR. YOUNGER.

He nods once, then sits stiffly in the back of the room, expressionless. Unlike his former jolly, warm self, he refuses to look at Ellen. Perhaps central casting sent a double?

I always knew the words "nice surgeon" were an oxymoron, observes Wiseass.

Rational Ellen decides to ignore Dr. Younger and soldiers on. "So—what do you think is causing it—the demyelination?"

"Could be antibodies, which are components in your blood that should attack bacteria or infections but in auto-immune diseases attack your own tissues—"

Yes, we know all about antibodies, Wiseass says, but only I hear her.

"—or it could be vasculitis," Dr. Lewis continues, "an inflammation of the vascular system. We thought you might have vasculitis, but Dr. Younger found no evidence in any of the biopsies."

"Of course, the biopsy could have just missed it by half an inch or so," Dr. Younger informs us. "There's no way to rule it out completely."

Thank you, Dr. Younger, Wiseass thinks; *that is immensely reassuring and clarifies matters completely.*

Just be quiet and listen, Rational Ellen says. *Why do you have to be so oppositional?*

Shut up, the other Ellens tell Wiseass.

"You're sure the damage is caused by antibodies?" Jim asks in the general direction of both doctors.

"Yes," they both answer.

"What kind of antibodies?" Jim asks.

Now Dr. Lewis leans back in her chair and relaxes a bit. I think it's because she knows she's on safe scientific ground, not in that slushy affective realm with messy human emotions. She's probably reassured that I have not wailed or rent my garments.

"We don't know," she answers.

"Then how do you know antibodies cause the demyelination?" Jim asks, ever the litigator.

"We can't actually see the antibodies, but we can see the damage they caused."

Oof. Damage. What an ugly word. Feels like a punch in my gut.

"So you don't have to actually see the perpetrator to know the crime's being committed?" asks Rational Ellen.

"Right," she smiles. She seems pleased by this question, which shows she's been fully understood. She relaxes even more now that she's reasonably sure Ellen will be brave; that no one will be forced to watch her cry.

Scared Ellen doesn't find this the least bit comforting. She hides her quivering lips behind Rational Ellen's *Thinker* pose.

Wiseass is on another tangent. *Dr. Lewis thinks I'm brave and clever. What she cannot know is that I have an overwhelming desire to burst out laughing. This desire is trying to take control of my lips and is totally disconnected from my thoughts or feelings.*

Observing Ellen notices, *I don't have any feelings at all. In fact, I'm just floating up here on the ceiling, looking down on everybody sitting there so solemnly, discussing what could be a disaster in such a civilized manner. But since none of this is about me, why not probe further?*

Interesting idea, thinks Rational Ellen, who now asks out loud, "So, uh, Dr. Lewis—what's the best and worst case scenario?"

Dr. Lewis stops playing with her pen. She takes a breath. "Well, the best case is spontaneous remission. You might get better without any treatment. Or, next best, you might have a very good response to very low doses of steroids." Now she sits very still and looks directly at me. Our eyes lock for a long moment. "The worst case is death."

Wiseass stifles a giggle.

Stop that! warns Rational Ellen. *No giggling.*

Wiseass stifles another giggle. *This is getting much too melodramatic.*

I don't like this scenario, Scared Ellen thinks. *I don't want to hear any more. I want to get my money back and see another movie.*

Rational Ellen ignores them. "But why, Dr. Lewis? It's not in the brain. It's not even in the spinal cord. You said it was peripheral neuropathy—in the peripheral nervous system."

Go, girlfriend, Wiseass cheers. *Pin that bitch doctor right to the wall. Doesn't "peripheral" mean "not important"?*

"If all the myelin on all your peripheral nerves is destroyed," says Dr. Lewis without flinching, "you won't be able to breathe. You won't be able to live. You'll die."

Wiseass can't help giggling a little. *I must be in the wrong room. Who is the poor bitch they're talking about? It can't be me. It cannot be. Me.*

CLOSE-UP OF JIM.

He's pale. His palms are sweating ice water. He opens his mouth to speak, but nothing comes out. Observing Ellen thinks, *Poor, dear Jim. He's so frightened. He must think Dr. Lewis is talking about Ellen.*

CLOSE-UP OF DR. YOUNGER AS RATIONAL ELLEN LOOKS TO HIM FOR HELP.

But he's frowning, studying the hairs on the backs of his hands and the buttonholes in his white coat.

Look at poor Dr. Younger, Rational Ellen thinks. *Even he looks depressed. Maybe "nice surgeon" isn't an oxymoron after all.*

Dr. Lewis clears her throat. "Now we have to discuss treatment options."

Oh, yeah? thinks Wiseass. *Forget it. I don't want to know about treatment. I don't want to think about it, worry about it, or make decisions about it.*

Scared Ellen turns away. *I don't care, either. I want to go home for a nap.*

But Rational Ellen sits up straighter and clears her throat. "I have—a lot of questions about treatment."

Oh, shut up, says Wiseass. *You just want to prove how fucking smart you are.*

No, YOU shut up, Rational Ellen snaps back. *I need to know.* She sits up even straighter and leans forward, biting her lips. In fact, she bites on this opportunity to take control of the situation the way a puppy bites a new slipper. And she won't let go.

"So what about treatment?" she asks Dr. Lewis. "What is it? When do we start?"

"Whatever happens, the decision will be yours—in conjunction with your rheumatologist, of course," Dr. Lewis states. "I will not be involved directly in your treatment."

You big bloody chicken, thinks Wiseass. *Not sticking around for the long haul, huh? Shame on you, Linda Lewis.*

Now Jim pipes up, voice a bit squeaky. "What are the treatment options?"

"She could do nothing and wait."

Hey! What's this third-person "she" shit? thinks Wiseass. *It's my privilege to deny and dissociate from now till kingdom come, but that doesn't give anybody else the right to talk about me as if I'm not in the room—even on my deathbed.*

You said it, chime in all the other Ellens.

But what did she say about treatment? says Scared Ellen. *Do nothing and wait? Sounds great.*

Sounds terrible, thinks Rational Ellen.

Yeah, let's start killing those cockamamie antibodies today. Right now, agrees Wiseass. *Where's the medicine? Can I take it right here?*

"And if I don't choose to wait?" I ask Dr. Lewis.

"You could take corticosteroids. If they work, they could not only halt the progression of the disease but help promote re-myelination."

"So then I'd be cured?"

"No. None of the treatments will result in a cure. This is an incurable and chronic disease. There is no cure. Only treatment."

There is a long silence. Nobody looks at anybody else.

Jim swallows hard, then speaks. "How do you know which treatment is best?"

"We don't. We're not sure precisely what causes this, so we're not certain how to treat it. We have to use our best guess."

"Can I take the steroids now?" I ask. "Can you give me some to take home? I want to get started."

"Wait, slow down. First we have to discuss the benefits and risks of steroids."

I'm not sure I want to hear this, thinks Scared Ellen.

Would you shut up and listen? says Wiseass.

This time Dr. Lewis talks without benefit of artwork. "Steroids work by reducing inflammation and cutting down your body's production of antibodies. But steroids only work about fifty percent of the time with peripheral neuropathy because there's not much inflammation. And you run the risk of major infections and other side effects when you take a big enough dose to suppress your immune system."

Does anybody else note the irony of cutting down on antibody production in the middle of the AIDS epidemic? Wiseass thinks. *Here's a possible plus: maybe I could help cure someone of AIDS by donating my over-abundance of antibodies.*

Be quiet! all the other Ellens insist.

"And you're not going to like the other side effects of steroids. Frequent infections, weight gain, water retention. Risk of diabetes and osteoporosis. Risk of cataracts and stomach ulcers. Possible agitation, depression, and other psychological reactions."

Jim and I look at each other, then down at the arabesque patterns on the rug.

"And, of course, you have to understand the purely cosmetic side-effects."

You mean there's more? I think, studying the rug again.

Dr. Lewis pauses till Jim and I look up, perhaps to be sure we're listening as we crush each other's fingers in a strange handshake. Then she continues without blinking her thick, un-mascara-ed eyelashes. "Most patients report thinning hair, chipmunk cheeks, and buffalo hump on the upper back."

"And what?" all the Ellens say in unison.

"Buffalo hump. Because when you take steroids, fat migrates to all the fattest parts of you, including the upper back, thighs, hips, cheeks, butt—"

"I get it," I say, waving her away, but wanting to punch her. Ugh.

Dr. Lewis sighs. "This isn't an easy decision, Ms. Schecter. This stuff is swamp water. You don't want to take it unless you absolutely must."

Another long silence—from everyone, including Dr. Younger, who still refuses to meet my glance.

"Are there any other options?" I ask, then try to lose myself again in the rug.

"Yes," she says with what sounds like regret, "and they're worse— though they may turn out to be better for treating your particular disease." She pauses a beat, then plunges in. "There are the cytotoxic drugs—the chemotherapeutic agents. They're much more effective in suppressing antibodies but cause temporary or permanent sterility, more extensive hair loss, and extreme nausea. They make you even more vulnerable to infections and, perhaps, in the long run, to cancer.

"Taking cytotoxic drugs is like having chemotherapy for cancer; it requires periodic hospitalizations while you puke your brains out," she finishes.

Oh, how we appreciate that tough-love honesty, Dr. Lewis, Wiseass thinks.

I wonder what Dr. Younger thinks about all this, but he is still counting the buttons on his white doctor coat.

Dr. Lewis starts pushing papers into my crowded file. She glances at her phone, which has been lighting up like a Christmas tree. We're moving into the final scene of this movie.

"All of this will be decided in consultation with the rheumatologist who treats you. I'd like you to see Dr. Israeli Jaffe, head of rheumatology here at Columbia-Pres. He's excellent, highly experienced. He'll know more about this than anybody. Why don't you see what he says?" She uncaps her fancy fountain pen, which I still want to grab out of her hand, and writes his name and phone number on her prescription pad.

"Isn't there anything else to try?" I ask, desperate.

"What about things like meditation," Jim asks, "and—and . . ."

"And—visualization?" I add. "Do you think concentrating on being well can have any real effect on a disease like this?" I'd always thought that stuff was hogwash.

"I think whatever you can do to put yourself back in control of your life will be of benefit," Dr. Lewis says. I can hear that she's just trying to be respectful of . . . hogwash.

That means no, Wiseass thinks.

Dr. Lewis continues, suppressing a sigh. "Who knows? Many of my patients say meditation and visualization help them."

"Perhaps prayer could help," Dr. Younger says softly from the back of the room. When I turn, he smiles at me with the same sweet gentleness I remember from the OR.

LONG SHOT: EVERYONE: IMMOBILE, SILENT.

There is another awkward silence, decorated with smiles.

"How's the leg healing?" Dr. Younger asks.

"Yes, let's take a look at it," Dr. Lewis says, rising behind her desk.

You want to look at my leg? Don't you realize my heart is breaking?

We all troop into the tiny white Chamber of Horrors the doctors call the Examining Room. The Ellens try to crowd in, but can only peek through the open door.

Our very civil conversation now devolves into a brief examination of my post-operative left leg, which looks to me as if it's been hacked open in two places with a rusty can opener. Both doctors, however, crow ecstatically over what beautiful incisions they are and how nicely they're healing.

We wind up with my brief review of all the things I cannot do with my left leg: sleep, place my heel on the ground, walk without a cane, go up or down stairs, put on pantyhose. When they understand how much pain I have, they prescribe crutches—for a week or so, not permanently, don't worry—and stronger pain medication.

Then our hostess ushers us back into her consulting room.

She closes my file and stacks it on top of her "finished" pile with what sounds like a sigh of relief. We shake hands all around rather cordially, as if taking leave from a cocktail party that never quite clicked.

The movie is over. There is no happy ending.

FADE OUT.

CHAPTER 4
Dr. Rheumatology

1988

JIM AND I SLOG THROUGH TWO LONG WEEKS UNTIL OUR APPOINTMENT with Dr. Rheumatology, scheduled like a bad joke on Halloween. Jim practices denial by losing himself in his legal cases. I don't have to try very hard to get lost in the details of my everyday life, either: the morning chaos of lost sneakers and burnt toast; packing lunches and backpacks; struggling to get Anna's socks on her sweet wriggling feet while electric shocks explode up my arms; trying to keep Alex from sprinting into traffic when I can't keep up with him on my painful, uncooperative legs. All this by 8 a.m.

Then my workday begins: script conferences, first drafts, rewrites, polishes, the occasional nervous phone interviews with LeVar Burton, star of *Reading Rainbow*, which always turn out to be a pleasure because he's so warm and collegial, so dedicated to the show. The series is always simultaneously in pre-production and production, so if I don't meet my deadlines, we're in trouble, and I often have nightmares of blank TV screens that keep me on schedule. What I do write—trips to erupting volcanoes, lighthouses and zoos; skiing, Indian pow-wows, and Caribbean islands—look easy on paper, but then people have to bring them to life, which takes enormous time and effort. So meeting my deadlines is essential to allow them time for their preparations.

With Halloween coming, our kids live in rapturous anticipation of pillowcases brimming with candy. The night before, Anna still can't decide between the Little Mermaid—"But how can I walk?"—or Super Girl—"Mommy! She can't fly with a blue towel; it has to be red." Alex is easy this year: Spiderman. He's been practicing for weeks in his Spiderman pajamas, zooming through our apartment trying to defy gravity, zinging webs against walls, crashing from chairs onto the ceiling of our downstairs neighbors, but since they're both profoundly deaf and adore the kids, they never complain. The kids and I get more and more excited about trick-or-treating as I finish inking black spider webs on red socks and gloves, then quickly assemble a Little Red Riding Hood outfit for Anna, at the last minute ironing the red felt cloak-and-hood I made her last year, finding a basket, washing her frilliest old-fashioned dress.

But life does not feel normal to me. If I pause, even for a moment, I realize that the ground beneath my feet feels like a thin sheet of glass—a fragile, transparent skin stretched over nothing. We could all smash through at any moment.

As our cab struggles up Broadway toward Columbia-Presbyterian Hospital, I glimpse tiny ghosts and witches parading in and out of stores, holding plastic pumpkins and adding surrealistic touches to our journey into the future.

I hold tight to Jim's hand while we wait in Atchley Pavilion till almost three-thirty for our two p.m. consultation with Dr. Jaffe. We probably look like the typical middle-class dual-career couple we are—Jim in his lawyer's pinstripes and red paisley tie Anna picked out for his birthday; I in my black suit with the crimson silk blouse I purposely put on to signal a defiance I don't feel.

Finally, the famed doctor appears, blissfully unrushed: crisp white coat, crisp white smile. Dr. Jaffe, the drop-dead handsome elder statesman of rheumatology, is chairman of his department. He's a sixty-something Jewish patrician with sterling silver hair and rosy skin as highly polished as alabaster. He greets us with a degree of disdain, as if—rank newcomers to his realm—we'll have to earn his respect.

As soon as we're seated in his cluttered office, he dispenses with preliminary pleasantries and poses a long skein of unrelated questions in carefully modulated tones.

Did you ever suffer a strep infection or rheumatic fever as a child? (Yes, and yes.)

A heart murmur? (Yes, at age 9; I still have mitral valve prolapse).

A false-positive syphilis test? (Yes, prior to my first marriage—mortifying, until a second, more sensitive test proved negative).

Joint pains? (Yes, since 1976.)

Muscle pain and weakness? (Yes.)

Unexplained fevers? (No; my temperature is usually below normal.)

Extreme fatigue? (Oh, yes.)

Muscle weakness? (Yes.)

Pain and tingling? (Yes.)

Refusing to be rushed, he notes my answers in my new chart with flourishes of his handsome gold-and-ebony Montblanc pen. Why do all these doctors have such beautiful pens? Writers should have beautiful pens like that.

Neurological damage is, of course, the $64,000 question, so I hand him Dr. Lewis's nerve-muscle biopsy report. I begin to covet his exquisite writing instrument with an irrational hunger, and as he reads my biopsy report with stern but leisurely attention, I have to clasp my hands together to keep from snagging it into my briefcase.

While he continues to read carefully through Dr. Lewis's notes I review the facts I've learned from the Lupus Foundation:

There is no single test or indicator for lupus. Instead, there's a checklist of eighteen common symptoms—as well as many more unusual ones—so the diagnosis must be pieced together like a medical mystery. For most people, the average interval between onset and diagnosis is nine to twelve years. The diagnostic process is made more complicated by the fact that nine out of ten people with lupus are female, and many studies show that their symptoms often are dismissed by predominantly male physicians as psychosomatic or the result of "depression." And "lupus" means "wolf," because many people get a red, butterfly-shaped rash over their cheeks and around their eyes which resembles the dark, masklike markings on the face of wolves.

Not waiting for the doctors, I tried to dismiss my strange symptoms on my own. Now, in the hands of a lupus expert, twelve years after my first painful and puzzling symptoms appeared, the answers begin to add up. The arcane neurological symptoms—found in less than five percent of lupus patients—are unusual but significant pieces in this puzzle.

Dr. Jaffe caps and puts down his pen, lacing together his impeccably manicured fingers. He stares at me with ice-blue eyes, then flicks his gaze over to Jim, who's holding my hand in a chilly embrace. The doctor takes a deep breath and lets it out slowly. He is clearly a man who will not be rushed by anything.

I watch him pick up his fountain pen, uncap it, cross out Dr. Lewis's noncommittal but neatly-typed diagnosis of "Autoimmune Syndrome" and inscribe "Systemic Lupus Erythematosus" right above it in shiny black ink. I watch the wet black words shine for several seconds before they sink into the paper. It takes ever so much longer for them to sink into me.

"Systemic lupus," he says. "I have no question."

The God of Rheumatology has spoken and continues to speak. "You have an unusual manifestation of lupus, and nerve involvement is very difficult to treat—if it can be treated at all. Nerve tissue does not seem to respond well to steroids. In fact, some physicians would say that you actually have two diseases—systemic lupus and peripheral neuropathy, a—"

"A disease and inflammation of the peripheral nerves," Jim interjects, trying to regain control over the conversation and thus over our increasingly uncontrollable lives.

"Yes," Dr. Jaffe intones with another crystal stare—one no doubt designed to inform his medical students that his classes are lectures, not Socratic dialogues. "Please do not interrupt," he says. "I have a great deal to say and not much time to say it. You'll have time to talk later, when I am busy with other patients."

Jim sits back, swelling with rage. Few people ever dare to silence him.

"But it doesn't really matter if you have lupus with neuropathic symptoms or inflammatory peripheral neuropathy with lupus symptoms. I still want to treat them with steroids, which can work well against inflammation. At least, that's my hope."

He pauses, and his message hangs in the air above my head like a nasty cartoon balloon. Or, like the sword of Damocles, ready to fall and cut my consciousness in two. I feel myself zooming toward the ceiling when Jim squeezes my hand and brings me back.

"There's only one treatment I would recommend. We have to go after a disease like yours with high-dose intravenous steroids—a thousand milligrams of intravenous Solu-Medrol per day, three days a month in the hospital for at least three months. I'll also put you on sixty milligrams of oral prednisone a day between hospitalizations to keep up the barrage. There's no point in starting more conservatively and you may know in a few weeks whether it's working."

A thousand milligrams? Ugh. Chipmunk cheeks, buffalo hump, weight gain—

"You will not like this, Ms. Schecter. No one does. Your face will get as round as the moon. But it's the only way I see to burn this out of your system before the antibodies do more damage. Nerves may or may not heal. That is an academic argument I would hate to see waged over your body. Your disease is spreading rapidly, as you well know. Let's try to get rid of those antibodies as soon as we can, before they damage more nerves."

He pulls a form out of a folder marked Hospital Admissions.

"When can you go into the hospital for three days and get this first treatment?"

I start to shake. Three days? The kids. Spreading rap—. My face. Script deadli—

"What about side effects?" Jim asks. He grips my hand, and we're in a sub-zero meat locker. I half expect to see frosty plumes of our breath fill the small, cluttered room.

"The worst side effects are all that really matter," Dr. Jaffe answers. "There are the cosmetic ones, but I have no concern about them even though you might. Many people get migraine headaches, and a strange metallic taste in your mouth when the Medrol starts to circulate. None of that matters. But you must know the larger risks and sign off on them, literally, before treatment. Though they rarely occur, I cannot guarantee against them." He counts them off: "Risk of heart failure, death from overwhelming infection, and psychotic breakdown. Heart failure occurs rarely, and then primarily in patients with serious heart problems prior to treatment."

"Mitral valve—?" I try to squeeze it in before he bulldozes over me.

"Mitral valve prolapse should not be a serious problem, though as I told you, I cannot guarantee that. Serious infection usually—usually—occurs in post-surgical patients in weakened conditions. Psychotic breaks? Entirely unpredictable, but we can treat you with drugs if we need to, and it would be temporary, caused by the steroids."

He uncaps his pen again and writes my name on the first line of the Hospital Admission form, continuing to speak as he adds my address, date of birth, and so on.

"When can you do this? We have Thanksgiving coming up, when I'll be away, and I must be around after the days of actual treatment in case of problems. So how about a week from Monday?"

"I—I need time to think about this," I manage. "Is there any other option?"

"You could do nothing, but I won't be responsible. You could take smaller doses of steroids, but in my opinion that's like sending mosquitoes to fight elephants. And you would have to find another rheumatologist if you exercise those options."

He fixes me with another ice-blue stare, then flicks once more to Jim, as if seeking an ally. When his eyes return to me, I feel them bore straight into my heart.

"This is no joke, Ms. Schecter. Dr. Lewis and I are very concerned about you. The sooner we start treatment, the better for you. But, if you like, why don't you give yourself some time to think about it and call me, say—first thing tomorrow morning?"

I nod numbly; Jim says something intelligent; we shake—my fist frozen, the doctor's alabaster skin surprisingly warm and satiny. Then Jim and I leave the office, walk through the waiting room, ring for the elevator, and get outside, into a taxi, and home from 168th to 72nd before saying one word. I stare straight through the costumed children we see on the streets as if they're wraiths.

Jim unlocks and very quietly pushes open our apartment door so we can listen.

No voices. Good. The kids are in the park with Mrs. Sarah Parker, our housekeeper. We tiptoe inside and shut the door. The words in our throats finally thaw, and we have one of the most important conversations of our lives right there in the foyer.

"I think we have to do it." Jim says, his beautiful dark eyes full of tears.

I nod, my tears frozen solid. "Before Thanksgiving, I think." I get out my date book and flip through the pages. I remember nothing unless I write it down. "A week from next Monday?"

Jim calculates meetings, trial preps, court appearances, all from memory.

"That'll work for me if I juggle a few things." He pauses, then looks down. "What'll we tell the kids?"

"The truth. But not too scary." I pause, thinking of my father's many mysterious disappearances into the hospital for surgeries after an accident when I was a very young child, and how they terrified me because I had no idea where he went or why. "But the truth. Maybe, I have go to the hospital to get—special medicine. They know something's going on—the biopsy bandages, the crutches, the cane. All the time I spend in bed. All the doctors' appointments." I draw a shaky breath. "I'll probably be gone just those three days. I'll tell them I can call them on the phone a lot, and give them my number so they can call me. Let's find out if they can visit, in a lounge or something."

"But won't the IV be scary?"

"Maybe. But we shouldn't lie about anything, or not explain. I write for kids; I should be able to come up with an honest but comforting explanation . . . like, "special medicine Mommy's body drinks through a straw." Or maybe I can get unhooked when they come. But it's better for them to see me with an IV than to imagine me dying or something awful like they see on TV. I'll wear regular clothes, so I don't look sick."

We still stand in the foyer, leaning against the closed front door as if we can keep the lupus wolf outside. I think maybe I should cry, get out some feelings, but I'm much too frightened. I need all my energy to stay calm and look strong.

"I'm sure he has to say all that bad stuff for legal reasons, don't you think, Jim?"

"Maybe."

"Maybe we can get your parents to do some fun things with the kids while I'm gone." My mind races to practicalities. "Movies, the zoo . . . maybe the Natural History Museum, depending on the weather. Make it fun for them."

"Mm." Jim looks distracted. "Listen, I'll come every day, but I can't stay. I want to put them to bed every night."

"I know, that's OK. Good, actually. It'll be good to have some time to myself, anyway. To read, do some writing. I've got deadlines. And I won't be sick or anything."

"Maybe not. Headaches—you'll probably get the headaches."

"Yeah, well, I get them anyway, so no big deal." I try to smile. I unbutton Jim's raincoat, then his suit jacket, and slide my arms inside, nestling against his white oxford cloth shirt, where I can feel his body heat and strong steady heartbeat. My head fits just under his chin, and we cling to each other for a while.

I pull away first. "I've got to get out of here before the kids get home. I've got a script conference in about half an hour, and I want to call the social worker at the Lupus Foundation before my meeting. You home for dinner?"

Jim sighs, picking up his briefcase as if it weighs a hundred pounds. "No, I'll be late—to make up for the appointment. And the waiting."

"Yeah, and we've got Halloween tonight. It's a shame you'll miss it."

We skulk out of our third-floor apartment, lock the door, and listen for sounds of our children's voices piping up from the lobby downstairs. Nothing.

We take the elevator down, holding hands, kiss lightly near the polished brass entry doors, then head in opposite directions. I'm determined to take control of my two new hard-to-spell diseases. Simple, I tell myself, thumbing my nose at terror. I'll just have to slip into a phone booth and turn into Superwoman.

CHAPTER 5

The Woman with Wings

1988

JIM HELPS ME TELL OUR FAMILY AND FRIENDS ABOUT MY TERRIFYING double diagnosis and scheduled hospitalization. My father sounds supportive, though silent—he hasn't always come through, lately, when the chips are down, probably because his new wife, Ina, is now the center of his life and decides what they do and when.

But in exchange for the bad news, each of my close friends offers me a gift: her help, an insight, a tip or suggestion, important information, a lead on a doctor or a person who can help. Perhaps best of all, my friends give me their tears and their time, a precious commodity for all these harried working mothers with their own struggles and fears. Each of these acts of love feels like an invisible jewel I can place in a mental treasure chest, to take out and cherish when times get even tougher. I know they'll be there when I need them.

The person I most dread calling is my mother. I have no idea how she'll respond, but I'm fairly certain it won't be helpful. I'm afraid to tell her myself, so I listen silently on the extension while Jim explains how serious my diagnoses and treatment are. There's an uncharacteristic moment of silence. Then she says, "Are you sure those doctors know what they're doing? How do you know they have the right diagnosis? Ellen should come home to Philadelphia. We have much better doctors here. And—that diagnosis is wrong, Jim. She has Lyme disease. Did they test you, Ellen? You'd better look into that. I read the newspapers. I know what I'm talking about."

"Ellen's been fully tested, Pearl," Jim says, his voice shaking with rage, "but I hear the kids, so we have to say good-bye now. We need to put them to bed."

"Well, if you don't want to listen to perfectly good advice." She hangs up on him.

I'm shaking so hard it takes a while to get up from my chair.

Almost two weeks later, a typewritten note arrives in a parcel post package. The note inside is dated the day after the phone call.

11-2-88, 10:12 AM

Dear Ellen:

Finally got to send this off to you. Enclosed find a crystal necklace and the yellow jade necklace. Sorry it took so long, but I am constantly dragging, physically. Now taking some iron with my calcium and hope my energy level goes up. Much love and we will be talking,

Love,
Mother

Additional handwritten notes are attached to each necklace, instructing me how to wear it—"*Crystal goes with anything. Yellow jade lovely with brown, green, white, etc.*" and are signed "*Mother (with much love).*"

I put the necklaces in my top dresser drawer and tape her letter into my journal, which is exploding with data from all my research. Maybe if I read her instructions often enough, I'll somehow come to understand that she's doing the best she can to comfort me.

Her package brings me the closest I've come to tears, bitter tears, since all this began.

❋   ❋   ❋

Jim buries himself in an avalanche of legal work, trying to finish up some cases and clear his calendar for the demanding days in the hospital and whatever the aftermath might be. I don my invisible Superwoman garb, trying to turn into steel and become an instant expert on My Dread Diseases. If knowledge is power, maybe I can transform it into control—and I am determined to take back control of my body, my life, and my future. I not only want to get a second opinion, but a third, fourth, and fifth.

Maybe I have moments during those first weeks when I feel sad, angry, panicky, or depressed, the way anyone might feel who doesn't hail from Planet Krypton. But I pay no attention to them. I institute a rigid no-tears policy and refuse to waste one second wringing my hands, moaning, mourning, or feeling anything but an arid intellectual curiosity unrelated to worry. After all, why should I suffer? Willfully forgetting Dr. Lewis's words "chronic" and "incurable," I convince myself that I'll be cured, or at least in remission, as soon as I find the best doctor with the best treatment at the best hospital—even though I need two magic bullets instead of one.

Once I jump to the conclusion that my body is the enemy and medicine will wrestle it back to health, I fly into the universe of modern medicine, trying to put my numb, clumsy, and trembling fingers on the facts, nothing but the facts. I give up sleep and lunches to do my research and still meet my script deadlines—Superwoman never misses a deadline. And if I haven't turned up any panacea so far, I just have not called the right phone numbers. Jim calls it crazed. I call it focused.

Jim has another approach to the diagnoses. He starts sifting through his feelings about how my illness and its ramifications might affect the kids, him, and me. He tries to talk about his feelings, but I refuse to have any. Superwoman is on a mission to knock my dread diseases dead—*Pow! Pow!* I can duck into another phone booth later and turn back into my soft, human self. But not yet.

Late one night, about a week after our initial encounter with Dr. Rheumatology, Jim trudges in from work at about ten-thirty as I doze in bed, finally finished with the fifth repetition of *Goodnight, Moon* and *Frog and Toad Are Friends*. He wearily tugs off his shoes, dropping them one by one on the floor.

"Listen, do you want to talk about this?" he asks, weary and pale.

"About what?" I yawn.

"You know what."

"What about it?" I answer, yawning again as I nestle deeper in bed, every demyelinated nerve sizzling.

"About how you feel."

"Not really," I say, forcing myself awake with an acid surge of resentment. After I get the kids to sleep, I consider myself off duty. "But do you want to hear what I found out from the Armed Forces Institute of Pathology? And I finally spoke to Dr. Hellman, the research neurologist at NIH. If Dr. Lewis sends my biopsy slides and a brief clinical history, for absolutely no charge they'll both either re-confirm or fine-tune the diagno—"

"Great. But I was thinking about your state of mind, Ellen, how you're coping."

"Well," I sigh, "I'm extremely worried about the kids while I'm in the hospital. So I spoke to that Child Life social worker at Mount Sinai. Remember, the terrific one I worked with when I was writing the film for kids who were having surgery? She gave me some great ideas about how to help calm our kids' fears while I'm gone, to help empower them to—"

Jim slams his shoes under the ottoman and stomps off to brush his teeth.

I cuddle down in bed, hoping to soothe my twanging nerves. And I take a moment, just a moment, to consider: How do I feel—really feel—about all this? I'm aware that I've buried my feelings down deep under my frantic scramble for facts about the latest: Research. Treatments. Clinical trials. Knowledge. Leading doctors in the field. Hospitals that specialize. I really can't be bothered with my emotions while I try to find out all the facts I can. And this scurrying around is so I can find some hope that these diseases are not incurable; that there are new treatments out there; that I have to find them and then everything will be okay. And finding those treatments is up to me.

That's how I feel: I have to be my own best advocate. I have to keep trying to find the facts, and then I will find hope. Real hope.

In my search for knowledge-as-power, the Lupus Foundation is an invaluable resource. I read in their various brochures that with systemic lupus erythematosus, SLE, the immune system produces antibodies against its own healthy cells and tissues. "These auto-antibodies ('auto' means 'self') contribute to the inflammation of various parts of the body, including the joints, skin, kidneys, heart, lungs, blood vessels, brain," and, "in only five percent of cases," the peripheral nerves.

In 1988, the year I'm diagnosed, the literature reports the average life expectancy of people with lupus as nine years after diagnosis—a statistic I try to erase from my mind after Enid Englehart, the sympathetic social worker at the New York City Lupus Foundation, tells me it's quite outdated. But I'm also troubled that she can't offer any updated statistics for life expectancy. She always changes the subject.

And what about my other disease, peripheral neuropathy (PN), which in the late 1980s was too rarely diagnosed to generate its own foundation? Dr. Lewis gives me a pass so I can use the medical library at Columbia's College of Physicians and Surgeons. There I pore over neurology journals and *Peripheral Neuropathy*, a cheerless tome the size and heft of a cinder block, which I read side by side with an equally ponderous medical dictionary. I find that PN is not one but many separate diseases. The book is rife with detailed descriptions of their possible causes, prognoses, and manifestations—all distinctly unpleasant. The data on treatment are scant, as Dr. Jaffe warned, perhaps because there is also very little agreement about causes. But one thing is clear: PN is not a diagnosis anyone would choose.

The neurology section of the medical library is several stories underground. Going down in the elevator feels like a symbolic descent far, far away from the grace of simple sunlight into one of the lower circles of Dante's hell. After deciphering as much as I can about acute or chronic, motor or sensory, autonomic, hypertrophic, demyelinated, teased fibers and the like, I decide to abandon my studies—especially when some of the terminology seems reminiscent of Dr. Lewis's biopsy reports and I read possible prognoses for my probable disease: increased muscle weakness of arms and legs, difficulty walking, facial weakness, difficulty swallowing and speaking, possible need for wheelchair. . . Ugh. Ugh. Ugh.

I shut *Peripheral Neuropathy* and rest my head on its faux leather cover. I stare with wide-open eyes at what we in TV call an "extreme close-up" of the pocks on the book's navy surface. They're blurred by fatigue and a thin skim of tears I cannot will or blink away. I'm so frightened by these possibilities that I don't share them with anyone or discuss them with any doctor. I try to forget them myself, except that what I've learned burns a small hole in the lower right-hand corner of my optimism—a hole that refuses to be sewn back together, no matter how carefully I mend, darn, or embroider. I rarely look at that hole, but I know it's somewhere at the farthest edge of my vision. I fear that I may someday fall through it into a bottomless Pit of dread.

Staying as far away as I can from that Pit, I'm determined to do everything I can to make the coming infusions work. Dr. Lewis's words from Diagnosis Day replay in my mind: "Whatever you can do to put yourself back in control of your life will be of benefit."

Scheduled for industrial strength doses of the most potent Western medicine, I also explore alternative ways of helping myself. I order tapes prepared by Peggy Huddleston, who has designed a method of meditation to help people facing surgery or other serious medical problems. As soon as the tapes arrive, Jim and I start practicing with them as part of our preparation for my hospitalization. We immediately feel comfortable with her simple method of quiet breathing, muscle relaxation, and anxiety reduction, which asks us to imagine that we can open little doors in our feet so all our nervous apprehension can exit our bodies, leaving us in a tranquil state of peace. Sometimes the children wander in and out, joining us quietly and even falling asleep. We feel convinced that these meditations will help me receive the potentially jarring drug more easily into my body, and help Jim support me and take care of the children in a more relaxed state.

In her last tape, Peggy encourages us to go beyond the practical techniques she's taught us, and to reach higher, into the spiritual realm. Jim and I wait till the children are sound asleep, then turn on the tape recorder, lie down comfortably, and listen.

"Let me help you go on a personal journey into a High Place of your own choosing," she suggests. "Imagine yourself taking a journey to a place that beckons you —a place where you feel safe and protected." I immediately find myself on an island off the coast of Maine.

"Close your eyes and imagine that you are climbing up to a place where you will encounter a benevolent Being who will share wisdom with you and give you courage. There is no reason to feel frightened—only curious.

"If you feel drawn to this, if you feel a need to be a seeker, keep your eyes closed, and make sure you're in a comfortable position. Take some deep, cleansing breaths and I will now help you go there. And if, for some reason, you decide this exercise doesn't beckon to you, just use the time to rest. Or take a break."

It beckons to me quite strongly, and Jim doesn't move either. I close my eyes, breathe deeply and make my own meditative journey.

I climb a steep, narrow path to my High Place—a pine-scented, dapple-green forest where nothing can harm me and pain is far away. The mountain peak vaults sharply up to my left; to my right, there is a sheer drop into a broad valley full of fragrant pines.

A radiant Image, shrouded in luminous mist, lit from behind by the sun or moon, appears above the trees. She approaches. She's been waiting for me.

She moves closer. Suddenly, She surrounds me.

Now she reveals herself as a robust, powerfully familiar Female Being made of light. Though not frightening, She awakens awe—loving awe. Gradually, I become aware of feathery wings—wings wide enough to fill the sky. Powerful wings to provide shelter. But I cannot discern Her face. Is She a bird with a woman's face? Or a woman with bird wings? Does it matter?

Her light doesn't merely shine on me, but through me.

I know I will search for Her presence forever.

Jim and I decide not to tell the children anything about my hospitalization until two days before, even though we set things up carefully with his parents, Doris and Stan: why make the kids worry until it's absolutely necessary? It's eerie how ordinary I can still make life seem on its vivid, energetic surface, while underneath time pulls me toward something so frightening. Each night, as I bathe the kids in turn, swathing their dark hair with iridescent shampoo bubbles, singing along with Anna's fantasies of being a Little Mermaid and re-living Alex's latest junior soccer league scores, I can feel John Irving's Undertoad squatting behind me.

Instead of dwelling on my fears, I seek refuge in details: rough towels stroking the velvety perfection of the children's skin; the comb parting their silky hair; the fruity scent of flesh the color and texture of summer peaches. Jim and I, as always, read a seemingly endless succession of nighttime books—*Goodnight, Moon* and *Wagon Wheels, Mystery on the Docks, Lyle Crocodile,* and the entire *Frog and Toad* oeuvre—then tuck them into separate beds in the room they share, divided for semi-privacy by two floor-to-ceiling bookcases. Every night, we all relax into our family ritual called "lie with me"—Jim and I taking turns snuggling beside Anna or Alex on their beds, singing lullabies, whispering answers to their endlessly inventive questions, luxuriating in the sweet fact of their childhood as they gradually become quieter and quieter, like birds twittering at twilight, finally fading into silence.

Then Jim and I drop into our bed, exhausted yet twanging with an energy we can't describe, pulled together by forces that won't—can't—let go. I feel Jim's unspoken vulnerability in the way he holds me with his whole body, as if he thinks I might get lost if he doesn't hang on tight; as if he somehow senses my unspoken fear that gravity no longer holds me safely to the ground. Then, like a tomcat curling on a cushion, he turns into his corner of the bed and drops like a boulder into soundless slumber.

Alone in the dark while everyone sleeps, my last smidgens of steel melt back into flesh. All a-jangle, I watch car and bus headlights sweep and weave like searchlights across our walls and ceiling. I think I can guess the colors of the cars by the tints of their headlights, the way it's possible to see the hue of an object contained in its shadow. I catch myself concentrating on anything—everything—but my own fears.

But my ability to keep my terror locked away often stops working in the dark, when fears and questions crawl out like bugs: fears about the treatments; about these damned twin diseases rising through my body like poisonous red tides.

How will I look and feel after three days of IV Solu-Medrol? Will the treatment work? And if it does, how will I look after three months of sixty mg of oral prednisone a day? After three years of lupus? Will I be able to take care of my children if the wolf keeps crashing through our door? How can Jim handle the children and his career and take care of me? It sounds impossible. And—will he still love me if I can no longer do my share? If I have moon face and buffalo hump and—all the rest of it? Can I handle disease and pain that's even worse than I feel now? Am I as gutsy as I like to think?

Of less importance but still crucial: Will my career stumble to a halt? Can I keep up this daily marathon of lover-mother-writer and add "patient"? I've been running on empty for years, trying to fulfill my triple role. How can I add a full-time disease—no, two—to my life? And how will this disease change me—not just the physical me, but the essential me, which is so entwined in my creativity?

Death is no longer the worst I can imagine—being helpless is, being in non-stop pain is. Even so, I wonder if I'll have to die too soon and leave behind everyone and everything I love? For the umpteenth time, I wonder why the hell I asked Dr. Lewis that damned worst-case-scenario question. And why she had to be so bloody honest and say it out loud: "You could die." Why didn't I just let that question float away like a silent word-balloon? Yet I know exactly why I asked: I had to know the answer.

One sleepless night, with these questions nipping at me for hours, I slide out of bed, ease the bedroom door shut, and walk quietly into the living room. The apartment feels full of sleep as I stumble to my desk, ready to explore the emotional landscape Dr. Lewis set out for me between spontaneous remission and death. Thinking about my own death—no, my life— against this bald new background changes everything. It's as if the colors I've seen all my life suddenly shifted and my world is drenched in startling new hues; perhaps the colors birds see, but we cannot.

I sit down at my desk—a polished wooden door resting on two black file cabinets—and switch on the hanging lamps with green-glass shades. Warm puddles of light push away a few inches of darkness as I open the battered black-and-white speckled composition book I use as my journal. Writing here keeps me tethered to earth. Without the gravity of pen and notebook, I might float up and up—not in the strong, free flight of Superwoman, but in the weightless drift and free-fall of terror. As if it were the first day of a new semester in a strange university, I'd brought this notebook when it was crisp and new to Diagnosis Day. Since then, I'd filled it with illness-related facts from medical consultations, hospital names and numbers, data from phone conversations with doctors and researchers; with many questions—and very few answers.

Now I need to answer my own questions. At the top of two fresh facing pages, I write *SPONTANEOUS REMISSION* on the left page and, very slowly, in very small, carefully printed capital letters, *DEATH* on the right. I circle these polar opposites, then draw a line, with little arrows at each end, across the two pages to connect them.

I sit and look at the words for a long time, thinking.

I begin to realize that big *DEATH* breaks down into many little deaths, so under it I write, *WHAT ARE THE LITTLE DEATHS?* I want to confront them by letting their impact flow from my brain, through my hand, and onto the page:

- the death of denial—no, many denials
- death of feeling graceful
- death of a leg without ugly scars

- death of painless walking—maybe permanently
- death of normal physical sensation—my left foot is so numb I wouldn't notice if a polar bear bit it; yet it's hypersensitive to the faintest flicker of touch where the biopsy scars are
- death of a casual, glorious innocence about my entitlement to a safe, healthy place in the world
- death of the illusion that I can control my life
- the death of walking alone—which translates into the reality of needing a cane, or worse: How can I accept this with grace instead of the terrible humiliation I feel?

I sit for a long while, but that's all the loss I can face at once.

So I turn to another page and write: *WHAT ARE THE GAINS?*

- meeting my Foul Weather friends: lovely people I meet through the Lupus support groups I've started to attend and even in doctors' offices
- the even sweeter, more piercing joy of music
- impetus and time to reassess my values—to decide what really matters to me
- my increased hunger for being, loving, reading, listening, looking—and seeing.

I know I'm unable to "make every moment count" the way some people say they do in the face of serious illness; there are still lots of ordinary everyday moments I have to get through before I get to the spectacular ones, though they do come.

I turn to the "pros and cons" about the planned treatment. I see my notes from an office consultation with Dr. Number Three, a sweet, very conservative rheumatologist who told me, "I've seen too many disasters from IV steroid pulse therapy to use it myself: seizures, congestive heart failure, overwhelming infections. I use it only in life-threatening situations, never for peripheral neuropathy." That page is decorated with heavy black question marks.

I turn the page to notes from a surprisingly tender and empathic follow-up telephone conversation with Dr. Jaffe. I can almost see him, smiling sardonically on the other end of the line. "I can guess who that other doctor is. He's a very nice guy. I know him, and he's also a very smart doctor. I'm not such a nice guy, but I'm just as smart as he is. We have distinct but valid differences of opinion on how to treat your disease. I want to do everything I possibly can for you, and as soon as possible."

Then his voice softened for the first time. "I know you're very frightened, Ms. Schecter. Try not to be. Let me take care of you. That's what I'm here for—to help you." His unexpected, genuine kindness brought me to tears in a way nothing else had.

I suddenly realize how much he's on my side.

Tears well up again as I sit alone in the dark. I feel relief flood through me: I know I made a good decision about both doctor and treatment. I push myself up from my desk, tuck my journal away on its shelf, and go quietly into the children's room. Alex is sprawled on top of his covers, positioned as if he's running a race in his sleep—so bold yet so vulnerable. His ultra-long lashes spread across his cheeks like fans. I stroke his face, so firm and soft. How can I protect him from what I know is coming?

I can't.

I walk past the bookcase divider to Anna's side, where she lies with one hand tucked under her cheek, knees bent, lips peaceful and slightly smiling.

These children are my anchors to this world, but I'm the center of theirs. I feel the profound responsibility that accompanies that privilege. And though I cannot protect them completely from all this, in some paradoxical way I feel that my love for them might protect me.

I go back to my desk, turn out the lights, slip into our bed, and curl around Jim's strong but slender back so we're like two spoons nestling in a velvet drawer. I feel the steady beat of his heart knocking at his chest and throughout his body with every stroke. I hear our apartment, the shell of our lives, tick and settle like a living thing, holding us within walls that lately have felt fragile. The slow heave of night traffic up and down West End Avenue feels frighteningly close to our warm bed that once felt so safe.

When sleep finally comes, dread chases me in dream after dream, taking the form of a giant, hairy spider. Sometimes it catches me and stings hard. Strange, because the next morning I'll have to fly high and fearless again. I'm still Superwoman, after all. Or am I?

CHAPTER 6
"Put on Your Pajamas"

1988

BEFORE DAWN ON THE MONDAY I'M DUE AT THE HOSPITAL, ALEX CREEPS shivering into our bed. I've been awake for hours, listening to Jim's steady breathing, trying to use it to calm my own.

"I have a pain, Mommy," Alex whimpers.

"Where?" I whisper. Jim is still sleeping.

"Here," he says, laying his hands over his heart.

"What does it feel like, sweetheart?"

"It feels like . . . I'm homesick."

I cuddle him close. "Oh, Alex, Mommy's right here."

"Daddy, too," Jim says, rolling over, thick with sleep. "We're both here."

"Why are you homesick this morning?" I ask, knowing exactly why.

"Because . . . I'm afraid that bad medicine will make you dead. Or it won't work, and you'll get dead anyway." He starts to cry and hides his face in my shoulder, so I have to strain to hear. "Or I'm afraid you won't be able to walk, and if you don't know how to work a wheelchair, then what can we do?" His tears trickle into my armpit.

I should have known, I think. The truth washes straight through children, no matter how hard you try to slow it, and even though you intend to tell them "in a little while." Barely six weeks after I became pregnant with

Anna, months before my belly swelled, Alex had a dream about a new bird in a nest.

"We don't think any of those things will happen, Sasha," I say, slipping back into his early nickname. "We think this special medicine is going to make me better. That's why I'm going to the hospital to get it. It's good medicine, not bad."

I swing Alex over me so Jim and I form a wreath of warm sleepy limbs around him under our fluffy quilt. If only we could snuggle for another hour.

Jim yawns, then patiently explains it to Alex all over again: how my body will drink the medicine through the special straw, how I can talk to him on the phone, that it's only three days, how Grandma and Grandpa will take him and Anna to the zoo and a movie. Before he finishes, Alex is back to sleep and Jim soon follows.

But I can't. Alex's fears flow through me as surely as the sweet warmth of his body. Somehow these fears soaked into him despite all the stories and metaphors we used to weave a protective cloak of reassurance. I feel stricken by the contrast between this sad little boy and the plump happy one who'd nuzzled a chocolate ice cream cone a few summers ago, while he waited for Jim to come back to Fire Island on the ferry during our vacation when he was three and Anna was newborn . . .

"When's Daddy coming back?" Alex asks for the fiftieth time. Jim had to leave our vacation to settle some emergencies in his law office.

"Tonight, soon, on the Daddy boat. Let's go down to the dock to meet him."

I push Alex in his stroller, with Anna riding in the Snugli baby carrier on my chest. As a fiery sun melts into the ocean, we line up at Unfriendly's Ice Cream to get a chocolate cone for Alex and a vanilla cup for me, with tiny tastes for Annie. I strip Alex down to his shorts, laughing as the ice cream drips off his chin and hands, and rolls down his chest into the folds of his tummy.

"Good, huh?" I ask. He smiles his answer, face awash in chocolate.

People gather around him, some licking their lips without realizing it.

"Don't you want to . . . clean him up?" someone says.

"Not now," I answer. "Let him enjoy his ice cream."

Alex finishes his cone just in time to greet Jim. My heart still gives a little jump as soon as I see him, first off the ferry. "Hey, big guy, looks like you had quite an ice cream there," Jim chuckles.

"Chocolate," Alex smiles as he tips his head to give a sloppy chocolate kiss.
"Mm," Jim says, licking his lips. "My favorite."
We hose Alex down on the back deck of our A-frame, the water warm after a
day in the sun, then dress him in clean PJs. The night is too perfect to go inside, so
we all sit on the front deck, swatting mosquitoes and listening to the wind chimes.

Oh, how sad I feel, comparing my homesick six-year-old to the joyous three-year-old who enjoyed such a carefree summer without clouds shadowing his life. How I wish I could take this disease out of his life and make it disappear.

Jim's parents arrive a little early, as always, and soon the kids are basking in their love. They're so well prepared, accept my medicine-through-a-special-straw story so casually that, despite Alex's early morning homesickness, they go blithely off without a murmur. We kiss them lightly and set out for Columbia-Presbyterian, barely four miles directly north along the Hudson River.

Our taxi takes the same route up Riverside Drive that we took for the spring births of both our children, when the trees were covered with white and pink blossoms. I remember thinking that they looked like bridesmaids in a wedding procession. But at this time of year, the trees are bare, stately and somber. I feel frozen solid with apprehension, my fist in Jim's, trying to use the new meditation breathing we've just learned, hoping it will keep me calm, the way I'd used Lamaze breathing to help me ride the tsunamis of labor—but this time, without the hopeful, fulsome drama of childbirth. This time, I feel as if gray moths are fluttering inside instead of vibrant butterflies.

Anna's birth was worthy of an ER episode—alarmed orderlies running me on a gurney through swinging doors back to the OR for a planned but now-emergency C-section because she was coming too quickly. My obstetrician, with his green face mask, beanie, scrubs and gloves already in place, barked orders while several interns struggled to insert IVs before it was too late and the baby's head slipped into the birth canal.

In contrast, this is a slow-motion, nerve-splitting series of waits. We wait in Admissions; we wait on the fifth floor for a bed; we wait in the room for four hours for the IV nurse. I keep my black leggings and long baggy blue sweater on, then we both climb into the bed. We kiss and hug for a while, then play with the fancy controls.

"I think we need to settle down," Jim says. "Let's do some meditation." He snaps one of Peggy Huddleston's tapes in our player. We cuddle as Peggy's calm voice fills the room. "Take some deep, cleansing breaths. Relax your body. Remember that little door at the bottom of your foot? Open it now, and let—"

Just then, the IV expert finally shows up, sticks me a few times, then plugs me into normal saline solution.

"Why can't I just drink a glass or two of salty water instead of all this rigmarole?" I ask Jim. The nurse tells him to get out of the bed and never cracks a smile. "Put on your pajamas," she says.

Another two hours pass, and no Solu-Medrol. Is this why health insurance costs are soaring two hundred percent a year? We both get raging headaches and decide not to wait any longer to meditate.

"Let's try again," Jim says.

"I'm sure the second we close our eyes and start to breathe deeply they'll come," I say, not quite sure who "they" are. Jim tapes the sign I made on the outside of our door:

> # WE ARE MEDITATING.
> You are welcome to join us.

Sure enough, the absolute minute we close our eyes, another nurse arrives. "Put on your pajamas," she says.

"I never wear pajamas," I say, and she lets it go at that. Jim climbs down from the bed again. She shrugs and announces, as if to the tune of distant trumpets, "It's time to hang your steroids." She shows me the clear five-by-five-inch plastic bag and points to each word as she says: "You are receiving one thousand milligrams of Solu-Medrol."

"This must be the way they avoid giving your krypton to some other patient," I tell Jim, trying to regain my sardonic Superwoman spin while my heart flip-flops.

The nurse hangs the little baggie filled with bright yellow fluid on my IV pole, connects it to the other line that's dripping clear saline into my wrist, adjusts the flow, counts the drops for fifteen seconds, then hands me the call button. "Give me a ring if you feel at all sick, and don't be shy. I'll be right back if you need me." She exits.

My mouth suddenly tastes as if I've been licking the insides of old car bumpers or sucking on rusty nails—no doubt that famed metallic taste Dr. Jaffe mentioned. I pop a grape sour ball in my mouth and offer the bag to Jim. He chooses cherry.

We suck our candies in silence.

I look at Jim and Jim looks at me. Is this all there is? Is this the drug that's supposed to rescue me from Crippledom and KO all those nefarious antibodies that are munching on my myelin? The stuff that can maybe give me heart failure, a psychotic breakdown, or runaway lethal infections? This tiny little baggie of something that looks very suspiciously like . . . the kids' pee-pee? I expected something lurid, red or purple at least. Or a substance that glows in the dark. Or maybe a bag full of tiny black spiders. But this? Spectacularly underwhelming.

"OK, Dad. What does this yellow remind you of? Think diapers. Think potties."

We burst out laughing. Jim almost chokes on his sour ball. I almost pee in my hospital bed. We laugh till we almost fall to the floor. Then we hug each other, still chuckling, and settle down again to meditate. Even with Peggy's calm voice emanating from our tape recorder, we keep breaking into wild spasms of laughter.

Then we settle down for real and go way inside into whatever entirely personal spaces always await each of us in our suddenly spacious inner worlds: places full of peace, and silence, and quiet breathing.

The Woman with Wings is there, waiting for me. She stays with me through that first hospitalization, and through many since, though not all. I'm loathe, even after all these years, to attempt to net Her with words. I only know that Her implicit brightness sustains me in dark times and places; that She consoles and strengthens me even though She never speaks in words. And I know that no matter what happens to my body, She will cherish my soul.

When we open our eyes about twenty minutes later, completely embraced by peace, we're amazed. We didn't hear anyone enter the room, but it's crowded with quiet people. There's the charge nurse who helped me get settled. And the internist who'd referred me to Dr. Lewis, just opening his eyes; he stopped by to wish me good luck and stayed to listen to our tape.

There's the IV nurse, and a nursing assistant who read our sign and stepped in out of curiosity. They all stayed to meditate with us and are just opening their eyes into that sweet silence. It's astonishing to see their faces without the masks of professionalism and fatigue.

They are very beautiful.

The hospitalization isn't so bad, despite our fears. I have wall-to-wall migraines, but we expected them. I can't sleep because of low-key but pervasive agitation, though the meditation helps while I'm awake all night. But I also feel as if lead is being infused into my veins along with the steroids. I feel bulldozed into the bed, under a blanket of iron fatigue more profound than I have ever felt. On one of his daily visits, Dr. Jaffe explains that some people feel this sense of depletion instead of the false energy, and that both are common reactions to steroids. My cheeks puff out like popovers and turn scarlet, then crimson. I have always wanted high color instead of my sallow, freckled pallor. It fools people into believing I'm healthy for the very first time in my life. Go figure.

Dr. Jaffe maintains his dignified, patrician stance, but takes excellent, even tender, care of me. At our behest, Jim's father brings a bottle of merlot for the good doctor's Thanksgiving table. The God of Rheumatology seems quite touched, and we can feel the icy surface melting to reveal the charm underneath.

I have lots and lots of calls and visitors—too many. I will have to learn to ration my visitors to one or two at a time, because "entertaining guests" in the hospital is exhausting. Friends and family shower me with scented soaps, lotions, chocolates, flowers, and lacy lingerie. This grand social event takes place around my bed, when all I want is to shut my leaden lids and cry leaden tears. I'm touched and grateful at this outpouring of love, but I'm in a deep low after the adrenaline of preparation stops pumping. And I'm deeply disappointed when I feel no signs of improvement at the end of day three, even though I knew it would take weeks, even months, for any improvement to manifest itself. If any. If ever. There's only one small sign that these massive doses of steroids affect my body: large swollen glands in my neck and groin that I have had for many years melt like ice cubes by the morning of the third day.

That's it.

I know nerves are very, very slow to heal, if at all, and that my disease might not respond to any treatment. I know. Yet I can't help but hope it might be different. Superwoman crashes and burns forever after the third little baggie of Solu-Medrol is infused. Not one baby step forward.

After I'm discharged, Jim and I sit, gray with fatigue, in the lobby of the hospital. Too tired, for the moment, even to go out and hail a cab, we agree with tears in our eyes that the only happy reason for going to a hospital is to bring home a healthy newborn.

PART 2

A Long Dark Corridor

I learn by going where I have to go.

Theodore Roethke

CHAPTER 7
It Is What It Is

1990

It.

I'm determined to outrun **It**, so I push myself relentlessly.

If I don't talk about **It**, maybe **It** isn't real.

It terrifies me, but I hide my terror from everyone, even my doctors. I hope what remains unsaid will remain unlived.

It causes pain and fatigue past all understanding, but I refuse to rest. I refuse to put my life on hold waiting for someone, somewhere, someday to create the magic bullets that will send It straight to hell. So I try to figure out how to live with **It**.

Meanwhile, new symptoms come calling, the worst being pericarditis: an inflammation of the transparent sac that surrounds the heart. It's almost unbearable when it first arrives in the middle of the night. I wake up feeling as if a sword is plunged into my chest and protruding out of my back. It persists for months, acute pain created by the rub of the thin inflamed tissue against my beating heart. It flares up, then recedes, leaving me short of breath and adding a new kind of pain to the rest, debilitating and frightening. More medications, almost enough to qualify as a small breakfast.

But unless I'm too sick to stand up, I never miss a parents' brunch or teacher's meeting, a school performance or a soccer game for either of

our children. We give carousel birthday parties, swimming birthday parties, and Shea Stadium birthday parties—with *HAPPY BIRTHDAY, ALEX*
or *ANNA* on the blinking scoreboard. And it probably won't surprise you
that I bake, dye, and ice the bright Mets-blue-and-orange cupcakes myself
while everyone else is sleeping. When Alex becomes obsessed with wolves,
we have a wolf birthday party at the carousel in Central Park. The kids play
pin-the-tail-on-the-wolf poster I find at the Museum of Natural History,
using the minimally wolf-like tails I draw and cut out; I trim the birthday
cake with little plastic animals that resemble wolves (they're dogs) and hope
the kids don't notice. Whether I die, end up in a wheelchair, or both, I want
to be sure my kids know how much I love them, and hope they'll someday
understand how hard I try to give them a relatively secure and carefree childhood despite my uncooperative body with its rampaging antibodies.

People ask, "How did you get so strong?" Strong? I'm not. I have no
choice. I push down my terror, grit my teeth, and keep marching. Am I trying to elude my worst nightmares about the future? You bet. Am I trying to
pretend **It** isn't taking over my body? Absolutely. I suspect I'm like a kitten
I once had—she hid her head in a brown paper grocery bag and thought no
one could see her.

My diseases and I are locked in a silent, relentless struggle, and my
overzealous antibodies always win. Pain and numbness crawl relentlessly up
both arms and legs, grip my trunk, and claw at my face. The steroids nearly
drive me crazy—I have moon face, chubby cheeks, gain weight, and suffer
from lack of sleep. Washing walls and alphabetizing my spice shelf while
everybody else sleeps is the least of it. The worst? The steroids don't work.
Dr. Jaffe finally has mercy and tells me to stop taking them.

What's next?

I accept a full-time job at the Bank Street College of Education. I've
worked with the Department of Publications and Media off and on as a
freelance writer and love the people and especially the college's educational
philosophy: child-centered and respectful of young minds; allowing students to develop at their own rates; challenging them with questions even
at the toddler stage. The department is famous for the creative, innovative
multicultural readers they wrote in the 1960s, which were a model of high-
interest, easy-reading materials featuring real children from cities, not the
suburbs—far more interesting than Dick, Jane, and Spot. The Director's job
attracts five hundred applicants, and when I go for my interviews I hide my

cane under my raincoat. I accept the position while I'm in the hospital with
a nasty flare, but I can't resist such an intriguing challenge. My mandate
includes refusing to make schlock even for big bucks, and I'm committed
to creating products that look like dessert but have all the vitamins growing
minds need. We've just moved up to 106th Street and Riverside Drive, and
the College is only six blocks from home. Both children are accepted at the
Bank Street School for Children, right downstairs from my office, so it feels
like winning the lottery. As always, I refuse to let my illness cut off my possibilities. High spirits, however, cannot keep the wolf away from my door.

So I become a secret whore in search of any potential for healing, East-
ern or Western, as long as it doesn't replace or endanger the traditional medical options I need, or seem so woo-woo that I feel foolish or frightened trying it. I use Peggy Huddleston's meditation tapes and keep that little door
in my foot wide open, trying to sweep out my anxiety along with as many
destructive antibodies as I can. I open my soul and, as a profound blessing,
sometimes meet the luminous Woman with Wings near the top of my inner
mountain. A lovely woman I meet through Peggy Huddleston comes to my
apartment now and again in her chauffeured town car. She gently mends my
chakras, the centers of spiritual power in the body, one by one; most vividly,
she helps me imagine a deep indigo ribbon flowing out of my throat like
a song. The Reverend Fanny Erickson, Founder of the Riverside Church
Healing, Health, and Wellness Program, visits me at home for the laying on
of hands; I am astonished at the intense and soothing heat generated by her
gentle touch. These encounters bolster my spirit, and I feel consecrated in
the presence of these luminous souls. I never tell my doctors or more than
a few close friends about these ministrations. In fact, I never tell anybody
much of anything about my physical, spiritual, or mental state.

And so I walk down the gathering years of illness as down a long dark
lonely corridor.

But I suffer beneath this can't-quit, won't-stop, gotta-be-a-hero stance.
My doctors may notice this madness, but never comment on it. They focus
on disease, not illness or its impact on me, my family, and my career. After
asking whether I'm still working full-time and nodding at the title of my
newest children's book, they quickly go on to list symptoms and medications. They're so busy discussing treatment schedules and nerve studies that

there's no time to talk about how I feel about living in double jeopardy and constant pain. Since I rarely discuss my illness and its impact on my life with anyone —a point of (false?) pride—it would have been comforting to discuss it occasionally with my doctors. But they don't ask, and I don't tell.

During this period, Dr. Lewis sends me a copy of the letter she writes to my insurance company to shame them into paying for the expensive drugs and treatments I must have. She lists various types of "itis-es"—inflammatory diseases I don't even realize I have. Then she writes, "Despite these symptoms and all the time Ms. Schecter spends in the hospital, she continues to work full time. This is evidence of her true grit. The least you can do is pay for the drugs that keep her functioning." The letter brings me to tears. I keep it close at hand, cherishing the words "true grit" so I can retrieve them when I feel especially worn out and low. Much to my own misfortune, it never occurs to me to seek any solace. I continue to believe that I am doing Jim a favor by not "complaining" about how I feel.

Then two friends—powerful and talented women who have illustrious full-time careers living with full-time, major diseases—tell me about a medical doctor who actually talks to them about coping with illness: one who knows how to treat pain—which my other doctors, skilled as they are, seem to know very little about.

Dr. Eric Cassell is in his mid-sixties, in practice over forty years, attending physician at New York Hospital, Clinical Professor of Public Health at Cornell University Medical College, author of roughly a dozen books on subjects ranging from medical ethics to the nature of primary care medicine, to how to talk to patients, to care of the dying. By day, he teaches in the medical school and runs a busy medical practice as an internist; by night, he streaks to the outer limits of modern medicine, using hypnosis and trance work to help severely ill or terminal patients deal more effectively and serenely with their diseases and the side-effects of their treatments. He not only helps his patients learn how to die, but how to live. I'm about to become one of those people.

When I call to make our first appointment, he explains in detail how he works. "I work only late at night after my office hours end, and I use hypnosis and trance to enable people to think about illness in new ways. I know it works, and my special patients tell me it does. So—is this a leap of faith you're willing to take?"

"I am," I tell him. "I'm especially interested in learning how to cope with pain. But—I'm not sure whether hypnosis will work for me."

"Well, let's give it a try, shall we? I think you'll do just fine."

My first appointment takes place near midnight at Dr. Cassell's East Side office—a weird hour for me as I'm usually asleep shortly after the kids conk out, around nine. It feels eerie to be in a medical office when the phones are silent and the waiting room is empty, but it also feels promising: I've never had the full attention of a physician for more than five or ten minutes. As he ushers me past several empty exam rooms toward his shadowy office way in the back of the large medical establishment, I feel a stroke of panic. What if this guy's a maniac? Am I in trouble, all alone with him? These worries dissolve the moment he turns, gives me a warm grin and says, "Feel weird all alone with me in this empty shadowy office? No need to be afraid, I'm perfectly safe. And I am very glad to meet you, Ms. Ellen."

Dr. Cassell guides me into his overcrowded, very dark office, lit by one low-watt lamp. The only other source of light is a large blinking computer that dominates his desk. Shelves crowded with books stacked any which-way overflow onto the floor, and files and more books are stacked every-where. He points me to an ugly black Naugahyde Lay-Z-Boy, but before I sit, I shake the bony hand of a full-size human skeleton that's hanging in a corner near the door. It feels droll rather than creepy.

"George keeps me humble," he says, nodding at the skeleton, and I can tell it's not a joke. "Want something to drink? Coke? Diet Coke? Water?"

"Diet Coke, please, Dr. Cass—"

"Eric," he interrupts, "just Eric. I know I'm a doctor; I don't need people to tell me all the time. Besides, I don't want all that white coat stuff getting in the way of our work together."

He pops open our Diet Cokes, and I sit down in the chair, which could hold two of me. Then he clips a tiny lavaliere mike on the collar of my yellow linen blazer. "I record all our sessions, so you can take the tapes home and listen to them again."

It probably protects him from all kinds of accusations from crazies, I think.

Taking sips of his drink, he starts asking me about my life. He wants to know about my family, my work, the people I love, my sex life, my heart, my soul, and how I feel about all of it. He listens intently to my answers, long fingers making a church, door, and steeple. I know he's listening not only to the words, but to what's between and behind them. I sense he can tell when I come close to tears but push them down. He asks me specifically about my pain, where it is and how intense, and how I feel about it, which none of my other doctors ever do. One question follows another in a gentle voice, slightly wheezy but melodic, with the narrow bite of western Pennsylvania in there somewhere.

I study him while he studies me. At first glance, Eric could look like a regular doctor: tall, rangy, a bit of a paunch, bent in the shoulders. Suit and shirt tasteful but rumpled, knot in his tie loose, creeping off-center and tangling with his stethoscope. Strong nose; generous, smiley mouth; whitish hair fluffing up like ostrich feathers. But when I look more closely, the resemblance to any-old-doctor ends. His eyes behind those smudged glasses are merry and kind, not distracted. He looks right at me, and it isn't once over lightly. He isn't rushed or looking at the time. He seems deeply interested—in how I move, where I hurt; in what my body language and expressions reveal or try to hide.

"Good, very helpful," he says when I finish telling him about my wonderful kids and how much I love Jim, how much I love my job creating all kinds of media for children based on the philosophy of Bank Street College, how I almost can't believe I'm paid for writing, I love it so much; how many resources I have for coping with my diseases—putting the best spin on everything, of course.

He leans forward. "And what would you tell me if I asked what you want, personally, to obtain in your life? Not in terms of Jim or your kids, but just for you? We'll be working together to reveal some of the most profound meanings in your life—your relationship to your illness; to pain; to your childhood. So what is it that you want from your life—just for you?"

It comes to mind right away, but I hesitate, not wanting to sound . . . pretentious.

"G'won," he says; "you can't be shy here. Your heart, your soul, your body—the all of you will occupy us."

Hell, I think, I don't want to hide behind fear here: it's a chance to grow. I want to be who I am, me—and my diseases. "Well, it came to me right away. In a snap. I'm . . . not sure you'll understand, though. And I never told anyone. I want—to gain a heart of wisdom."

He sits straight up in his squeaky desk chair.

"I think it's in a psalm, or maybe Proverbs . . ." I say. "I'm not sure where I heard it . . ."

"Psalm ninety," he says with no hesitation.

"You know it?"

"I do. Go on." He leans back again.

"Well, it's haunted me, this idea, since I've gotten sick. Since Dr. Lewis—Dr. Linda Lewis up at Neuro—said" tears well up—"the worse case scenario is that—I could die. Those words keep rolling around inside me. It's something like, 'Teach us to number our days, so we may gain a heart of wisdom.'"

He looks at me, dead serious. "Ellen, dozens and dozens of people have sat where you're sitting, many of them dying, all of them with serious illness. They have wanted fame, wealth, more time—a lot of them want more time, until I try to help them understand how to cherish the time they have.

"But not one of them want what you want." He rolls his chair over to me and envelops my icy hands in his large warm ones. "Let's work toward that together, shall we? And, along the way, we'll also help you learn how to be sick without suffering; and how to deal with the pain I see all through your body, though you're pretty clever about trying to hide it; and how to live with your illness as a smart young woman instead of a fearful child.

"Oh, and that incredible piece of wisdom? It's Scripture, Psalm ninety, verse twelve: 'So teach us to number our days, that we may gain a heart of wisdom.' I think that's right.

"Now shall we get to work?"

That first night, I discover it takes me ten seconds to go into a trance.

Eric pushes *Record* on the tape player, and says, "Okay, Ellen, lie back in that chair—you can push it all the way back and put your feet up, that's right, just like that. Now close your eyes. You'll find this is really quite easy, really quite breezy, all we do is count to ten, not even back again, and whoosh! You'll be in a trance." Eric's voice becomes more melodic and playful as he eases me into the trance. I close my eyes as he speaks, even before he counts backwards from ten to one.

"Now, loosen the muscles between your shoulders till they're soft and fluffy as skeins of wool . . . and loosen the muscles between your ribs, shedding that suit of armor you usually wear around your ribs for protection: you don't need protection here. And take a deep, relaxing breath to see how wonderful it is to breathe when your chest is no longer bound by that corset of tension . . . and try to feel some relief from your pericarditis. It shouldn't pain you so much now, when you're in a trance."

"Now loosen the muscles of your face and jaw, that's right, especially the muscles around your eyes, which can be tight like the drawstrings on a little purse, or loose as can be—loosen them now. That's right. I can see the tension leaving your face.

"Now find your own way to go deeper into your trance." While Eric's chair squeaks as he takes a sip of Coke and sighs to relieve his own tension, I do a swan dive off the back of my brain, my own way of disconnecting from the "real" world, and . . . there I am, in a trance: peaceful, relaxed, but totally conscious of everything going on inside and outside the first-floor medical office on 82nd Street and York Avenue. I can still smell alcohol swabs and hear taxi horns bray outside the window, the snoring old air conditioner, Eric's wheezy breaths. But I feel myself let go of tensions I thought were with me forever.

FAQ? Yes, I can do anything in a trance that I normally do—drink Diet Coke, cook dinner, write a script, swim laps. We're not talking about Svengali here, so forget everything you ever heard about hypnosis. Our work has nothing to do with gypsies or crystals, tick-tocking pocket-watches, or lifting your hand to prove you're "under." It's just tranquil; relaxed; wide awake.

"Okay, now we're ready to work," he says kindly. "How about we explore your general feelings about being sick, hmm?"

"Well . . . I hate having these diseases, but I don't consider myself sick. I don't even like to talk about it, actually."

"But isn't that why you're here? So we can talk?"

"Mm—yes. But I want you to know from the get-go that I'm doing very well. I work full time, and take really good care of my kids, and I try not to pay much attention to being . . . well . . ."

"Sick? Even when you walk that way? I can see it hurts."

A scalding blush sweeps over me.

"Why are you so embarrassed?" he asks gently when I don't answer.

"I don't want anybody to know," I whisper. "If no one knows, then maybe **It** isn't. . . quite . . . real."

Tears prick under my eyelids, so I clench them closed.

"What's so wrong about having a disease? Two, even?"

"I hate it. I don't want people to be sorry for me. I don't want it to change me. I love my life just the way it is. I love my career, and I don't want to give it up. I'm trying to be a great mother, and I want Jim to lo–"

"Whoa. Who says you can't be a great wife, mother, and writer—and be sick?"

I don't answer. He's gotten to pay-dirt in less than five minutes.

"Are you afraid you can't hold it together? That it's getting harder and harder?"

"Maybe. Yes. Maybe." The tears push out. I turn my head and try to wipe them away surreptitiously on my sleeve, but my mascara leaves tell-tale blots on the yellow. "I don't want anyone to think I'm weak. I never, ever want to be seen as weak. Be weak."

"Is that why you're hiding those tears? Tissue?" He holds out a box.

I nod yes so he won't hear tears in my voice; so big sobs won't take over. But I take the tissues. I discover I can stay in the trance if I open my eyes and blow my nose.

"Well, when you work with me, girlie, tears are a sign of strength. You'll see me cry, too, and I'm a medical daktuh . . a he-man. To me, tears are a sign that you're being honest with yourself—and me."

"Please don't call me 'girlie.'"

"Ah. And I assume babe, missus, missy, chick, lacy lady, and all like no-menclature are likewise off limits?"

"Yes," I say, snapping the bait. "But I, in turn, promise not to call you pig, fat pig, male chauvinist and other like nomenclature—as long as you desist."

"Fine, I stand corrected, sweethe – Ms. Ellen."

"Terms of endearment are not out of the question, Dr. Cassell."

"Eric to you." He sighs. "OK, Ellen, let's forget this nonsense and work. Let's try something new to you. While you're in a trance, let's go back to the time when you first learned to hide your tears. All that you remember will be absolutely real. But instead of just talking about it, you'll go there. And I'll be right here to protect you. Are you ready?"

I think for a moment, then nod. We both take deep breaths.

Comforted by Eric's presence, at the snap of his fingers . . .

I am five years old and in Children's Hospital—a new and scary place, yet it feels as if I've been there for days and days. When I wake up, it's visiting hours. The ward fills up with mommies and daddies, grandmas and grandpas. But where's my mommy?

I wait and wait, but she doesn't come. Johnny's mommy comes over from the next bed and offers me cookies, but she doesn't count—she's not mine. I curl up under my covers so nobody sees that I have to cry. The big mean nurse, Miss Oliver, squeaks over on her white shoes.

"Your mother just called, Ellen. She will not be coming to see you today."

"Tonight?"

"No. She's very tired and cannot make the long trip from your home."

Home.

Just thinking of Mommy putting a bowl of red Jell-O on our white kitchen table makes my heavy tears spill over.

"Now don't start crying. Have some pity for Mother. She'll come tomorrow."

Miss Oliver turns like a soldier and squeaks away. I want to smash her white cap that looks like a cupcake, but no cake inside.

I pull the covers over my head and make-pretend I'm under a white-sheet tent in my very own bed at home. I hug my pink calico elephant Mommy sewed and stuffed for me. I pretend Mommy's climbing upstairs to read me a story and tuck me in. But I know she's not coming. Not all the way till tomorrow. I'm alone by myself. All lonely.

I cry all night, every time I wake up. The little boy beside me with the red tube in his arm shivers and calls his mommy all night, too.

"Coldy, coldy," he moans; "Mama, come," he wails. "Mama. Come." But no mommies come, just nurses and doctors. Then a doctor unhooks his red tube, covers the boy's face with his blankets, and wheels his whole bed away.

Why does he stop shivering? Why is he so still? I cry more, but now I'm afraid to put any covers over my face.

My mommy doesn't come the next day, either. It takes two whole tomorrows till she comes back. By then, I learn to cry myself to sleep so nobody hears me. By then, I'm so tired of waiting that I don't care, even when she finally hugs and kisses me.

I forget how to care.

I open my eyes. Eric is watching me with pain on his face.

"Good work, Ellen," he says. "You took us right back to the advent of your 'tears equal weakness' equation as the age of what—six?"

"Five, at Children's Hospital in Philadelphia." I wipe my eyes, glad to be back in the present.

"And why were you there?"

"I kept having stomach pains."

"And Mommy didn't come because she was tired."

Tears spill again. "That's what she said."

"Damn her," Eric says. "Such a hard, pointless lesson. It would have been so easy to comfort you. But can you think about how counterproductive it is for a woman with major disease—and small children—to live with a no-tears policy? Why do you think you've nixed tears, my dear?"

Now I let the tears roll freely down my cheeks. "I think I'm afraid. . . that if I start to cry, I may never stop." My tissue shreds but the tears keep flowing.

"I can help you with that," Eric says. "I can help you love your tears as real and true and healing.

"But please believe me, Ellen. Until I can help you deal with your present illness as a woman, without a child's misunderstandings, I cannot teach you how to be sick without suffering. And I would so love to help you do that. It's the only way you can gain the freedom of knowing that your illness is what it is: nothing less—but nothing more."

CHAPTER 8
The Body Speaks

1994

"GO, BULLETS! GO, ALEX, GO! BUT—WATCH! WATCH BEHIND YOU—"

Be careful how you yell, I warn myself.

My bladder's full of all that coffee I drank to get going so early this Saturday morning—and to keep warm on this nippy October day. Hope I can make it through this game. I hate to miss a minute. I shiver into my scarf and wrap it tighter as the wind whips off the Hudson right into my face. This must be the coldest soccer field in Riverside Park, but the day is perfect: flawless sky, blazing gold and pumpkin and scarlet leaves.

Now a feeling surges up that has little to do with soccer-mom pride. I often feel it when we watch our kids play sports, win or lose. Tangled, incomplete, lovely phrases from "Fern Hill," the poem by Dylan Thomas, well up in my mind. There they are, I think—"young and easy, green and carefree . . . on the fields of praise . . . in the sun that is young once only . . ."

Coltish and gangly, the boys run and play with such innocence and abandon; though I suspect my son isn't completely carefree. Both my children know fear. They've been brushed by the shadow of losing me, even though we rarely discuss the Blue Hippopotamus of Illness that pushed into our apartment years ago and radically changed our lives. It moved with us, of course, from 72nd Street up to Riverside Drive and

106th, and takes up just as much emotional room. Maybe more.

"Go, Silver Bullets, keep it up," I scream. It's hard to contain myself—our team is two goals up, and they have a chance to win. The Barracudas are tough to beat, but—"Hey," I grab Jim's arm, "did you see that?" He's linesman today, running up and down the sideline with the red flag, but he stops beside me just in time to see Alex kick the ball right into the goal. Beautiful.

"Yay, Alex!" we yell, dancing up and down, hugging other parents—and that's when I know I have to head home right away, even though we're only in the first half—that, or I'll pee in my pants. "See you later, sweetie," I say, pecking Jim's cheek. "Gotta go, and you know what I mean. Please apologize to Alex?"

"OK, I will, sorry, see you later." Jim is off already, running with his flag.

It's just over two years since my diagnosis. I started tripping over my own feet maybe two months ago, but my walls of denial are sturdy. Now my body suddenly feels so tired that the path along the edge of the soccer field looks endless.

As I trudge toward the distant Riverside Park exit at 108th Street, my left leg feels heavy, more and more like a foreign object—Captain Ahab's peg leg, perhaps. I start to limp so badly I have to use not just my cane—which has become my constant companion, but the backs of park benches, railings, and the water bubbler to push myself ahead. I start to pant harder than the joggers speeding past me.

Part of it is panic: Can I make it home in time? I can see our brown brick apartment building soaring above the trees at 106th and Riverside, one block—one vertical block—away. It seems as distant as the Chrysler Building over on the East Side. By this point, my left foot seems to be dragging. I begin to burn with shame and a strange guilt.

As I struggle, time gear-shifts into super-slow-motion. Each brilliant autumn leaf twirls into my path with exquisite grace—achingly beautiful and far removed from my escalating panic. To help me keep moving forward, I will myself to cherish those leaves: to name their colors precisely—crimson, honey-gold, nutmeg, scarlet, pumpkin. Twenty minutes later, I pull myself to the top of the stairs at 106th Street, then into our building elevator and into our apartment, just in time to crawl to the toilet in a cold sweat.

I get an emergency appointment the following Monday with Dr. Lewis, who gives me a careful exam then scrawls a prescription on her pad with particular ferocity. When she hands it across the desk, it says "FAO."

"A spaceship?" I ask.

"A Foot-Ankle Orthotic. You've got a foot drop."

Doctor-talk for what I felt—the muscles in my left foot and ankle are no longer strong enough to pick up my foot properly.

"The brace'll keep you from tripping over your toes and knocking your front teeth out," she continues, with her usual mince-no-words approach that I usually appreciate. I'm not so sure this time. "My husband has one— post-polio syndrome. Nothing, really. With your prairie skirts and jeans, nobody'll notice. It'll just make walking easier. But you've gotta see Doug Ey, best man in the brace business."

She hands me his number, snaps another predatory-style clip around my expanding file and stands, presumably satisfied that she can do something specific to help me.

"Come back in a couple of months so I can check your progress. This should help a great deal. Sorry I didn't do it for you sooner."

We shake hands as usual, but this time I don't feel like thanking her. I'm more than a bit annoyed at how cavalier she is about my downward skid into a world I don't want to enter; a step I feel turns me into more of a cripple than I want to be. Somehow I "forget" to schedule another appointment, having little appetite for returning so she can duly note the stages of my downhill slide. Feh.

But I do make an appointment with the brace genius as soon as I get to my office: I don't want to knock out my front teeth and add cosmetic insult to neurological injury.

Later that week, wearing my best lace-up ankle boots and a bravely colored "prairie" dress, I wait in East Side Prosthetics on Madison Avenue for Doug Ey. Who could imagine this grotesque establishment tucked in among all the glamorous boutiques and salons? I sit tight as a fist, chilled by an array of colorful life-sized posters glorifying gorgeous young athletes skydiving and hang-gliding like multi-colored butterflies, slaloming down snow-covered peaks—all with absent arms and legs replaced by stick-like metal prostheses. They seem to yell, "I'm amputated and I'm proud." Ugh.

I want to whack myself for complaining about getting a little FAO when these dazzling young people are winning medals for bravery while missing crucial body parts. I've never skied on a black-diamond trail or jumped out of an airplane, and probably never will . . . yet here I am, whining over (almost) nothing, while these nearly-perfect poster people are performing feats of athletic prowess after someone cut off an arm or leg—in some cases, one of each. The Technicolor posters are so vivid I almost expect to see my breath in frosty plumes. To top if off, the athletes' quotes say things like, "I'll never give up skiing, and my prosthesis keeps me going where I want to go."

And here I sit, four limbs intact, trying not to cry and rend my clothes because I need a teeny "assistive device" to keep from tripping over my toes on perfectly flat sidewalks. I decide to take a cue from the posters and act ever so bright and cheerful when the brace genius finally appears and leads me toward the inner sanctum.

Oh, dear. More posters of brave but mutilated athletes, many signed with personal messages of gratitude to the very same Doug who now asks me to sit in a chair with a foot-rest just like the ones in shoe shops. There also are quite a few smaller photographs signed by celebrities I never knew wore prostheses—including a predictably large selection from the Kennedy son whose leg was amputated because of cancer. There he is, slaloming down-hill, wind surfing, para-sailing, and so on. Those bloody Kennedys—can't they ever do anything wrong?

Doug is a big, beefy guy, quite gentle, very matter-of-fact about the brace and fitting. He's clearly been through this many times and no doubt sees right through my stiff, chirpy, nauseating bravado. Fortunately, he's all business and not overtly kind, or I might have to do the tears thing. He takes a long while to fit an extremely unattractive, phlegm-colored polyurethane device on my weak-but-still-attached left leg and foot.

It has a plastic footprint a bit larger than my real foot, and continues up the back of my heel, splitting above the Achilles tendon into a wishbone-shape so it won't touch the ever-painful biopsy site. The two flat pieces of plastic, each about an inch wide, continue to rise all the way up my calf to just below my knee, where they meet another two-inch-wide horizontal plastic band, which curves around the entire back half of my leg. A wide band of Velcro, adjustable for comfort, wraps around the front of my leg to grip onto itself. Once fastened, the band and brace make a complete circle that will keep me from tripping by holding my entire foot and ankle at a firm ninety degree angle to my lower leg.

Ingenious. And hideous. Worse than I'd expected. My heart contracts into a limp raisin of disappointment. My lips begin to tremble from too much forced smiling as the Incredible Mutilated Athletes in the Technicolor posters still perform their feats of prowess. Doug doesn't seem to notice their heroism or my cowardice.

"Are you going to be wearing your brace with a boot like this?" Doug asks. The b-word makes me cringe.

"Yes," I manage.

"Okay, put it on then, and tell me how it feels."

"It feels fine," I say, lacing my boot with wooden fingers, "just great. Thanks a lot, Doug." I start gathering my things to leave. I can't wait to escape this weird, unwelcome world.

"Whoa," Doug says, "this takes a while. I have to make sure the brace fits comfortably. Get up and walk around the room a few times. See if it rubs or feels funny. I want to make sure you're completely comfortable."

Comfortable? I stagger obediently to my feet, feeling for the first time how strange it is to have one foot immobilized in the shape of a golf club. I grab for my cane and start walking—hobbling—around the stuffy little room, feeling so much more crippled than I ever did before that I want to lie down on the floor and sob. Or, better, to take off the goddamn brace, throw it against those accusing posters, rip them with my cane, bolt from the shop, and never return.

Instead, I obediently take a few turns around the small room, barely paying attention to where the brace does or doesn't feel right.

Because something strange is compelling my attention: a feeling of deep, physical insult surges through my body, almost knocking me down. An overwhelming feeling of pain—and something else—is flowing through my body, emanating from the mouth of my cervix. I know it's my cervix because of childbirth; it's the same place deep inside where the waves of pain began as my cervix opened and opened to let my babies out. But what's happening there now? And why?

I take a few more steps, trying to concentrate on how the brace fits . . . and as soon as I even think the b-word, there it is again: a contraction half-way like labor, halfway like the beginning of an orgasm, yet with no pleasur-able pay-off. Is this some profound physical corroboration of the wound my psyche is feeling because of this brace?

Again. Is this a humiliation so deep, so profound, that it's striking me in the very center of my female self? That's what it feels like. A wound to my sense of my self as a woman—no longer a healthy woman—and now a discernibly crippled woman, because it's impossible to walk anywhere near like a normal person with this thing on my foot.

It suddenly occurs to me: as bad as it feels wearing this "assistive device" in this odd little inner sanctum for the mutilated and crippled, I'll soon have to walk up Madison Avenue dragging this social stigma with me; with all those stares, all those ugly words slapped like labels on top of the real and original me: me and this—no, my—brace.

And my cane, don't forget the cane: visible signs and symbols of—helplessness, weakness, old age. Which should be decades away at my age. All symbols of can't: can't walk without a cane, can't walk without a brace. Branding me as a crip—

Whoops! Is that an orgasm? Should I laugh? Or cry? Both?

"Stop that," I silently tell my body; "please behave. Please.Be.Quiet."

"How does it feel, Ellen? Does it feel good?" Doug asks. "Does it hurt?"

What? How could he know—?

The brace. He means the brace, says the Rational Ellen.

"Oh, it's fine, Doug, really fine, it feels perfect." And, pretending to look at my watch, trying to still my body with attention to details, "Listen, I have to go now."

"Walk a little more, and let me watch you," Doug insists gently.

Watch me? Why do all these bloody people want to watch you sink into disability all the time? Neurologists, rheumatologists, physical therapists, brace people—just when I need to be invisible, they all want to watch me hobble.

Get out of my face, brace man, I want to snarl. Git. Just git.

At the same time I want to lay my head on his big broad chest while he gives me a very big, very gentle hug; a hug I can never ask for or get. I'm not used to this, I want to sob; I don't want this to be happening to me. I'm not brave like the poster people. I have no desire to soar off cliffs like a human butterfly. I will never, ever jump out of an airplane. I'm just an ordinary barnyard chicken; all I want to do is walk down the street like a normal person. Please: take back this brace and the reason I need it.

But of course I can never say any of that.

Instead, I practice a kind of tripod waddle on the faded blue carpet blotched with coffee stains, bald spots, maybe tears. The pinch and rub of the ugly plastic makes me feel sorry for horses. This must be what a bit feels like in a colt's mouth, I think; something hard and unyielding that doesn't belong there.

I want to run out of here and hide the brace forever in the back of my closet.

Then I start to think about why I'm doing this. I don't want to be helpless. I don't want to be at the mercy of my weakening body. I don't want a five-minute walk out of Riverside Park to take half an hour. I don't want to miss any more soccer games. So I grit my teeth and try to walk as normally as I can with this gruesome thing on my leg. And I notice, aside from the weird sensations and the awkwardness of my never-bending foot, that it's easier to take steps. Maybe it will help. Maybe it will get me where I want to go.

"Good," Doug says. "Now you're getting it. Sure it doesn't hurt anywhere?"

"Well, a little bit, here, on my ankle where the wishbone thingie separates. And here on this side. And here, at the bottom."

Doug helps me take off my boot and I point to the hurting places. Then he takes off the brace, heats it up in the back room, and molds it more closely to fit me. When I put it on again, I can feel the difference. For better or worse, it feels more like mine.

This time Doug lets me go, though I can tell he's still suspicious, that I'm not giving him time to fit it properly. "Come back in a week so I can check it—sooner if you feel any discomfort." He tilts his big shaggy head and gives me a gimlet look. "Most people come back four or five times, Ellen; it takes time to get the fit perfect. Once it's right, you won't notice you're wearing the brace. Except, it'll make life easier for you."

I'm busy lacing up my boot.

"That's why you're wearing it: to make life easier," he repeats, "to make it easier for you to walk. And it will."

"Really?" He does get my attention with that.

"Really," he says, as my eyes finally meet his. "I promise."

I breathe for the first time in forty-five minutes.

"Now don't walk more than five blocks today. See where it's uncomfortable. If it doesn't feel right, come back tomorrow. It'll only take me ten or fifteen minutes to make an adjustment, and I'll always make time for you. If it's fine, go ten blocks tomorrow. Then fifteen the next day."

"Oh, I'll go as far as I can," I say, trying to stare down the blond hang-glider with the missing lower left leg. "I like to challenge myself. I don't know about jumping out of airplanes, but five blocks? Piece of chocolate cake."

"Five blocks is enough," he says, frowning. "Don't be a martyr." Then, probably sensing I'll ignore him, he shrugs and says, "See you next week."

I limp out into the sunlight on Madison Avenue and awkwardly try to join the flow of pedestrians on the sidewalk, half-waiting for everyone to turn, point, and yell in unison, "Cripple! Cripple!"

They don't, of course, though I do notice a few people shoot sideways glances of pity and, sometimes, obvious distaste behind their Christian Dior sunglasses. As I watch the fashionable crowds rush past me, the overwhelming sensation of my cervix opening and closing sweeps over me again. At Madison and 63rd. If they only knew, I think with a sly inward giggle. All they see is a crippled woman, and here I am having a delightful bit of an orgasm in broad daylight. I chuckle again. But I'm still puzzled. What the hell is going on in here?

I lurch into Central Park, vaguely keeping Doug's five block limit in mind, and sit on a bench with my head tilted to catch the forbidden sunshine. Lupus, you know. Sun is the enemy. I decide the hell with it. I deserve a treat. I love sunshine.

I close my eyes partway then peer at the rainbows on my eyelashes as I think serious psychoanalytic thoughts, along with some of the ideas I've learned from Eric about listening to my body. These are the feelings of childbirth: of my cervix opening and contracting. So perhaps I'm giving birth to my new self as a disabled woman. And, yes, now I remember: I had the same sensations after the nerve-muscle biopsy when I had to use crutches, another episode of disability. Then, again, when I had to start using the cane more or less permanently. It makes sense that I'd be giving birth to a new sense of myself now, with this new, concrete symbol of disability.

But there's more. I think my body is also reminding me that I am still a woman—a youngish-looking, and dare I say still an attractive one, despite all this illness. I think perhaps my body's reminding me it is still a source of pleasure, not just of pain and humiliation. Good. I get the message, gratefully.

As I sit in silence, eyes still closed, I hear Eric's voice: "What else is your body telling you?" And, "Listen to the body's wisdom." And, "Don't be afraid of tears."

A deep sadness floods through me. It is time to accept that my illness is now more severe; that I need to adopt new ways to cope with a physical reality I had so dreaded, but is now upon me: that a cane and a brace are no longer just symbols but necessities.

I open myself to other feelings I've been pushing down, focusing on the brace instead of them: my fears about the future and what will become of me; the new losses of glamour and strength the brace signifies; the fear Jim and the kids will feel when they see this concrete symbol of the fact that I'm getting worse. As I face these deep sorrows, feel these realities and the pain they bring, I listen compassionately to my body and its losses. Rather than turning away, I let my body speak. I listen.

The contractions slow, then stop.

But the New Ellen is not quite finished.

As I sit there in Central Park, eyes clenched, I take a chance and allow myself to touch bottom, to grieve my lost self. It's terrible to be sick. It brings constant and relentless loss. I hate it. I let a dark red, gargantuan rage crash up out of the Pit where I bury my feelings, and explode into the sunlight. I hate this damned disease. I want to rip it out of my body. But I can't. I can't do anything about it.

Except—I can. I'm doing it. I'm mourning my losses; palpating the dimensions of my rage instead of burying it. And I know I can do something even more powerful. I can decide how to step forward out of this moment into the next.

I take a long, quavery breath. I open and wipe my eyes, and look up. All around me, in a day vibrating with fall colors, men and women and children run, skip, and hop; walk dogs, ride bikes, and hold hands; argue, smooch, explain, and giggle; read the *New York Times,* and fill in the crossword puzzle.

I watch life burst and rustle all around me—sunlight golden and luscious as honey, leaves scarlet and nutmeg and pumpkin, just as they were that day at Alex's soccer game. This time, I revel in them.

I feel a borrowed exuberance just seeing and remembering all that motion. And I'm suddenly but unmistakably flooded with a fierce joy that simply will not allow me to be dragged down into that deep Pit, but instead pushes me up and up into the light.

CHAPTER 9
Body Language

1994

BY THE TIME ERIC AND I MEET AGAIN, I'VE CONQUERED WALKING WITH my FAO, enhanced its benefits by another trip to the brace genius, and downplayed its risks by tinkering with my wardrobe. While he fetches our Diet Cokes and pins on my mike, I make important small talk. "Well, Jim has done it again—surprised me with his tact and lovingkindness." Tears come again. "These are happy tears, Eric."

"Yes?"

"Soon after he learned about my brace, he came home and threw dozens of colorful brochures on our bed that said, 'Welcome to Greece.' He's taking me there for my birthday. Do you think I can do it, Eric?"

"You're the one who keeps telling me you can do anything you want."

I take a deep breath. "I can. And if I have to do it more slowly, I'll still do it."

"Good, gi—uh, woman. Now let's work." He counts me down into a trance, and I'm right there, relaxed and waiting.

"Let's set out on one of our most essential adventures, Ellen: reconnecting you to your body; the body you cannot escape; the one I think you try to reject because it's now so often a source of frustration rather than an instrument of your will. Sound right?"

"Sad but true," I sigh.

"Is it? Has the body you once loved and cherished, decorated and displayed, flaunted and flirted with, become one giant disappointment?"

"Yes." I realize my body—that slim, tanned, 101 pounds of fun, the one I love to dance and make love in, dress stylishly in capes and jewels, velvets and silks; in boots of Spanish leather, spike heels, ballet slippers, or no shoes at all—is gone.

"Yes, it's true, Eric. This body Jim and I make beautiful love with; which miraculously gave us our two perfect babies—that body has been stolen by disease and replaced with this one, which hurts, and makes me stumble and look like a cripple, and I'm beginning to hate it."

I can feel a combination of rage and regret gathering in my body.

"Except, you're stuck with it, Ellen. No matter how much you like to believe you exist separate and independent of your physical self, you can't. You're wed to your body from first breath to last, and there's nothing like an illness—or torture, starvation, or those thousand ills flesh is heir to—to make that fact indisputably clear."

He rolls his chair toward me and leans in close. "In fact, when one is fit and able, it's far easier to enjoy a casual and thoughtless relationship with the body—to maintain the illusion of mind-body dichotomy. It's one of those luxuries only the well can afford. You say, 'Walk!' and it walks. You command 'Eat!' and it does, along with all the wonderful details of biting, sipping, chewing, swallowing, digesting, and eliminating."

I feel sharp regret, remembering how I ran up and down stairs, often two at a time—because I was late, or just because I could.

"But. As soon as something goes wrong with just one of those finely tuned systems, you're slammed right back inside your body with the gates locked tight. Does this ring a bell?"

"Too many bells. The whole idea of it makes me feel furious . . . and hopeless."

"Why don't we use the trance to help us work with some of those bells?"

I sigh. "I don't really want to, Eric. I know the examples. I live them, and I don't really want to go into them again."

"But I'm right here with you to soften the irritation. And maybe we can figure out how you can do something about them. I'll get us some more Diet Cokes while you think about it, okay?"

He comes back. "Okay, I'll do it," I say, "but I'm not happy about it."

"It's called resistance, my dear. But you are very brave and flexible enough to give it a try." He wheels close and kisses my forehead. "And I mean that: very brave."

He turns the tape over and pushes record. "Now, where should we go?"

"Well . . . it seems that no matter where I turn, I keep running up against another manifestation of my own mind-body trap." I run through a handful of infuriating examples in my mind. "Okay, here's one. I close my eyes, go into a trance, and I'm there:

"I'm riding the M104 Broadway bus uptown to pick Alex and Annie up from school. Wonder of wonders, I'm on time; I even have a seat. But I'm in secret agony. Because of the demyelination of my nerves—no insulation—the vibrations of the motor drill through my feet, up my legs, into my thighs, and smack into my spine—as if some Neo-Nazi concocted an invisible torture just for me.

I grip the chrome rail in front of me with both hands, which creates pain in my hands and arms, and try to concentrate on the pleasure I'll see on my kids' faces when I surprise them in the delicious hubbub of the school lobby. But the painful vibrations distort those happy images like snow on a TV screen.

"Damn!" I want to yell, "I hate you, body." I want to throw my arms and legs out the window. I want my real body back. I squeeze my eyes to cut off the bitter bite of tears.

✵

Here's another one:

Jim and the kids and I are packed into our Rent-A-Wreck, headed for our August rental cottage in the Berkshires. We're all singing "Sugarpie, honeybunch, You know that I love you..." as loud as we can, to a tape of "Motown Sounds of the Sixties." The constant vibrations from the car are even more painful than last year, but I plan ahead. I'm using self-hypnosis and a double dose of Demerol to introduce layers of mental cotton-batting between me and the road. And I have pillows under both feet.

Jim's hi-jinx keep the kids and me in stitches as he morphs from the Big Bopper to Marvin Gaye to Stevie Wonder to Diana Ross and all four Supremes, moving from deep bass to ultra-falsetto in his utterly tuneless warble. But when he becomes a Teenage Mutant Ninja Turtle zooming his Turtle-Mobile hither and thither on the empty country road, I laugh so hard that the combination of nerve damage and pain medication makes me lose bladder control and—ugh. I pee in my brand-new Gap Classic jeans.

"Ugh, WAR," he grunts with Edwin Starr. "What is it good for?"

"ABSOLUTELY NOTHIN', YAH, yah, yah, yah, yah," we yell back.

And I'm thinking—my body's good—for ABSOLUTELY NOTHIN'.

Fighting shame I haven't known since potty-training days, I open the window wide and pray I'll dry out before we hit Lenox.

I open my eyes. Eric is looking at me with his face full of compassion.

"I hear you," he says. "I hear and see how terrible it is to have your happy heart and fierce soul in your painful, breaking-down body." His eyes are shiny with unshed tears. "But I think I can help you. And even though it sounds so completely counter-intuitive, I think I can do that by helping you learn to love your body again."

"Mm," I grunt, distinctly underwhelmed.

"And what does that mean?" he asks.

"It means I don't believe you, Eric. You don't have to live in my body, but I do. How would you like riding the cross-town bus in my neuropathic carcass? Losing bladder control? Would you like to hear what it feels like to turn over in bed at night? Or—"

"I get it, Ellen. Nobody would like any of those things, and I'm sorry you have to suffer them. But how about if you start by making friends again with your left leg? I can help you call on your body to help you if you give it a chance. You could ask it to help you with some of these indignities."

"Mm." I say without enthusiasm. "Maybe."

"How can I help you learn to rely on your body for help when you act as if it's no more than a flawed flesh-and-bone chariot that exists for the sole purpose of ushering your brain and soul through the world?"

Eric sighs. "Your body is essential to your very being, yet you treat it like a servant; a second-class citizen." His tone becomes dead serious. "We need to work on this, Ellen, because you cannot be whole or healed until you start loving the all of you again."

I don't answer, but I know he has a point; I have to find some way to call a truce in the war between my body and the rest of me. Since I'm realistic enough by now to know I can't be cured, I'm switching my focus to being healed—a different, yet wholly possible, goal. And I don't think of it in a New-Age artsy-fartsy way with crystals and instant success. I'm beginning to understand that curing is a purely physical matter involving flesh and bone; but healing involves the intangible and ineluctable—the spirit and the soul—and I believe that I can be healed, even though my body cannot. I'm also beginning to understand that learning how to love my body again—even though it still hurts like hell and malfunctions in more and more ways—is an essential element in the healing process. And because my diseases are chronic and incurable, and my body will malfunction again and again, I'll have to make peace with it over and over again.

My work with Eric now focuses right where the mind and body meet. He assumes that mind-body are one, even if not precisely the same, and that they must, should, and will be allies in the search for healing. "I'm going to teach you how to ask your body for help so you can understand how the body-mind connection works on the simplest level," he says in our next session. "Western medicine—doctors—aren't calling on the body to assist sick people and help them heal, but I'd like to teach you. We'll start small, so don't get all nervous and twitchy. Do you ever burn yourself when you're cooking or baking?" Eric asks.

"Sure, though I'm not much of a baker."

"Next time, ask your body for help. Don't get all flustered and expect pain and blisters. Stay calm. Go into a trance, which you know you can do while you're cooking. Immediately ask your body to help. If you can, put the burned spot under cool water.

"'Body,' you can say in your own words, 'please help me with this burned place. Please heal and repair it. Please do whatever you can to make it better.' Do not tell Body what to do. Don't tell Body to imagine cooling the spot with ice cream or ice cubes, et cetera. Just ask Body to help. See what happens."

I do, the next time I accidentally touch the hot rack in our toaster oven. I close my eyes, relax in a quick trance, calm my breathing, and ask my body to help me. And this is what happens: Nothing. No burn. No blister.

I do this routinely now when I get burned, and there's no pain. I never blister. My body does the work once I extend the invitation. Simple. But it isn't simple to make peace with my entire besieged body. It's an enormous struggle to bring body, mind, and heart—and, in time, my soul—back together, but this is an essential step toward healing.

One night, Eric says, "Tonight, you're going to make friends with your body, Ellen. Tonight, you're invited to have a conversation with . . . your left leg. Oh, I see that look on your face. That left limb is not your favorite. It's there that your disease first manifested itself. It's the leg so cruelly damaged by the diagnostic biopsy that, to this day, it never stops hurting you; it was the first to acquire an inconvenient foot drop and thereby to require the brace you find so ugly but which gets you where you want to go. No wonder your left foot is the unfortunate lightning rod for your rage. But tonight, tonight"—he sings the opening bars of the song—"we hope to change all that."

I'm pissed by this ploy, but know Eric is right. I have to stop the civil war inside me. So I start a conversation with my left leg. It turns out she has quite a bit to tell me.

Now, I don't actually hear her talk out loud like Charlie McCarthy or a voice from outside me; but her words sound quite clear inside my head, the way you hear a song you love when the radio isn't playing, or the voices in a dream emanating from inside you.

"Yes," she says, (she shares my gender, which shouldn't surprise me, but does), "I hurt terribly, and I never get a smidgeon of sympathy from you. You hate me for being clumsy and having to wear this brace. But I get you where you want to go, even when I feel like screaming."

To my surprise, I begin to feel sorry for her.

"I've been hurting the longest," she says, "because I got sick first. And what do I get for all my pain? Nothing. Not one bit of TLC. Just grumbling and disdain."

She's right.

"And it's not my fault, you know. The disease isn't me, any more than it's you. It's something attacking both of us. I wish you'd understand that I'm in the same boat—uh, body—as you are, and stop hating me so much. I hate being hated."

I'm utterly flummoxed by these revelations. They begin to change the whole picture of what's happening in my body—the whole meaning of what disease is and where it's located. It's not something my body is doing to me—it's something disease is doing to my body and to me, which means something entirely different.

I immediately feel a flood of affection for my left leg, which after all, was always an essential part of me till I decided to banish her. I'm surprised at these warm feelings, but—there they are.

"So, how do you feel about your left leg now, Ellen?" asks Eric. He hasn't heard this dialogue, which was completely internal. But perhaps he's heard reports from similar reunions.

"I feel . . . I'm amazed. But—strange, I feel a little of the same kind of love welling up for my leg that I feel for Annie," I answer, astonished.

"Yes?" he says, obviously pleased.

"And if Annie were sick, I wouldn't abandon her. I'd take care of her, even if she got cranky and difficult to deal with."

"And?" It's an upward glissando.

"Well . . . since my hurting left leg is actually part of me, just the way Annie feels part of me through love. . . I guess . . . I guess . . . maybe I should show my own body the same kind of love and compassion I would show my little girl."

Eric smiles. He looks beatific.

"Can you do that, Ellen? Can you show your leg that compassion and love? Can you gather it to you, just the way you gather Annie to you when she's sick and hurting? Even if she's been mean and cranky and kept you from doing things you really wanted to do for a long, long time?"

"I . . . I would have to gather Annie to me; I love her too much to push her away, even if she's sometimes a giant pain in the butt."

"Well? What about loving something that's part of you?"

Long pause.

"Well . . . maybe I can gather my leg to me again . . . Maybe I can love my body again. Maybe."

I lie there on that sticky Naugahyde chair with the air conditioner wheezing out tepid air, watching the images under my eyelids of me taking care of Anna when she has a high fever and throws up all over me; how I clean us up and put her to bed in a fresh nightie, smoothing her hair with my hand and her face with a cool washcloth. I listen again to the feelings of sadness from my rejected hurting leg . . . and wonder if I could really stop hating my body and start—well, perhaps not loving it all at once, but maybe feeling compassion for her. Maybe . . .

And so I imagine gathering Annie, well now, with her cap of dark shining hair into my arms. I feel her nestle under my chin as her arms slide around my neck. I feel the peace that always floods me when I inhale the freshly-baked-bread and slightly salty smell rising from her flesh. And I dwell in that feeling—that expansive, warm, connected feeling that flows from me to her and back again—that feeling I call love.

I try to flow that same feeling toward my hurting left leg, to gather her to me. And suddenly I feel a strong, slow flow of electricity throughout my body, including my legs and vagina and womb—a feeling I usually experience only while making love with Jim. It feels as if my whole body is fully connecting to itself, making love to itself, rejoicing in itself. I haven't experienced that energetic wholeness for a long time. And of course my leg is once again part of the wholeness of my body, and I feel like laughing out loud, or crying in a kind of deep rapture, and I just stay with that electric joy as long as I can.

"Did anybody ever have an orgasm in this chair?" I finally ask Eric.

"Nobody I know of," he says, "but don't let that bother you. You just enjoy yourself, my dear, and I will go get us some ice-cold Diet Cokes."

He gets up, then pauses at the door.

"Can I take that to mean that you've made friends again with your body?"

I nod and smile without opening my eyes.

I am lit up like neon.

CHAPTER 10
Just a Syringe

1992

I'M THREE, SITTING ON A COLD WHITE IRON STOOL IN A COLD WHITE doctor's office that smells cruel and sharp as dread. And just as I dreaded, Dr. Borak, my pediatrician, stubs out his cigarette and picks up a very large, very long, very sharp needle.

My tummy squeezes into a hard, hurting fist. Dr. Borak is going to stick that big sharp needle in me. He always promises it won't hurt, but he lies. Needles always hurt.

The glittering third eye in the middle of the doctor's forehead mirrors everything backwards and upside down. I see myself, tiny and sitting on my head. I want to shrink smaller and smaller. I want to run and hide, but Mommy holds one hand and Daddy holds the other, and they both tell me to be a brave girl—a good girl. Good, brave girls do not run away when doctors want to help them, they say.

I think maybe Dr. Borak wants to hurt, not help. I think maybe needles won't hurt good little girls, just me. I think it's because I'm bad, not brave. I think if I could be really good, and really brave, maybe needles wouldn't hurt at all, the way grown-ups say.

Maybe.

But now Dr. Borak leans closer, pretend-smiling with crooked yellow teeth and cigarettes-breath. He tells me to climb up on the doctor-table and lie down on my tummy. He pulls down my private panties and scrubs my tooshie too hard with ice-cold cotton that smells too sharp and spiky-clean. Then he comes too close with that too-long needle.

No! NO! I do not want his three eyes to see my private self, even though Daddy pats me and whispers, "Please don't cry, Nelle," and Mommy says, "It's just like a mosquito bite. Count one-two-three and it's over."

But it's past two-three and the needle bites way too hard for mosquitoes, and I'm screaming hard. I'm mad-mad-mad and very sad-sad-sad, crying because it always hurts, and they lied again, and there's nothing I can do, nothing at all, 'cause they're so big and I'm so small. I'm only me, only one-two-three, and only me.

Sickly sweet cherry lollipops don't help. Do they think they can stop my mad-mad-mad with lollipop hiccups and cherry tears? The needle is over, but I will never ever forgive. Even when I am grown-up, I will never forgive that they lied to me when I was only three, only three, only one-two-three . . . and no one helped me.

Forty-eight years later, neurological disease stomps through my body wearing heavy boots. My treatments become more toxic. Drugs I've taken orally will now be given in larger doses by injection to enhance their wallop. One, methotrexate—a chemotherapeutic agent used to treat breast cancer—also is used in much lower doses to treat my neuropathy for some of the same reasons: it kills fast-growing cells. In my case, it targets not cancer cells, but the destructive antibodies churned out by my immune system.

My weekly injections, which take less than five minutes, begin to cost more time, and as the Director of Publications and Media at Bank Street I'm incredibly busy. I'm in various stages of editing a dozen books; producing a video on immigrant children called "We're Here: Young Newcomers Tell Their Stories;" and scheduling at least two meetings a week with publishers or TV producers to seed new projects. Best of all, I'm writing children's books myself. I usually can't settle down at the computer till the office gets quiet after six. By then I'm desperate to rest and want nothing more than to go home to enjoy my family. When I have to take more than two hours out of my week to get a shot and pay $90 for the privilege plus taxi fare, then fight my insurance company to collect reimbursement, it drives me straight up the wall. I'd rather give myself the shots. I make an appointment with Eric to learn how.

On that humid summer night, Eric begins my lesson by lining up a handful of wrapped sterile syringes and two bottles on the counter in his treatment room. The first is a tiny vial of jaundice-yellow methotrexate; the second, a large bottle of sterile water. I sit rigid at the edge of the exam table, swinging my legs and trying to look casual. I push away all thoughts of Dr. Borak, my pediatrician, with his cigarettes breath and third eye—and, especially, his promises that needles won't hurt.

"Let's start with sterile water," Eric says. He pats my face with one hand and holds out a syringe with the other. "Why don't you get started?"

I've watched so many injections that I think I know what to do. I unwrap the syringe with shaky fingers, flip the metal cap off the sterile water, and wipe it with an alcohol swab. I try to stab the needle into the very center of the tiny rubber bull's-eye on top of the vacuum bottle.

It isn't as easy as it looks. I have to pierce it directly in the center or the rubber is too thick. The first needle bends into a C-shape.

"Try again with a fresh needle," Eric says, handing me one. "And be sure to cap the first one before you stab yourself—or someone else. Never put the same syringe into a sterile bottle of medication twice. If you miss, or ruin the needle, throw it away. It's no longer sterile and will contaminate the whole kit 'n caboodle. I'll give you plenty in case you make mistakes. Now try again."

I try again, and bend the second needle exactly the same way. I cap it, and he hands me another. When I insert the third needle properly, Eric shows me how to invert the bottle and slowly pull back on the syringe until I fill it with water exactly to the twenty-five mg line. I have to try several times, pushing fluid in and out till I get the proper amount. I withdraw the needle from the container with a tiny pop! that breaks the vacuum. But now the water in the syringe has a fluffy necklace of little air bubbles around the top.

"OK, now point your syringe at the ceiling and push out those little bubbles. Very slooowly, so you don't lose any medication."

I loose control and squirt bubbles and water straight onto his eyeglasses.

"That could have been fifty dollars worth of methotrexate and toxic chemo in my eye," he says, grinning almost gleefully as he wipes his glasses with a paper towel.

I take a shaky breath.

"It's okay, no harm done. That's why we're using H_2O. Just try again."

I pull more sterile water—and more bubbles—into another syringe.

"I have to get rid of every single bubble, right?"

"Right, but please forget all those murder mysteries where the greedy, nefarious doctor kills the wealthy heiress by injecting bubbles into her blood," he says. I'm still trying to push the last few air bubbles out the tip of the needle without losing more water.

"Those stories are bullshit. You'd have to fill the entire hypodermic with air, and then inject it directly into someone's bloodstream in order to kill them. And you won't be injecting oxygen directly into your bloodstream. I'm going to teach you not to do that."

"But look how many little bubb—"

"Forget those stories and watch this." He shows me how to flick the hypodermic with my finger to get rid of the bubbles. "They're fiction. We deal with facts."

So I practice pulling in exactly twenty-five mg of water again. I do it several times to get the feel of it. Each time, I practice thwacking the syringe to loosen the bubbles, then pushing the plunger toward the ceiling to push out whatever little bubbles are left. I start to feel ever so slightly like I'm an actress playing a nurse in a movie.

"Good," Eric says. "Now you're ready to give yourself your first injection."

I stop feeling even remotely like a nurse.

He looks at me. I look back, terror seeping into my bones. It's summer, so my thigh is bare, right there, waiting.

"Where's the orange?" I ask.

"What orange?"

"They always have an orange in the movies."

"But we're not in the movies."

Long pause.

"You've watched this a thousand times," Eric says. "Don't you think you could give it a try just once?"

"Does it hurt?" I ask.

"It hurts a little tiny girl who feels very helpless a lot. It hurts a grown woman who feels a little helpless a little. Very little. And it hurts very much less when that same woman takes full control and gives herself the shot."

Pause.

"I promise you. Now could you please try? We'll use sterile water the first time. I'll talk you through it."

Because this doctor has never lied to me about anything—always telling me whether procedures hurt or not, or whether new diagnoses are "not worth worrying about," "merely inconveniences," or "real problems"—I believe him.

Eric's voice holds infinite patience, but also a hint of "get on with it, girlie," which I know he'll soon say if I dawdle much longer.

Longer pause.

"I'm not ready yet," I say. "I think I have to watch one more time."

"Okay, watch."

He takes the syringe and wipes my thigh with an alcohol swab. "I very carefully miss any veins. I go in at a forty-five degree angle. I pull up on the syringe a little to make sure I'm not pulling blood, which says I'm in a vein. Then I push the plunger down slowly or quickly—your choice. I make sure all the medication is out of the syringe. Then I maintain pressure on the plunger and pull the syringe straight out so you won't bruise. I use my other hand to press the puncture with a fresh alcohol swab. When there's no bleeding, I use both hands to cap the syringe. And that, my love, is that."

He sits back and looks at me through those smudgy glasses that make his eyes look even bigger than they are. The look is not unkind, but does not contain even one half-note of coddling.

"Got it?"

"Got it."

Without missing a beat, he unwraps a syringe from the counter and hands it to me.

Trying not to miss another beat, I take the cap off the bottle of sterile water, wash the top with an alcohol swab, push the needle exactly into the center of the bull's-eye on the rubber top, tip it up, fill the syringe, and pull it out with that funny little pop! I flick the syringe, push out all the little bubbles, and take a very deep breath. My hands are shaking, but I deliberately go into overdrive. One more deep breath and my hands calm.

I wash what looks like a vein-free area on my other thigh with a fresh alcohol swab. I set the needle against my skin at the correct forty-five degree angle. It looks much longer than it ever did before: almost two inches long because methotrexate has to be injected deep into the muscle. I'm distinctly aware that the tip of the steel needle is cut on the diagonal. I can see the hole where the medication enters and exits.

I stop breathing. Time stops ticking. I don't know if I can make myself push that wicked-looking needle into my own soft flesh. I don't want Eric to think I'm a weenie, but I am. I also don't want to waste two hours and ninety dollars plus double cab fare every week. I don't want to wound myself. I—

Oh, hell, just do it. I push—too tentatively. I push again—but stop when the needle meets the resistance of my flesh and makes a slanty little pocket, like a peg against the taut surface of a tent. I push again, harder—and the needle slips past my skin into my flesh, into my muscle. I feel very little: virtually nothing. Now I press on the plunger and very slowly push the clear water into my body.

I do not feel a thing as the syringe empties. I gently pull the needle straight out, pressing on the plunger, and still feeling nothing. I cap the syringe and hand it to Eric. My fingers vibrate as I tear another alcohol swab open and press it against my skin.

Amazing. It hardly hurt. Much less than when anybody else does it. Much less.

"Good girl," he says. "Now do it again, this time with the medicine."

"Hey, give me a freaking second, would you?"

"Do you want to give yourself the medication or not?" he says almost cruelly, bearing down on me with that little bottle of yellow methotrexate. "Do you want to stop being dependent on doctors and nurses all the time and learn to do it yourself? Or do you want to keep spending hours and hundreds of dollars letting them do for you what you can do for yourself? Do you want to be the one in charge of your disease?"

He hands me a fresh syringe as if we're assembly line workers. "We're not just playing doctor here, sweetheart."

Without a word, I take the vial, unwrap a new syringe, and repeat the procedure. This time it's much harder because the methotrexate is so viscous. I draw the fluid up and push it out several times before I have an entire dose safely in the hypodermic without what still looks like a murderous collar of bubbles. I flick it with my finger and then it's perfect.

I take a deep breath, swab another veinless area on my thigh, and wham-bam, inject the methotrexate.

"Flawless," breathes the good doctor.

"Hmm," I say, trembling but proud, watching a little blood dribble out of the pinprick. "I can't believe how much less it hurts when I do it myself."

I scrub at the spot with another alcohol square and it stops bleeding. Not a twinge.

"Dr. Cassell, emergency, pick up line three," squawks the intercom.

As Eric punches the flashing red light and asks a skein of quiet but urgent questions, I let the spiky-clean scent of alcohol whisk me back to when I was Nelle, sitting on a cold white iron stool in a cold white office that smelled cruel and sharp as dread. One last time, I see myself reflected upside down in my pediatrician's glittering third eye: helpless, powerless, caught in a charade of sickly-sweet cherry lollipop lies that—though intended to protect me—left me feeling utterly alone and uncomforted, impaled on my own ineluctable truth: needles hurt. Especially when they look very large and sharp to a very small girl.

But back then, I was only three, only one-two-three, and no one helped me.

Now, I'm in charge. Now I know that "being good" has nothing to do with illness or pain. Now I can take control of one small part of my medical care.

Sometimes a syringe is just a syringe.

CHAPTER 11

The Paradox of Pain

*Find a place inside where there's joy,
and the joy will burn out the pain.*

Joseph Campbell

1993

"HALLELUJAH! HALLELUJAH! HALLE-LU-JAH!"

Two thousand people jump up and join Handel's Hallelujah Chorus. *Carnegie Hall, the sharp smell of evergreens everywhere, pulses with the call of trumpets and the rumble of organ, drums, and voices. The music has never been more stirring. But, surrounded by hundreds of warm bodies, breathing the same over-breathed air, I feel utterly alone. Pain keeps me prisoner, trapped inside an invisible glass box that lets the music in, but keeps everyone else out.*

Stripped of my identity along with my black lace bra and panties, I shiver on the narrow operating table in a thin hospital "gown." I try to ignore the sharp instruments lined up on a nearby tray with glittering precision. A doctor I've never seen ties a mask over her Colgate smile. The closer I get to a familiar painful procedure, the more alert I become to what's lovely: a triangle of blazing blue sky beyond that unwashed window; the sweet, piercing whistle as an orderly passes in the hall. Watching the doctor come nearer carrying pain in her hands, I force myself to snatch tiny handfuls of joy even as pain and terror

chase the essential me into the tip of my little finger.

Pain is a paradox. It both gives and takes away. It's a fickle, double-fisted force that can reveal or conceal, bless or curse, galvanize or paralyze. At best, pain wakens me to fierce joy: an electric awareness of the breath of life moving through me and every blade of grass; to the rapture pouring from cellos and flutes. With pain as my reminder, I am conscious that I stand on holy ground—but only if I allow myself to realize how precious life is.

At best, pain goads me to grab hold of my life with both hands; to push the flame of my soul higher. Pain galvanizes me to write with heightened energy that kicks in when I struggle hardest against it. I refuse to let pain beat me down, even when I have to write lying down with a yellow pad or laptop perched on my legs. Pain snapping at my heels propels me faster, so I won't miss a beat, a breath, a word, a moment to connect with the people I love. At its worst, when it's too overwhelming, pain sucks up all my energy, paralyzes me, steamrolls me into my bed, and pushes me up against a glass wall, with everyone and everything I cherish on the other side.

Most people picture pain as an enemy: a heavy-breathing Darth Vader that stalks, pounces, and always wins. I did. But after more than thirty years of living with twin auto-immune diseases, I've found ways to live almost peaceably with pain as my dark shadow, an unwelcome doppelganger. I've learned to outwit, outthink, and overcome it—most of the time. I don't love pain, but I try not to hate it anymore. Hate requires energy and attention I would much rather spend embracing life.

It wasn't always this way. I had to learn to control pain instead of letting it control me. Pain medication helped, as did making pain an "object"—something not-me. Learning self-hypnosis from Eric was key—that way, I could go into a quick trance and imagine pain as a greasy-green icon I drag to one side of my computer screen each morning. Then, I can try to use the same twenty-six letters of the alphabet to write something no one else has said before. Sometimes, I can also try to gain power over pain by writing about it—taming it by naming it, word by word.

I struggle with a paradox: How can pain, and the fear of pain, morph from curse to blessing? Why, when I'm alone in a taxi, terrified, having a stroke, racing to the Neurological Institute to meet my neurologist, with the entire left side of my body stone cold, pain crushing my face—why does dawn breaking over the Hudson River never look more lovely? And why do the blooming cherry and pear trees along the median strip make me think of bridesmaids in a procession toward the altar of morning? Why has the sleeping city never looked more valuable? These are more than simple distractions.

When I find myself trapped between the calipers of terror and exultation, I snap awake to anything beautiful, or that I can construe as beautiful. My eyes become microscopes or telescopes, finely focused on the emerald-and-ivory arrangement of my spine on the fluoroscope; the network of veins on the back of my hand, the warm gold of my slender wedding ring. And as a thick needle enters close to my spine, I experiment: how many colors can I find if I squeeze my eyelids tight? Scarlet; tighter—lemon; tightest—purple.

For most of my life, I avoided medication, including herbs, even aspirin, even (gasp) vitamin C. It takes many sessions before Eric can teach me how foolish this is. "Not taking medication is a luxury only the temporarily well can afford," he says, peering over his smudged glasses and under his scraggly white eyebrows. "And you, my dear, are not one of them, nor will you ever be again. I know you're strong and independent." He crosses his arms and rivets his eyes on mine. "But if you want to keep going and enjoy your life, you have to take pain medicine. Otherwise, you'll fall by the wayside."

I already feel as if I'm falling apart and it terrifies me, but I glare at him anyway. I know he's a specialist in pain management, the first doctor I've found who fully understands my dilemmas, frustrations, and rage when it seems my whole life is being stymied by disease and pain.

He looks at me tenderly. "I look at you and watch you move, Ellen, and I can see pain in every inch of your body. Don't you want to feel better?"

I'm afraid painkillers will fog up my brain, but I don't say it.

"And tell me, are you still living three lives—with three full-time jobs—working at Bank Street College, taking care of your family, and going to the hospital for four days of infusion every month?" There's an edge to his voice.

"Um."

"Why are you so against it, Ellen?"

Silence.

"Well, if you won't tell me, I'll tell you," he says, "because I've heard it a trillion times: I'm strong. I don't need medicine. I want to be natural. I don't want to be: a coward, a baby, a chicken, an addict."

I still don't say anything.

"And there's more," he continues, "I want to be a good soldier, a good patient"—and he nails me right between the eyes with this one—"a good little girl. It will make me stronger if I overcome my pain. It will make me feel weak if I rely on medication. It will undercut my moral fiber. I want to be part of the wild frontier, Davy Crockett, the American dream. Blah-de-blah-blah-blah."

He leans forward and engulfs my icy hands in his warm ones, saying softly, "It's just blabber, Ellen. I hear these excuses all the time. And I respect the anguish behind these feelings. But they do not take away pain. Medicine takes away pain." He sits back suddenly and slams his fist on his desk. Everything jumps—including me.

"Medicine will free you to do whatever you are capable of doing, and then some. You'll be happier. You won't have to get that steely, unattractive look I see on your face when you're pushing against pain.

"And as for becoming an addict? I'm sure you've thought of that, hm?"

I avoid his gaze.

"People in serious or chronic pain do not become addicts—research proves it. They take their narcotics on a regular schedule for as long as they need them—that's what you'll do, dearie, take them just before you need them so you're not playing catchup. I'll help you do that. And then, when and if your pain gets better, you'll easily taper off—sometimes simply by forgetting to take your doses.

"The false bugaboo of addiction keeps people in pain from getting the adequate and necessary relief they need." He leans even closer and says softly, "I promise that you will not become a drug addict, Ellen. You'll take what you need and forget the rest." He sits back in his desk chair, wheezing.

"So shall we try? It will be such an enormous relief for you not to walk around, sleep, make dinner, write childrens' books, and love your husband and family when you don't feel as if your arms and legs are attached to live wires."

Tears crowd into the back of my throat at the very thought of relief.

"People have sat in that chair where you are sitting now, Ellen, who are dying. They have very little time left. But they don't all suffer the pain you do. And you live with it every single day. Don't you think it's time to help yourself?"

I cry big, kindergarten sobs, imagining how it would feel. "But—can you make sure it doesn't take away my mind, Eric? Won't make me fuzzy and sleepy? I am so afraid of hurting my mind. It's the only thing I can count on."

"If the first one makes you foggy, we'll go on to the next, and the next, and the next. Your mind is too beautiful to waste. Let's try it, shall we?"

He scribbles on his prescription pad, then pulls me gently to my feet.

It takes some maneuvering, but we find a medication that doesn't create a buzzing, gray fog in the middle of my brain, make me sleep till noon, or keep me awake all night. I have to be patient while we titrate up and down to reach exactly the right dosage. But then—I feel released from the painful prison of my body. I'm part of the world and far more energetic. I no longer have to fight deep aching pain to walk up a few stairs, or endure fireworks up my arms to pick up a pencil, or write or edit a manuscript. I don't waste most of my energy just to push through the day.

Eric also makes audio tapes I use to take my familiar swan dive off the back of my head into protective trances that lift me above the pain that remains. Once the meditation is familiar, I can induce it anywhere in a few seconds, then go right on with what I'm doing—chairing a meeting, having a treatment at the hospital, or writing my new picture book—based on a true story about a Hopi girl who uses cleverness rather than violence to save her people from the warring Apache.

What a relief to no longer experience pain as an enemy relentlessly pursuing my body and me; to realize it's possible to forge a truce and make the best peace we can. Otherwise, I'd go on living in a constant state of siege. Trading war for peace gives me much more energy to live joyously and fully, even though my diseases are incurable and may be getting worse.

Send your tired, your poor to New York City, and they turn into taxi drivers. I love talking to these men, and our conversations are a great way to take the pulse of public opinion on elections, war, peace, terrorism, and the president—of any country. They come far-flung from Kashmir, Siberia, Senegal, Uzbekistan, Mongolia, and other more predictable places, and offer perfect opportunities to compare America's hostility toward illness and disability with the kinder attitudes of other cultures. And I can do it sitting down.

Many Americans seem to become blind and deaf in the face of chronic illness, and I see them quickly turn away from my disabilities—too inconvenient? too embarrassing?—and consequently refuse to see me. Crutches and canes usually don't register on their radar and seem to be viewed as awkward and irritating when they do.

Not so with cab drivers—those from overseas, not native New Yorkers—and they almost always ask, "What happened to you?" which at first makes me want to gnash my teeth and growl. I bristle at their incessant queries about my "condition" and try to get the best of them by snapping preposterous answers to their innocent questions: "I broke my legs on a flying trapeze." Or "I took a fall jumping my mare—or was it the stallion?"

But as time goes on, pain wears me down and I become humbler, more open to sympathy—as long as it doesn't tip into pity. I begin to understand their questions as expressions of concern and good-hearted attempts to help, especially when they so often jump out of the cab and graciously open my door, gallantly helping my packages, my crutches, and me in and out. And though polyneuropathy isn't likely to be cured by diet, part of me feels healed by their nutritional suggestions. My sarcasm feels tawdry in the face of their compassion.

I learn that my simple answer to their "What's wrong?" or "How did you get hurt?"—"a neurological disease"—almost always elicits energetic promises of prayers for my recovery in a babel of languages and home remedies sure to cure. My favorites:

"Wodka. Lots of Wodka. For drink, and for rub on chest."

"Beets. Eat only beets. It cured my aunt in Ghana, who once walked crazy like you. I hope it cures you, too. For you I will pray all the time."

And my all-time favorite, from a Punjabi driver: "My brother, he once walk veddy, veddy bad like you, and now he walk wonderful just like me. You must rub alcohol and marijuana on your chest once every day, and you, too, will be cured."

Either that, or I will no longer care.

After I tuck myself into a corner of the cab and listen to slivers of stories from faraway places, I feel healing seep into my heart. The warmth of these well-intentioned men flows through the protective plastic barriers into the back seat, past the networks of my damaged nerves, and deep into me. At times, their kindness even sets loose a few of the tears I steel myself never to shed—which, to my surprise, also makes me feel better. I come to vastly prefer their good-hearted intrusions to the all-American crippled-woman-of-glass syndrome that tries to erase my very inconvenient existence.

Each time disease creeps into another part of my body, I can't help moments of panic and despair. Then I take a deep breath and remember all I've learned about taking care of myself. I make an appointment with my rheumatologist or neurologist to find out what's going on and what we can do about it; then I go to the St. Luke's-Roosevelt Hospital Center for Pain Management to repeat the procedures that help quell pain, and to explore new ways to curb it. In addition to using a banquet of painkillers, they also use a variety of procedures: a series of epidural steroid injections for sciatica and lower back pain; radio frequency ablation to block the transmission of pain from either leg to my spinal cord and brain; and morphine patches to turn down the shooting neuropathic symptoms. I'm calmed by knowing there are many more options.

I used to kiss my pills before I swallowed them, but now there are twenty-six every day, not counting the patch, to welcome into my body—almost enough for a small breakfast. I use every resource I have—spiritual, pharmaceutical, psychological, physical—to gently push aside the iron fists of pain. I exercise as often as I can in a heated swimming pool, relishing the aquamarine water, and inviting help from my body's natural painkillers, the endorphins.

And I trust that my pharmaceutical saviors will continue to give my body back, including whatever physical freedom is possible—one dose at a time.

CHAPTER 12
Third Opinion

1994

"MS. ELLEN, YOU DON'T LOOK WELL," ERIC SAYS ONE NIGHT. HE INVARIABLY notices what I deny, even to myself. He scribbles a name and phone number on a prescription and hands it to me. "I'd like you to see Ed Parrish. He's an excellent rheumatologist and clinician—young, but very bright. I have a lot of respect for him." Coming from Eric, who picks bones with so many doctors, this is high praise.

Dr. Parrish is affiliated with the Hospital for Special Surgery, one of two premier institutions in the country for treating rheumatic disease. I like him at once: he peppers me with shrewd questions and fully answers mine. In his late thirties, he's vigorous and muscular, bristling with energy—one of those men who look especially attractive with a shaved head. His vociferous, take-charge manner frightens me a bit at first, but I'm impressed with his rigor.

After a flurry of tests, he decides on a new treatment with a drug recently approved by the FDA—intravenous immunoglobulin, or IVIG. I'll receive my first infusions over three days in the hospital, and sped the nights there, which makes our kids, now twelve and nine, rather anxious, but will force me to act like a patient for a few days—not a bad idea. I have to sign a release after he tells me about the possible adverse side effects: difficulty breathing, tight chest, rash or hives, or anaphylaxis—a sudden, severe, and potentially fatal allergic reaction, which is why I have to be an in-patient for the first infusion.

I don't take the warnings very seriously.

When I get to the hospital around six, the nurse tapes a large syringe of adrenaline to the foot of my bed—the antidote for an anaphylactic reaction. "Just in case," she says, pinning a call button to my pillow. Then she hooks me up to the IV.

"Don't hesitate to use this," she says, pointing to the call button.

"I won't," I say. "My father almost died from an anaphylactic reaction to a shot of penicillin, so I won't be shy." I start to get a bit anxious and try to push it away with a joke. "Hey, am I getting an infusion of IVIG or TNT?" She doesn't laugh.

I use Eric's relaxation tapes to calm myself. I want to welcome the drug into my body and, as a matter of pride, to show my new doctor how strong and calm I can be. If I can't control my body, at least I can control my behavior. I also suspect this infusion will prove to be a lot like my initial treatments with IV steroids: a big bang ending in a whimper—nothing at all.

Dr. Parrish stops by to wish me good luck a few minutes after the IVIG, almost as expensive as liquid platinum, begins dripping into my arm.

"I feel fine," I tell him. "Just fine."

"Good," he says, and rushes off with a smile.

And I do. Until about nine p.m. I'm dozing off . . . and damn, my chest begins to feel tight. Maybe that big syringe isn't such a bad idea. Still, I fear that once I push that call button, my treatment will be in jeopardy. I don't want to cause a fuss—but much more important, I don't want to lose this drug. I desperately want it to work—to KO those damned auto-immune marauders. I convince myself that I'm just imagining the tightness, that it isn't real, but just to play safe I push the call button.

The nurse comes immediately.

"My chest feels a little tight," I tell her. And, once I admit it to myself, I realize it feels as if someone's tightening Scarlett O'Hara's corset under my hospital rag, making it a little hard to breathe. My head feels tight, too, probably from the tension.

"Sit forward," she says, cranking up the bed. "Lots of patients feel this way because the medication is so viscous." She checks my vital signs, says my lungs sound fine, and goes for more pillows to help me sit up more comfortably. She also must have called Dr. Parrish, because by the time she gets back and we finish fluffing and rearranging my bed, he sweeps into the room. After a cursory greeting, he listens to my chest. Carefully. And again. "Any rash? How's your throat?"

"No rash," I say, checking my arms, "and fine."

He checks it. "Looks fine," he says, thumping and listening to my chest again.

"You're fine," he pronounces, sounding relieved. "Try not to worry. Just rest sitting up. Keep monitoring your reactions, just the way you did, and let the nurses know if anything feels wrong." He fiddles with the IV, then taps my shoulder and leaves with a jaunty wave. "Sleep tight, and keep up the good work."

Around eleven, I begin to feel a strange pressure from inside, near the middle of my back, but it's so peculiar I decide not to say anything. My breathing is better sitting up, no itch or rash, but I never really go to sleep; too nervous, I guess. I'm still debating whether to say anything about my back when I hear a commotion at the nursing station.

"What do you mean you haven't checked? What are you here for?" Dr. Parrish marches into my room, followed by a small gaggle of nervous nurses and interns.

He's angry, and I immediately feel guilty. "Just checking," he says. "How's your breathing? Do you itch? Let me listen to your lungs."

"Well . . . my back hurts a little, here and here," I point, "but I'm fine otherwise." I feel even guiltier when I confess my discomfort. As if I'm failing some sort of test.

He whips around to confront the medical contingent. "This is why you need to check, whether or not a patient is sleeping." He turns to me, face red but speaking more softly. "Again, where does it hurt?" I point, and he presses the spot. "There?" he asks. I nod. "And there?"

"Yes."

He listens to my chest again. Again. Fiddles with the IV. Again.

"I'll check you again in a few minutes," he says.

By the time he comes back, I feel better. A little. Less worried, maybe, because he's there.

"How's the back? Headache?"

"Back pain's better but still there. And yes, I'm getting a migraine."

"Okay. I'll order something for your headache, then try to sleep."

I never sleep, but morning comes quickly. By then, the migraine bloats, filling my entire head, with a chartreuse ribbon of nausea that connects my eyes to my stomach. Light—any light at all—is an assault. When Dr. Parrish comes in, he looks as tired as I feel.

"That went well," I say cheerfully, trying to ignore the light and the ribbon. "I'm so relieved we can continue this treatment."

"Went well? Are you kidding?" he says. "It was a nightmare. We had to slow the drip twice and you still had chest pains, shortness of breath, and now you have a raging migraine. I almost had to stop the treatment."

"You did?" I'm shocked. "But I got through it. And I get migraines anyway, so this may have nothing to do with the drug." I'm so eager for this drug to work.

"Well, you got through this one. Let's see how you do later today. We'll slow the drip even more and see if that makes it any better."

It does. My hospital stay is a day longer, but I get the full enchilada. And I have a new doctor I know I can trust to give me the best possible care. That feels very good, having him there to protect me.

Soon, new cost-saving measures from my health insurance plan require me to continue treatment in the new Infusion Therapy Unit at the hospital, initially for two days a month. I'm one of their first patients. After a highly unpleasant bout of aseptic meningitis, a well-known side effect of IVIG that produces painful and potentially dangerous inflammation in the brain and spinal cord, Dr. Parrish increases my treatment to four days each month so the drip can be twice as slow.

When I go home every night after a long day of treatment, it's easier on the kids but harder on me. I have to be a vivacious and loving mommy, even with my migraines in full bloom. On the other hand, being a part-time patient allows me to continue my full-time career. It allows me to pretend to everyone—especially myself—that I'm not sick. Not really.

PART 3

Stay Within Yourself

Simply the thing I am shall make me live.
William Shakespeare

CHAPTER 13
Easter Seal Poster Girl

1996

IT MUST BE THOSE CRACKS IN THE NEW YORK CITY SIDEWALKS; that's why I'm tripping again. But I feel like Dorothy in Oz, when she stumbles over the invisible iron bar set out by the Wicked Witch of the West. Maybe there's a Wicked Witch of the West Side who's casting spells on me, I tell myself, trying to be jocular. But it isn't funny; it's scary. I don't want to fall. I don't want to break bones or my two front teeth. I look bad enough with the cane and leg brace that keep me from tripping over my infamous left foot.

Even worse than tripping is the escalating nerve pain that jags up and down both legs. That pain reins me in as surely as the sense that my muscles are weaker. They feel like rubber bands with no stretch; walking through ordinary air feels like slogging ankle-deep in wet cement. But I'm not quite alone as I stagger through this gauntlet: I hear a stream of agitated internal chatter as the Ellens return.

Why can't I walk one lousy block without resting five times and getting out of breath? asks Scared Ellen.

Don't be such a worrywart, answers Wiseass. *You're just imagining it.*

I'm not. I walked this far easily—well, more easily—last month, Rational Ellen replies. *I know when I'm going downhill. My right foot is weak now, can't you see it?*

    Damn, whispers Scared Ellen. *I hope nobody else notices.*

    Shut up and stop complaining. Don't be such a weenie, complains Wiseass.

    No, listen: definitely worse in the right leg, insists Rational Ellen. *Call Dr. Parrish. Maybe he can help. Or call Eric—at least get help with the pain.*

    Oh, great, thinks just plain me. Great. I already take industrial strength doses of IVIG, one of the newest drugs on the planet, more expensive than diamonds, when I can convince our insurance company to pay for it. If that doesn't help, what will?

    Who gives a bloody damn what the doctor thinks anyway? And screw the insurance company—you always win the fights. If the disease is worse, I don't want to hear about it, says Wiseass.

    Just forget about it and maybe it will go away. Scared Ellen, of course, always hiding from the truth.

✸   ✸   ✸

Denial can be sweet in its season. But while I procrastinate for a few more weeks, things get worse. Sometimes I lose my balance because it's hard to feel the sidewalk under my feet. It gets even more difficult to walk that one block from my apartment on Riverside Drive to West End Avenue.

    But I refuse to let pain blot me out. At the door of our building, I greet Arturo, our tall, handsome doorman, who always says "Good morning, Ellen," and smiles back. I walk onto the sidewalk and catch my breath, looking through the just-green trees at blue flashes of the Hudson River.

    Then I pace myself by resting under each tree, which stands in its own flowerbed.

    Every time I'm forced to pause, I concentrate on one thing, anything, rather than my humiliating weakness and the lack of control implied, or stated, by pain. Then I take a deep breath and press on to the next bed of flowers, fifteen paces east, where I gaze into the black hearts of the crimson tulips. Their stamens bear heavy heads of golden pollen, and within each black heart burns a yellow star. Only by deliberately looking down into the chalice of the tulip am I privy to this hidden sacrament.

    Another deep breath, another twenty paces, and I lose myself in a branch of golden-green leaves in the very act of unfolding. If I stop long enough, I will see the buds explode into leaves. This is it—the very edge of spring—and I am bearing witness.

Pace and pause, pace and pause. I move slowly down the block and stop, out of breath, in front of a trio of butter-pecan brownstones where a pair of pigeons court and coo on the steps, his iridescent neck feathers aflame in the sun above an immaculate white ruff. Riffling and ruffling, desire burbling like a spring from his throat, he sidles up beside the female. She awaits him, shuddering in subtle shades of salmon, beige, and brown until, at the very last moment, she side steps him and whirls high in the air with a sound like shaken canvas. Now their courtship continues in another dimension as they dance in the air, whirling above my head with a flurry and sheen of feathers.

I balance the curse of pain with these small blessings. Life and death are set before me. I choose life.

I finally call Dr. Parrish.

"What's up?"

Even over the phone, his melodic voice bristles with energy and a warm current of concern. There are sparks of impatience, too. He treats so many people who are so much sicker, I tell myself. Get on with it.

"Hi. Mm, havingtroublewalking," I mumble.

"What?" The "t" is sharply bitten. "I'm having trouble hearing you."

"I keep tripping . . . over my right foot," I half-whisper. I don't want to hear myself say it out loud, but know I have to be explicit.

"Be careful you don't fall," he says. "You don't need broken bones on top of everything else." He runs through a few quick questions, then pauses so long I think I've lost him. "Make an appointment to come in sometime in the next week," he finally says. "Be sure to give a buzz if things suddenly get worse. And make an appointment at physical therapy before you see me."

More procrastination. More flower beds and pigeons. I finally make back-to-back appointments.

Inside the Hospital for Special Surgery, I blend in quite nicely as we all limp, lurch, roll, etc. past the antique "Hospital for the Ruptured and Crippled" insignia near the elevators. But instead of the creepy Frankenstein fears I get at the Neurological Institute, I've spent so much time at HSS that it feels a little like home. So many people are hauling themselves around on crutches, walkers, and wheelchairs, wearing ornate casts and weird contraptions with little medieval-torture-type pins and wheels sticking out, that I feel strangely normal with my garden-variety cane and brace. I can hardly remember walking without them.

It's also homey because I know so many people—Mr. Feeney the doorman, the admissions ladies, dozens of doctors, nurses, and technicians by sight if not by name, and they often say hi. I don't love coming here, but I don't hate it, either. I'm taken care of with kindness and compassion, treated like a person, not a disease. It's a relief to stop trying to pass as "Normal" in the world of the well. Sometimes people I don't know recognize me from *Voices of Lupus*, the video I produced with the hospital that features patients, with a few token doctors. The idea was to hear what people who have lupus feel—what their lives are like—rather than the usual spiel from doctors, no matter how empathic. Roberta Horton, a social worker, and Laura Roberts, Director of Education, were key colleagues in creating the video, with independent Producers Steven Mantell and Harriet Fier. It's strange: there are many people here who know crucial, personal things about me that some of my friends and colleagues in the well world never will.

I say hello to a couple of nurses who took care of me on inpatient floors as I squeeze into the crowded elevator and go up to physical therapy on two. Then I wait with the broken and ruptured of all ages, tiny tots up to the elderly, until somebody finally calls my name.

"What's the problem?" asks Maura, who's named on her badge. She's young and blonde and astonishingly beautiful, with large green eyes and thick golden lashes. But she's all business and aluminum-clad. Explaining my "problem" to graceful young Maura means, of course, that I have to say out loud what I don't even want to think. "I'm having trouble . . . walking. I—keep stumbling over— my toes. Losing my balance."

"Have you fallen?"

"A little."

"Do your legs feel weak?"

I nod. "Weak" is a word I cannot pronounce.

"What's your diagnosis?"

"CIDP." I like medical talk; it knocks away the personal edges.

"What?"

"Chronic inflammatory demyelinating polyneuropathy."

"Ouch. How far has it spread?"

"Pretty much everywhere."

"Okay, get up and let me watch you walk."

Another effing watcher. I knew it was coming, but I still hate it.

She watches only a short time. "The cane isn't giving you the leverage you need," she says matter-of-factly. "Let's try two canes."

She pulls them out of a bin. Stainless-steel old-lady ones. At least mine is beautiful: cherry wood, brought from Australia by our good friends Terry and Jeff.

"We" try walking with the two ugly sticks, but Maura quickly frowns and shakes her head. "That won't do it, either."

She disappears into some hellhole and reappears with hideous metal crutches with arm cuffs. "Underarm crutches will hit too many nerves in your armpits, right?"

I nod, rendered mute by the crutches, which are far uglier than ordinary wooden, broken-leg crutches. They practically scream cripple. I thought my leg brace was ugly? Well, these crutches make that Velcro and mucus-colored plastic device look like a buttery, high-heeled Chanel boot in comparison.

"No basic black?" I ask.

"Sorry." Maura smiles briefly for the first time. Score one. "Canadians—that's what these are called—only come like this."

"So I'm stuck with these flashy steel numbers? You'd think they'd give some French designer a crack at an updated version."

Maura doesn't answer. She's busy sizing those—things—down to fit me.

Flash! I'm six years old, staring with reverence, revulsion, and terror at one of the Easter Seal Posters that pop up like crocuses every spring. This year, a darling little girl smiles bravely back at me. She wears a ruffled dress in Easter-egg blue that froths out around her ballerina-style. Her shining hair curls in crisp ribbons, and her radiant smile lights up her perfect skin, perfect teeth, perfect eyes—everything's perfect except the wretched braces of metal and leather buckled like cages around her legs, and the hideous crutches with metal arm-bands that circle her dimpled elbows.

She's the child I never want to be: a child who thinks she's beautiful but is, in my eyes, just an ugly polio-child begging for dimes. The big, bright-red words at the top and bottom of the poster prove it— FIGHT POLIO, at the top; and at the bottom: BUY EASTER SEALS FOR THE MARCH OF DIMES

This adorable little girl is crippled, an object of shame and humiliation that makes my skin shrink. Her crippled-ness makes my stomach heave with an oily pity, and I feel soiled. More than anything else, I feel deeply afraid that what happened to her can happen to me. And, though I couldn't have said any of this at the time, that bottomless fear makes me despise both her perfection and her terrible weakness.

❀

"Follow me," says Maura.

I slip my arms into the metal cuffs and put my weight on the hard, rubber-coated hand rests for the first time. They feel strangely warm under my grip, and the metal bracelets make my arms look skinny and unfamiliar. Part of me watches myself as if I'm watching that poster, but I can't endure the stirrings of my own self-contempt. So I close my eyes and fast-forward through a series of quick movie clichés in lurid 1950s Technicolor:

❀

Shazzam! I wrap myself in a wizard's soft satin invisibility cloak and Poof! disappear in a shower of silver stars.

❀

I fold up thin as a sheet of notebook paper—assistive devices included—and slip through the cracks between the dreary linoleum tiles.

❀

I pick up these hideous sticks, throw them at Maura, and mangle her good.

❀

I crash the crutches aside and fling myself onto a narrow bed nearby, sobbing hyperbolically like the poor heroine in every cripple movie I've ever seen—until all the handsome doctors rush over to a) cure me, and/or b) fight over who will marry me first. Then I stop the projector and tell them all to go fuck themselves.

I run home and grab Jim, and we make wild, rhapsodic love. When we catch our breath, he promises to take me back to Greece for another honeymoon, the way he did when I got my leg brace.

What I really do is open my eyes and clump obediently behind Maura, trying to get the hang of walking with four legs instead of two. She grabs a pair of ordinary crutches and demonstrates how to walk with them: right foot-left crutch, left foot-right crutch. I secretly start planning to wow my kids by swinging along like a chimpanzee, but Maura brings me right back to earth. "Later, when you need even more leverage, you can go to the four-point walk: right crutch, then left foot; left crutch, then right foot." I stare at her, stupefied. Does she mean it can get worse—even worse than this?

"Forget it for now," she says, looking away. Is that a smidgeon of compassion in her eyes? Am I beginning to love or loathe her?

We walk over to a fake wooden staircase that leads nowhere. Maura demonstrates how to use the crutches to climb up and down, which is a bit counter-intuitive: crutches first going down (Egad, how do I keep from falling?); crutches last going up (Will my arms be long enough?). This seems to maximize my awkwardness in both directions.

She suggests I walk around the physical therapy room, which feels safe enough, as everybody needs help with some aspect of ambulation.

Soon I have to admit it: love or hate these big steel babies, they do the job. They make it much easier to get from A to B, just the way my first lupus friend, Carmen, told me: "It doesn't matter how you get there, girlfriend; just get there." She'd gone from dancing on her toes with Alvin Ailey to creeping with a walker, so she knew.

It makes me feel braver, thinking of Carmen, and I stand up straighter. She'd have guided me away from the quicksand of self-pity. Instead of mourning these new symbols of disability, she'd have taken me out to celebrate my greater mobility with a stiff double-scotch and a movie or art museum—at our own tortoise pace. Yes, maybe I should think of these that way, Carmen: mobility instead of disability. I will; I will try.

Maura gives me the insurance slip to sign. I can't believe these hideous things cost way more than a luscious pair of sexy suede spike heels. I try my best to thank her, and then reluctantly leave the relative safety of the noisy PT room, trying to keep Carmen on my mind. But as soon as the double doors swung shut behind me, those weird sensations start: the childbirth-like contractions in my cervix which show up every time I confront a frightening new diagnosis or a deeper level of disability. What do they mean this time: self-pity? humiliation? No. Am I giving birth to yet another new self? Again? I think so.

At the moment, I feel too besieged to care.

The downside of having so many friends and acquaintances at the hospital is the way they all pop up when I want to be invisible. I desperately need to escape people's stares, to get used to my new status as Easter Seal Poster Woman. I want to imagine Carmen walking beside me, helping me absorb this new blow with her humor and gusto. My need to find a new internal balance, grapple with this greasy sense of self-loathing, maybe even locate a new wellspring of inward beauty, is so intense that tears prick my eyes. I have to stop and squeeze my eyelids shut to keep them from breaking free.

But before I even get to the elevator, I run into people I know—Wayne, the be-bopping assistant in the OR who held my hand through a second muscle biopsy in my thigh. Carmine, the kind phlebotomist who always tells me the latest shenanigans of his little boy so I don't feel the tourniquet or the pinch of his needle in my vein. And there's Joanne, Dr. Parrish's beautiful, brainy secretary, a lovely woman I've come to think of as a friend, and who shows her sensitivity with a quick smile before she tactfully turns away. I see too many people too fast, all wanting an explanation of my new status as a full-fledged cripple. I want to turn to the wall, find a place to hide.

Then, best or worst of all, comes my dear friend and former social worker, Roberta Horton. She got me through the first frightening few months after my diagnosis, and we worked hand-in-glove on the lupus video. Now she has no time to slip on a mask of professionalism to hide her confusion. Her discomfort makes me want to disappear.

"What happened?" Roberta whispers, love and shock merging on her face. She rests her hand on my shoulder, but I shake it off, as if it scalds.

"Nothing happened," I snap sullenly, feeling the nearest thing to adolescent rage I've felt in decades—perhaps because that kind of anger springs up as armor in the presence of someone's fiercely protective love. My rage entwines with a deep sense of shame for causing the pain I see on Roberta's face. I try to tighten my heart so I won't cry, and think a reference to Carmen, whom we both loved so dearly, might help both of us feel braver. Knowing she'll hear the echo of something Carmen said in the video, I blurt out, "I'm just trying to get from A to B."

It has the opposite effect. Roberta's eyes fill. "Oh," she says. "I see." Her tears spill over. Then her professionalism rises; she wipes her cheeks, waiting quietly to see what I'll say next.

"Listen, do me a favor?" I say, my throat strangling again. I look down at the floor as if something helpful might be written on the scuffed, no-color tile. "Could you take my cane for me? In case I need it again? No one needs three assistive devices." I thrust my battered, suddenly beloved wooden cane towards her.

Tears spurt out of my eyes, squirting almost horizontally. I quickly turn and try to shake them away. It's my bitter first lesson that, with crutches, I'll never have a hand free while I walk to wipe my nose, brush away a fly, or hold an ice cream cone.

'Listen, I'm late for an appointment with Parrish, so I gotta run. So to speak." I try reaching for some black humor I can't quite manage. "I just can't talk now, Roberta; please understand," I choke.

"I do understand, Ellen. I'll keep this till you need it." Roberta's voice is soft and quavery, her tears a gift I can't accept.

"Why don't you give it to Linda Leff, the nurse in Outpatient Infusion? I'll be there all next week." Then I scuff away on four legs with no goodbye. The elevator opens and then mercifully shuts behind me.

When the elevator opens on seven, I run smack into Dr. Parrish himself, a blur of unstoppable energy bustling down the hall waving a fistful of papers. He stops dead in his shoes and booms in his most authoritative tones, "What happened? Are you all right? What's going on here?"

With my usual cowardice at moments of confrontation, my mind jump-cuts to a fantasy, this time the moment when Sleeping Beauty touches the spindle and even the fire stops mid-crackle in her castle. Everyone in the rheumatology waiting room, jam-packed with patients, turns and stares at me. Then everyone freezes into a weird TV-hospital-show tableau: Dorothy, the receptionist, her pen poised above a list of names; Ms. Green, the skilled nurse who often helps me in the Infusion Room pauses mid-greeting; Angela, the phlebotomist with the Mona Lisa smile; lovely Pilar, a gentle nurse who helped me through a bout of meningitis; Dr. MacKenzie, Dr. Ye: they all stop mid-gesture and stare at me.

"I said, what's going on here?" Dr. Parrish thunders again.

Then, just as when Sleeping Beauty wakes, everyone goes back to their tasks. Pilar calls the next patient; Ms. Green checks a medication order; Dorothy types in her computer. Dr. Parrish frowns at me and my flesh shrinks beneath my skin. I feel the same shame I felt with Roberta: that I have somehow failed him and all his devoted doctoring. I manage to say quietly, "Please, Dr. Parrish—I'm embarrassed in front of all these people. You told me to go to PT, and I just came from there. I'll explain everything in your exam room."

He leads the way without a word. Mortified, I clump behind him into an empty room, where I explain without a single tear how Maura in PT gave me these crutches and why.

For a long moment, he doesn't say a word. Just as I had, he looks down at the scuffed, no-color tiles, as if something interesting might be written there. Then he sighs, makes a brief notation in my chart, and says, "Let's go over your meds."

I don't say anything, but I need him to say so much more. To explore, even a little, how I feel about this new level of disability. It doesn't occur to me that his shock and outrage might indicate how much he cares about my well-being. It also doesn't occur to me that he could possibly be as disappointed as I am that my disease has done so much damage.

I think we both know we've lost a major battle, but we have no idea how to bind up each other's wounds. We know neuropathy is incurable, and that he's done everything possible to treat it. He's sent in the foot soldiers, the cavalry, the cannons, and the nuclear warheads—the biggest, newest medical weapons available. I in no way blame him; how could I? I know he's used the art and science of medicine as well as his enormous personal gifts of intelligence, perseverance, and passion. What more could he do?

But in addition to my own strange sense of failure—maybe I didn't try hard enough to get better?—I need him to acknowledge what's happening to me; to acknowledge this deep new wound to my psyche and self-image as a woman. It would be so simple for him to say, "I'm sorry." Or, perhaps, "How do you feel about this?"

He doesn't say anything.

Neither do I. A sense of—false?—pride enforces my silence. Once again, I force myself to swallow my tears.

I accept that a cure is not possible. But what about healing? Simply acknowledging the impact illness has on me, on my life—especially in the face of a terrible new blow like this one—would have a deeply healing impact.

But in the two years he's taken care of me, despite our burgeoning sense of partnership over my care, we've never explored the vast differences between healing and curing; at this point in time, neither of us has the vocabulary or concepts at hand. It doesn't occur to either of us to say what we feel.

The wall between patient and doctor remains insurmountable.

I've never felt more alone in my life.

CHAPTER 14
The Cocktail Party

1996

I LICK MY LIP GLOSS AT PARTY INVITATIONS THE WAY A CAT GLOATS above a bowl of cream. I love the allure of party lights glowing ritzy and golden in the dark, the warm buzz of voices that pull me inside, the pleasure of wondering who's there. I never tire of meeting new people and hearing their stories; of watching someone assemble in the smoky air before me as they speak, like an image swimming to the surface of a developing Polaroid.

That's why I relish the chink of ice, the first rough burn of scotch on my tongue, the frisson when the warm delight of anticipation rubs against the cool stroke of momentary stage fright. And so I take an eager breath, bypass the shallows at the edges of the room, and plunge deep into the center of the crowd.

But not anymore. Wading into an elegant, softly chatting crowd dressed in basic black and ancestral pearls doesn't have quite the same cachet when I also don leg braces and metal crutches that fit like ugly bracelets around my forearms. These new facts of my life are becoming as routine to me as brushing my teeth, dabbing Chanel No. 5 in the hollows of my throat, and tucking house keys into a glittery evening bag. But they seem to repel strangers as much as saying, "Good evening. I think I have bedbugs."

That Christmas, as I career downhill ever faster into disability, Jim and I are invited to a housewarming cocktail party by Nancy and Robert—a couple we met many years before when our son fell in love with their daughter on the first day of nursery school. It was a cordial but hardly intimate relationship, massaged by years of pleasantries, an occasional brunch, and the joyous havoc of children's birthday parties. At the very last minute, Jim's legal case blows up, so I go alone. Eager to partake of holiday cheer, I dress my deteriorating silhouette carefully in flowing black silk and pearls, then set out into the bitter wind sweeping across Riverside Drive. I can't resist the chance to peek at their newly renovated townhouse, no doubt the height of Upper West Side elegance.

Shortly after the butler greets me at the heavy oak door, Nancy herself appears, red hair gleaming against emerald velvet. She gives the air a kiss in the general direction of my cheek, bids me a brief hello, then watches uneasily as the butler helps me off with my coat—an awkward bit of business which requires him to hold my crutches. She looks startled by them, though far too demure to acknowledge it. Last time we met, I'd used a jaunty Irish burled cane that could still pass as a fashion statement. The ugly metal certainly doesn't harmonize with the beautifully refurbished decor.

As our conversation limps to a halt, I take a deep breath and look up at the long oak staircase that leads upstairs to the party on the parlor floor. Beautiful. Daunting.

With a stiff smile, my hostess escorts me to this curving masterpiece, which I acknowledge with genuine admiration. Arriving ahead of me at the foot of the stairs, Nancy's hand rests gracefully on the polished banister, her diamonds glittering in the light of the polished period chandelier. We both admire them.

"Can I help you?" she says in carefully dulcet tones.

"Yes, you could help, Nancy." I answer gratefully. "You could take one of my sticks while I climb the stairs."

With a slight twitch of her delicate, possibly renovated, nose, Nancy takes one crutch with the very tips of her fingers, as if it might be infected with contagious material. She regains her taut smile and keeps up a skein of chatter while I wait at the foot of the staircase. The moment goes on a bit too long.

"Is there something else I can do for you?" she says again, her left hand still resting on the banister—the very banister I require in order to haul myself up to the parlor floor.

"Yes," I say. "I need to use the banister."

She finally understands and moves to the wall side of the stairs, while I heave myself, step by step, to the top. I'm breathless and sweating by the time I get there. By then, I suspect Nancy can't wait to get rid of me. She gestures toward a dark, empty room at the far end of the hall. A Christmas tree sparkles in one corner, but otherwise it's crowded with shadows.

"Why don't you go in there, out of the crowd, and I'll get you a drink," she suggests. "White wine or red?"

"Scotch, please," I answer, "on the rocks," looking from the shadowy room to the drawing room at other end of the long hall. It's filled with golden light, and laughter and the murmuration of people. As I turn toward it, Nancy tries to steer me toward the dark room.

"It will be so much easier if you sit down back there." she says, her jaw a bit tight.

"No," I insist, "I'd really rather wade into the crowd. You don't have to worry about me," I say, my jaw as tight as hers. Our eyes lock and I win. She turns toward the bar.

She returns with a glass of white wine. I take it with a small sigh of thanks then turn immediately toward the golden room. Two people try to squeeze past me in the hallway but have the decency to be introduced briefly when Nancy snags them for the obligatory hand-off. Then they quickly excuse themselves and disappear for the rest of the evening—as does Nancy herself.

Holding my wine glass in my left hand, I let that crutch dangle loosely from my arm as I inch my way down the hall into the well-lit room, only to find myself at a wall of backs. Several people at the far side of this impenetrable circle catch a glimpse of my face, begin to smile, then notice my crutches. An iron mask on each face slams shut.

After waiting a polite interval, I say, "Excuse me," to the backs. When there's no response, I excuse myself again rather insistently, then work my way along the near wall to the right merely to enter the room, being careful not to knock the ancestral portraits askew, wondering whose ancestors these really are. I try several times, and fail, to start conversations with elbows and

backs festively attired in velvet, silk, or tweed. I try to squirm my way into
the center of the room. I try to smile at people over several shoulders and
backs, hoping that might haul up a portcullis or make the widening moat
between everyone else and me disappear.

It does not.

Every time someone starts to smile at me, the grin extinguishes like a
match on a wet wick as soon as they see the crutches.

I look for familiar faces from yesteryear, from my kids' preschool and
birthday party days. I sip, then swig, the white wine I do not want. I scan
the crowd again, hoping someone will spot me and wave and say, "Ellen!
Hi! Wait, I'm coming over."

I wiggle my way along another wall, looking for an empty armchair.
Perhaps it will help if I can sit and stop balancing so many items; perhaps
then I could lose the tension in my face, flash a warm smile, and find an
answering grin or two. But the few chairs are occupied, and the delicate
dowagers and pregnant Junior Leaguers clearly haven't the slightest interest
in relinquishing their Chippendale roosts. Nor should they, I feel. In truth,
I really don't want to sit; I want to talk. But as I gaze around the center of
the room, I see that there are no familiar faces; just more backs or closed
conversational clusters. As soon as someone spies my sticks, a profile swivels
into a back.

I will myself to turn iron as my throat thickens with tears of outrage
and disappointment. I turn those tears iron, too; I will not shed one tear in
this place where there is no place for me. For a moment, I long for Jim at
my elbow, but only for a moment; longing will turn me back into flesh. So I
withdraw inside my own iron mask. I set my sweating wineglass on a highly
polished, inlaid wood table, resisting any impulse to cushion the goblet with
my napkin so it won't leave a white ring.

I turn around and clomp with all the dignity I can muster past all the
elegant backs toward the entry I used into the golden room, then finally
down the long hallway. But just before descending the stairs, I peer into the
shadowy room at the end of the hall. It's still dark and empty. Then—

No. It isn't empty. There, by the window, amid all the well-polished
oak, gazing out alone at the night, sits a silent figure in silhouette. The room
is so dim I would have missed it if not for the multi-colored smear of Christmas lights along curved steel wheels.

A seated figure. In a wheelchair.

A halogen flash of rage snatches my breath away. So that's it. Dear Nancy wanted me to disappear, along with the other skeleton at the feast. Well, I have no intention of being segregated into the cripple room. I came to this party to meet people and hear stories and laugh—not to commiserate.

I struggle down those elegant, curved stairs as fast as I can, barely resisting an impulse to gouge the oak banister with the steel bracelet of one crutch. I find my coat, struggle into it—the butler having disappeared—and haul open the heavy oak door by pulling all my weight back on it with both hands.

I relish the rough burn of a double scotch when I reach home, thank you very much. But as I sip, turning from iron back into flesh, I realize with horror: I did exactly the same thing to the person in that wheel chair that Nancy and her guests had done to me: I turned away.

Why?

CHAPTER 15

Stay Within Yourself

1996

NANCY'S MIX-UP ON MY DRINK MERELY IRRITATED ME. BUT WHAT burned the living hell out of me was her attempt to segregate me in the dark cripple room, away from the golden lights and away from the other guests—one cripple, one "problem" entertaining another. But that event, that attitude, is about far more than it is about me. And I need to understand what lies beneath what happened. Why did my hostess and her guests treat me like Typhoid Mary?

Before I was visibly disabled, I'd never gone to get-togethers where nobody but the hostess spoke to me. It happens all the time now in rooms full of strangers, even though I'm just as interested in meeting new people and hearing their stories as I've ever been. I've never been the luscious, long-stemmed blonde who draws every man in the room like bees to nectar. I'm the good listener who nods at all the right places in the story. Why doesn't anybody give me a chance now? Why do I find myself the leper in certain types of formal and semi-formal social situations? I want to find the meanings at the bottom of this social conundrum—not just for me, but for all of us.

Perhaps people fear I'll regale them with some sob-sister tale of woe. Are they reluctant to chitchat for fear they'll get stuck with me for the rest of the evening? Do they think that physical disabilities are bundled with mental deficiencies? Are they afraid I'll attack them for being whole-bodied? Are they so insecure about their own self-image that they're afraid it might be damaged if they're seen in close proximity to a (gasp!) cripple? At best, their distance might be a form of kindness: a fear of offending or hurting me if they say something "wrong."

Sad, all these fears. The last thing I want to do at a party is rehash my difficulties—or even think about them. I go as a person, not a poster child; I want to have fun, not wring my hands and weep.

So I suspect that many people don't speak with me simply because they're embarrassed. They're not sure what to say, so they say nothing. Probably they were taught as children to say nothing; not to ask any questions for fear of being rude or intrusive. It's a shame they learned those childhood lessons so well. For if they felt free to ask a few simple, direct questions, most of the discomfort on both sides would dissipate, with disabilities quickly pushed aside to make room for natural conversation. Now, as adults, many people turn away from me entirely. Not wanting to stare, they look the other way, just as they were taught as children that it was the "polite" and "right" thing to do. This makes me invisible—which is even more painful than collecting stares.

The fact is that I'd prefer a few honest, straightforward questions, like "What happened?" Or, "Are you okay?" I'd give a few straightforward answers—"Neurological disease, but I'm on top of it." Then we could go on to more interesting and festive topics.

People don't just pull this complex of feelings—dare I say prejudices?—out of the closet and put them on with their party clothes. It takes lots of training to embed them in their social interactions. And it could disappear in one generation if children were taught differently. In my experience, children are fascinated, not repulsed, by crutches, canes, wheelchairs, and electric scooters. Of course they notice my crutches or cane—even toddlers in strollers sit up and take notice that I walk differently—but their first response isn't hostility or repulsion. It's curiosity about something new.

Kids, especially kids untainted by parental fears, aren't afraid of me. They're either indifferent or fascinated. They actually think it's cool to walk with a cane or crutches—for about twenty-five seconds. Then they get it and get bored. Given the opportunity, they might try swinging on my cane or crutches, then turn them into swords, spears, wands, or periscopes according to the twists and turns of their imaginations. And they ask lots of questions—"What happened to you? How come you need those? Will you always need them?"—questions I don't at all mind answering, unless I'm in a hurry, and even then it takes less than half a minute to satisfy a child's curiosity. "They help me walk" usually does it. Once they get an answer, they go back to their ice cream cones, play, and parents, seeing me as one tiny part of their fascinating world.

This satisfying interchange, unfortunately, rarely happens. What happens instead is that their embarrassed or frightened or guilty parent whisks them away with a sharp, tense command to "Stay away from that lady"— the one with those strange sticks. I see their curious little faces close like fists, and can imagine the questions behind their eyes. "Are those sticks weapons? Would she use them to hurt me? Is that why Mommy's acting so strangely? Is that why Daddy acts so upset as soon as he sees her?"

Then, whamo!—the interesting stranger turns into the Other. With a sigh, I watch one more curious kid being dragged up Broadway by the elbow, looking back at me with fear, suspicion, or even dislike in her eyes, when before there was curiosity and the excitement of "Oh, look, here's something new I want to find out about."

The behavior of the alarmed parent—"Don't hurt the lady! Hold my hand, now," when said lady is all the way across the store—is so preposterous that it easily boomerangs and gets interpreted by the child as "Don't let that crippled lady hurt you." Even if it's well meant—some strange effort to protect me—that's not what the child remembers. So I watch the child learn to fear the Other from a tense, frightened mom or dad who learned this behavior from tense and frightened parents. And when the children are grown up and sophisticated, they'll put on "fear" along with their silk or velvet clothes when they go to chat with the "right" people at the Christmas cocktail party.

The same attitude is also made manifest in a more outrageous form in the behavior of some total strangers who go way out of their way to apologize profusely—"Sorry! Oh, I'm so, so sorry!"—when they barely brush me on a sidewalk or at a theater intermission. "Sorry!" they say, in a highly dramatic, almost amusing overreaction.

It happened recently in the checkout line at the supermarket. I was waiting my turn, reading the headlines on the *Star*: "Nun Gives Birth to Quads in Convent Chapel," when a cart ran into mine—but not into me.

"I am so very sorry," the woman said, looking at my legs, then at my crutches, but never once at my eyes or face. "I'm so sorry!" she repeated, shaking her head with pity in her eyes. She didn't knock me down or graze my baby toe, so what was all that apology and pity for? She wasn't sorry she hit my shopping cart; she was sorry for me.

I wanted to say, 'Look, lady, I'm not sorry for myself, so why should you be? This is just who I am. I don't need your pity. I'm a happy person, happier than most. I like to walk down the street in the sunshine, and go to the supermarket or my writing class without being flooded with the unwanted treacle of a stranger's pity. I'm having a very good life, and the last thing I want or need is pity because I walk funny." Of course I didn't say it; I never think of the perfect response until days later.

But you don't have to take my word for all this. Monitor your own reactions. Wait till next time you brush close by somebody crippled or blind or homeless or visibly mentally ill or retarded. Do you apologize a lot, or try to pass by in an elaborately circuitous route while whistling at the clouds or craning your neck to examine the shop windows? Do you get a kind of oogy, embarrassed feeling in your stomach? And if you dig down under that discomfort instead of running away from it, do you find guilt?

And if you dig down under the guilt, is there something else? Is there a smidgen of rage? Take a deep breath and observe yourself for a few minutes, quietly and honestly. See if you can figure out what's there, and I'll bet you the New York State Lottery Jackpot that you'll find a strange anger. Anger that you have to confront somebody like this.

And then try to take the next step. I'll bet that underneath your anger is something that feels worse: fear. Fear that it could happen to you. Perhaps you also feel some weird, secondhand version of "survivor's guilt"—some perfectly personal echo of "there but for grace go I." And perhaps you want to turn away because you are afraid to see; because looking at "those" people awakens your own vulnerability and deep fears.

I think that's why Nancy wanted to control where I went and what I did at her party—because if she could control me, perhaps she could in some magical way also control her own fate. Perhaps she could unconsciously pretend that she could control the universe so that what happened to me could never happen to her or the people she loves.

That's the fear that's covered by anger. And being near me can be too close for comfort for some people. I can represent the fear we cannot control; those people that we—including me—want to turn away from, whether it's at a posh party, or in the park, or on the street: the old people trembling and drooling in wheelchairs; the homeless people (though sometimes we leave out the word "people" when we talk about them) who sleep on cardboard beds over the hot vents from the laundries that dry our clean clothes; the blind people tapping their red and white canes in front of them in their daily act of heroism we call walking down the street. We turn away because it's the only way we can pretend we're in control. We think being in control of our eyeballs and our field of vision will somehow, magically, control the course of our fate. But obviously we can't control our fate or our fear, and turning away is really turning away from our own vulnerability.

I think that's why people sometimes turn away from me.

Here's the ironic coda: I do it, too. I treated the person in the wheelchair as the Other. I share those same layers of guilt and rage, transfer them to the Other, and hide under my own shield of resentful not-noticing. And even more: fear and disdain of the Other contributes to my own self-loathing. That party was so painful, in part, because other people's reactions to me reinforced my attitudes toward my self.

I looked in the mirror before I left home; I knew how I looked. I knew I'd gone from a size four to a size eight, sometimes ten, with a face grown round as the moon from steroids, my body swollen and flabby because of my inability to exercise. I suspect I looked almost as crippled, ugly, and old to other people as I did to myself—my harshest judge by far. Even if Nancy didn't want to shunt me aside, a large part of me already wants to hide in a closet, or to stay home and punish myself for looking the way I do. I mourn the fact daily that I no longer look like my "real" self. I had to force myself to dress up and get out that evening, especially without Jim. Nancy's perhaps unintentional unkindness added insult to my own self-inflicted ego injuries. I've internalized my society's distorted cultural lessons only too well: I know I bear the stigma of the Cripple that separates me from all those Normals.

And, of course, I could see nothing of the scars and vulnerabilities carefully hidden beneath the other partygoers' elegant clothes. It took me a while to realize my hubris in thinking I was the only wounded person in that room. How arrogant of me; how tawdry and lacking in compassion.

Despite suffering social frostbite at the cocktail party, after a while I decide I'll be damned rather than see myself as any less valuable than the next person because I can't run for the Broadway bus, kick a soccer ball, or spin a pirouette the way I once did. Analyzing what happened is the beginning of a process of healing myself from the hurt inflicted by other people's judgments. Because I realize I can't change them—I can only change myself.

One way I could try to protect myself is to hide behind a shield of anger; to say "the hell with them, who needs them?" But anger wears me out; it makes me feel cut off in ways I hate. It makes me feel as if I'm digging a moat between me and everybody else. I'd rather shed the anger and find a way to have their pity slide off me, as if I'm made of Teflon.

Jim gives me a way to shed pity and other kinds of ugliness.

"Try to stay within yourself when people objectify and hurt you," he says.

"What does that mean?"

"Athletes talk about staying within themselves when they want to concentrate their inner focus; when they want to ignore the fans, and the other players, and all the brouhaha."

Stay within myself. Focus there. A good idea. Can I do it? I try it out. I go inside myself and listen to what I feel and think when people avoid me. Or when they stare at me with pity, which makes me feels so soiled. I stay within and pay attention to my own concerns instead of all those nasty intrusions.

With practice, I create a quiet refuge inside, where I can look out and observe. And I realize that these people are strangers I care nothing about—people who know nothing about me. What they feel belongs entirely to them; it has very little—no, nothing—to do with who I am. It's their discomfort, their fear, their embarrassment that informs their actions and reactions—it doesn't belong to me. When I learn how to remain quietly within myself, I can stand apart from their pity, their judgments, their disdain or refusal to see the actual me. I shed their feelings the way window glass sheds rain. It doesn't take away all the pain, but eases it considerably.

When I no longer care about the static from strangers, I'm free to look at myself honestly: Yes, I'm changed by my illness and its manifestations. The way I walk bears heavily upon the way I live. But it's not possible to measure the power of my intellect or imagination, or the depth of my soul, by assessing the strength of my muscles. The reach of my curiosity is not tied to the amount of medication I take, or the strength of my legs, or the canes or crutches that help me get where I want to go. I can stay within myself and know I am still Ellen, no matter how transformed I am by disease or circumstance. I begin to understand that no matter how I look, I am still and always will be myself—changed, to be sure; but still and always exactly who I am.

CHAPTER 16
Sanctuary

Without music life would be a mistake.

Friedrich Nietzsche

1996

The prescription in my hand says:

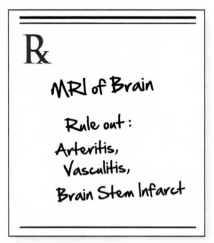

Rx

MRI of Brain

Rule out:
Arteritis,
Vasculitis,
Brain Stem Infarct

I hand it to the technician in the MRI suite. He points to the narrow bed; I lie down, trembling.

You can do this, says Rational Ellen.

Just stay calm, Observing Ellen adds.

But they're examining my brain, answers Scared Ellen.

There's nothing wrong, says Rational Ellen. *Nothing serious.*

You hope, Wiseass taunts.

The technician straps me down on a narrow pallet: knees, trunk-and-arms, forehead.

Like Dr. Frankenstein's monster.

"Don't move," he commands, voice colder than the room.

I forget and try to nod, but I'm now completely immobile.

Like a quadriplegic. Ugh, the Observer says.

Nose itches. I have to scratch.

Tough luck, Wiseass points out.

"Can't you hold your feet together?" he asks.

"No."

He straps them.

Too tight, Scared Ellen complains. *It hurts.*

Shut up, all the Ellens tell her.

"Keep still." He's irritated.

"I'm shivering."

"The machines need it cold."

He wraps me in two sheets. Both cold. Like a mummy.

Like a baby, whines Scared.

He punches the green button. "Let's go."

"Wait! Can I lis—"

"No."

"Do you have music? Headphones?"

"Not today. System's broke."

The MRI hums. Green and red lights blink.

Slowly, I enter the flawless white sarcophagus. It presses down around me, much too close. Strikes me snow-blind.

"We're starting. Total time, forty minutes."

Ugh.

MRI. Sounds like . . . sneakers in a dryer. Nuts chasing bolts. Like . . . robots, learning to dance . . . the polka. The man with the hook scrabbling at the roof of Teddy's car, midnight, down by Pennypack Creek.

No. Too scary. Start again.

OK, then . . . Let's write a cartoon. Think *New Yorker.* Carnegie Hall:

MRI machine mid-stage. Heads of audience, seen from behind. Conductor lifts baton. Over shoulder of audience member, we read the program:

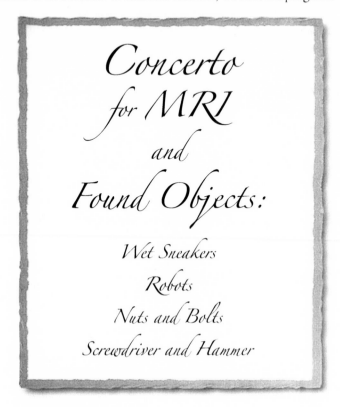

Concerto for MRI and Found Objects:

Wet Sneakers
Robots
Nuts and Bolts
Screwdriver and Hammer

No, I can't think.
Can't breathe.
Let.Me.Out. Feels like death.
Don't want to die.
Help me. Let me out.
Help me. Oh, please—help me—and—

Suddenly, rising up out of the living hollows of my bones and brain, out of that deep wellspring of joy seated near my soul, vibrating right inside my breastbone, soars: the Bach *Double Violin Concerto*.

The first few notes promise me this dingy lab painted the color of despair is merely one tiny corner of the world; the next strands of melody lift me above my slowly exploding composure; and now the elegantly braided golden chords of the violin fugue lead me away, into a flash of sunlight where I breathe green air and fly free of my body. Unseen musicians play my bones like violins. The music lifts me up as glory floods in like a rising tide.

My work with Eric helps me understand how important it is to go exploring in my past to look not only for the frightening parts of what I learned through my father's illnesses, but for the peaceful interludes and positive ways our family found to get us through the wrenching times. Whenever I have to go into the hospital, to endure spinal injections or another painful treatment, it's no accident that I think of music as a portable sanctuary that goes with me almost anywhere.

Terrified in the middle of a stroke, after Dr. Lewis calls Jim, I use my one allotted call from the ICU to phone my dear friend Sarah.

"What can I do?" she asks.

"Help Jim and the kids," I say. "And please, bring me music." When she arrives with a shopping bag full of Brahms, Dvorak, and Bach, I somehow know I can make it through the spinal tap and other hideous moments.

Where did I learn that habit of solace?

My childhood was drenched in music: my mother sang and played the piano beautifully, and when I begged to play, too, she promised that as soon as I could sit on the piano stool and touch the pedals with one foot I could begin. So at four, after lots of stretching, we put on white gloves and pretty dresses and took the trolley car to Miss Haynes' white house for our lessons. We played duets at recitals, curtseyed to applause, then enjoyed tea cakes and lemonade. When my mother went downtown for her voice lessons, I lay in the crimson twilight under the grand piano, music vibrating in every bone.

It's a Technicolor Sunday morning. I dribble honey on my pancakes and it catches stars of sunlight. Daddy conducts the Philadelphia Orchestra with his fork. The golden notes of a violin drizzle down around us in the sunlight, thick and sweet as honey.

Belly warm and full, I sprawl on the floor in front of an ancient mahogany record player much bigger than I am. The booming magenta chords of the War- saw Concerto *vibrate deep inside my chest. Magenta*—my favorite color in the sixty-four Crayola crayon box.

When the record ends, I wait, suspended in velvet silence, till the next heavy disk flops down. The needle starts to hiss-ss-ss, then notes unfurl from the record's circling ridges. I count on those notes, every time the same, not like Mommy, who can be happy one minute, angry another. The notes wave over me like a large white banner that shelters me, for a time, from the big black spider that jumps out on black-and-white days when Mommy gets mad and when Daddy disappears for a noperation.

What is it, a noperation?

I am a little girl of three, living in our Rosebush House, where my daddy calls me Nelle—Ellen-backwards. Daddy has been away a long time in the hospital for another noperation. I still don't understand what a noperation is, but he's finally home.

Maybe it's Daddy. There's a bandage on one eye and the other won't smile. His face is white as our fridge and his lips are skinny. His whiskers make his face gray. His hands shake, even when he's resting on the couch.

"Hi, Nelle," he says, kinda whispery. Way back, he showed me Nelle, Nell- E, Ellen-backwards, with a pencil on paper. So it must be Daddy. He's wearing Daddy's maroon bathrobe and scuffy maroon leather slippers. Maroon is another one of my favorite Crayola colors. I go closer to hug and smell his good daddy smell.

"Don't hug Daddy hard," Mommy warns. "Don't you dare jiggle him."

She pulls me away.

"Sit over there," she commands, pointing to a brown leather hassock across the room near Jack Scarlet's window.

I won't.

"I said go!" Her words scald like too-hot soup.

I stomp over, but I won't sit.

Daddy closes his one eye I can see. Does the one under the bandage close, too?

"C'mon, Daddy, let's go outside and play. Let's mow the lawn." He has a big *green mower, and I have a toy one.*

"Maybe tomorrow, Nelle," *he answers, and his eye closes again. I see fat white bandages sticking out: one wrist, two arms, three throat.*

"Daddy's too tired to play. He has to sleep now, Ellen."

"Want to cuddle then? Just a little? I missed you so much." *I can't help crying.*

"He can't jiggle, Ellen; you'll hurt him too much. And stop crying or I'll send you upstairs to your room. Big girls—good girls—don't cry and nag."

I plop on the hassock, and put my head on my knees. I feel tears down my legs. I'm afraid she'll send me away from Daddy after I waited so long to see him. I want to be a big good girl, but it's hard to stop crying once I start.

I jump up, but stay away. "How 'bout music, Daddy? Want to listen to music?"

Daddy turns his face and opens his eye. Now it's smiling, and I see my very own soft Nelle-light and smile-crinkles at the corner.

"An excellent idea. Pearl? The Sibelius Violin Concerto? It'll do us all good."

Mommy puts the records on the spindle and clicks the starter. I see the Jack Scarlet rosebush climbing up the wall outside, all big thorns now; no roses till summer. The first fat black record flops down, the needle goes hiss—ss—ss, and I rock to the rhythm in my little rocking chair by the window. In a few heartbeats, the creamy satin song of the violin lifts us up and up, then binds us loosely together in a momentary peace.

Whenever Daddy's home, the world floods with music. Daddy and Mommy and I sing The Mikado *as we wash and dry the dishes. We are Gen-tle-men-of-Japan, or Three-Little-Maids-From-School. Daddy is the Wand'ring Minstrel, starring and conducting the orchestra at the same time, singing the words I remember:*

"A wand'ring minstrel, I,
A thing of shreds and patches;
A man of songs and snatches,
and dre-ee-mee lu-u-la-by-eyes,
And dreamy lullabyes."

He draws out the notes with glee, curling his pinky fingers, his unruly eyebrows lifting with his voice, and I love him down to his toes. Clowning under our tent of music creates a safe space that makes me feel nothing can hurt me as long as Daddy is near.

Each morning begins with singing at the small William C. Jacobs Elemen-
tary School in Bustleton, PA in 1952. The building is a hundred years old and
holds barely a hundred students. After attendance each morning, we slide back
blackboard sashes between the classrooms on the second floor to create one large
room that becomes our auditorium. The little kids file upstairs and squeeze in
beside us big third-graders on the seats of flip-top desks so old they still have flakes
of dried-up ink in the glass inkwells.

After standing to salute the flag and sitting "still as statues" for the Bible
reading, we open fat, sand-colored copybooks that crackle with sheets full of typewritten, pale-purple words. The books reek of the dizzy smell of ditto ink and
flour paste. Mrs. Crissie, the stern teacher who wears garish orange pancake
makeup and magenta lipstick that oozes outside her lip lines in dark threads,
bangs out sour but enthusiastic chords on a rickety piano.

As sun shines through the wavy old window glass, we all sing to greet the
day:

     "This is my Father's world, And to my listening ears

     All nature sings, As round me rings

     The music of the spheres."

I was sure in second grade that the hymn was about my father. Although I
know by now, in third, that it isn't, I can't help pretending it still is.

My father pushes back the dirty dishes on our kitchen table and
scrubs a clean space with his napkin. Then he draws a diagram of the sun
and planets on a piece of my loose-leaf paper. I always feel a shiver, a kind
of exultation, when my physicist-father tries to help me understand something about how the universe works, even though I'm only ten. When he
rotates an orange under the lamp above our kitchen table to show how
the earth circles the sun—how night becomes day, then gives way again
to night—I feel connected to the planets and stars. Knowing about gravity
and centrifugal force not only makes me feel subject to their power, but
also in possession of that power in some small way.

Now Daddy explains Johannes Kepler's theory of the "music of the spheres." My mother keeps clearing the table, half-listening. I know she's both happy and jealous that my father is so patient and gentle with me, when her father was always so cruel.

"Copernicus proved that the planets orbited the sun," Daddy says, still drawing the solar system in his precise way. "Then Kepler plotted the orbit of each planet. He believed that each planet, or sphere, circling in its orbit, created its own musical tone."

"Like when you run your finger around the edge of a wine glass and it sings?"

"A little like that. Well, Kepler thought each planet had a different tone because of its size, and the size and shape of its orbit."

Daddy finishes sketching the dotted lines of the orbits in his drawing, then turns each line into an arrow. "When all the planets moved through their orbits, he thought they made music together—a kind of celestial, crystal chord. He called it "musica universalis." But you can't actually hear it—it's more of a theory. Even so, I like imagining it."

"Me too."

We sit quietly. "Hey, let's go outside, Daddy—maybe we can hear it."

"Well . . . we could try. Want to come, Pearl?"

"No, that's all right. I'll just finish up here, then relax with my book." Mommy smiles a little sadly. "I'm not as imaginative as you two."

Daddy and I walk into the starry suburban night and sit on our front step. The air feels chilly after the steamy kitchen and dew twinkles orange on the grass, tinted by the light over our front door. I feel bombarded by the normal night sounds: the pulsing shrill of tree frogs and crickets; moths and June bugs bumping on the screens; faint clinks of silverware and glasses from the house next door. Daddy clicks off the bright light.

It sounds quieter in the dark. I try to hear the silence: to strain away the tiny sounds of tiny creatures that hug our tiny planet, including us. Sitting quietly with my father, I feel huge and infinitesimal at the same time; a tiny speck, yet connected to his large ideas.

The stars are perfectly silent way above us, but I think maybe—just maybe—I can hear the deep, thrilling pulse of the planets because of what Daddy told me. It seems both impossible yet entirely fitting that we two can listen together to an unheard music struck from the universe by our knowing. Maybe we're the only two people in the world except Kepler who will ever hear this glassy harmony, I think, and just because we have faith enough to listen. How lucky we are to trust each other, and the universe, so completely.

❁   ❁   ❁

Both the bull and the bullfighter know how to find their *querencia*— their place of sanctuary within the ring. Smelling blood, hearts hammering, fighting for breath, facing death, both find places of rest before the battle continues. I, too, must find my own sanctuary—and music and memory help me.

As an adult, I move through years of illness, lighting one match at a time to find my path through a dark forest full of pain and confusion. Even when I'm most frightened, music offers radiant, inviolable moments, no matter what pounces on me out of that darkness. I carry it everywhere I can. It offers protection in the sterile boredom of a doctor's waiting room or a desolate underground hallway, when I lie on a gurney waiting for a procedure, staring at the water-stained ceiling with my bladder bursting.

Though my father's frequent disappearances for surgery taught me terror, he also showed me dignity and strength in his responses to infirmity and disability. During World War II, my father—a research physicist—was excused from military service so he could work on crucial army weapons, helping to invent, then test, the recoilless rifle, which would be used all over the world in sharply different climates. About a month before I was born, he tested the gun in a special sub-zero laboratory, neglecting to wear protective gear. The gun exploded in the cold, spattering metal all over his body, immediately destroying his right eye and threatening his left. For weeks, he lay in Wills Eye Hospital, packed in sand bags so he wouldn't move and endanger the left optic nerve. My mother sat beside him every day, feeding and encouraging him, making a pink-and-brown calico elephant for me, stuffed with surgical cotton the nurses supplied. His vision was saved, and as soon as he could, he picked himself and went forward, to work on the first pilot ejection seat, still used by pilots when their planes go down. We christened it the Schecter Ejector.

It wasn't until I was an adult, grappling with my own physical losses, that I understood how difficult it must have been for him as a handsome young man to maintain a positive self-image and pursue his daunting career facing a lifetime of living with a glass eye that was extremely obvious and frequently infected. He also endured, with equanimity, the dozens of surgeries necessitated by the shrapnel wounds all over his face and body. Yet he never gave up, and because of his example, neither do I.

Even in my most despairing moments of illness, I try to spend my time well instead of wasting it. I heal my soul with the sunny dazzle of Mozart flute concertos; invite the passionate elegance of Brahms' violin and piano duets to remind me why I want to be alive; and ask the Brahms *Clarinet Quintet* to bind me to a Presence with wings I have come to know as God.

No matter where I hear it, even on the bleakest black-and-white days, even snowed into a white MRI sarcophagus, music still brings me back to those Technicolor Sunday mornings when my father conducted the entire Philadelphia orchestra with his fork, and I could almost taste the violin melodies flowing through our kitchen.

Music brings back the warm sunlight that shone on us like a blessing and sings of the evenings in a tiny, faraway kitchen when I was one of Three Little Maids from School, drying dinner plates till they shone as bright as moons.

It still holds the promise of a mysterious, crystalline harmony ringing out between the silent stars, and unfurls above me like an immaculate white banner bestowing sanctuary.

CHAPTER 17

Climbing Down the Mountain

1996

ONE SUMMER, JIM, ANNA AND I MEET SOME FRIENDS IN NORTHERN Italy. In resplendent sunshine, the others set out each morning to hike in the soaring Dolomites. My walking is poor despite the crutches and ankle braces, but Jim is entirely gracious about skipping the alluring peaks, which must be difficult, as he's been an ardent mountain man since his teens. He became an Adirondack Forty-Sixer at sixteen—meaning he climbed all forty-six Adirondack high peaks. He's also hiked the Sawtooths in Idaho, the Cascades in Washington State, the Wyoming Tetons, the Colorado Rockies, and the French and Swiss Alps. But he's hardly shown a flicker of disappointment about stomping along with me at a slow crawl down in the lowlands. He assures me that it's easy to be gracious after three days of hiking in Val Gardena with our friend, Jeff.

Day after cloudless day, Anna and the rest of the hikers set off early into the high cobalt sky and return in late afternoon after exploring another rugged peak. Jim and I walk on flat grassy trails below the rocky slopes. We stroll between rocks the color of sheep, and sheep the color of rocks, meeting droll cows that eye us warily as they stand knee-deep in wildflowers.

On Sunday, at end of our stay, the other families set out to explore

Sassolungo, another beautiful peak. A cable car whisks Jim and me to the top of a mountain called Col Raiser. The flat meadow is crowded with older couples and young families, out for a day of hiking in the beautiful weather. The trailheads leading down the mountain are clearly marked, beginning with "very easy."

It's a perfect day: hot sun, cool wind crisp as white wine, a few harmless, silky clouds driven into grand shapes that change every minute in the playful breeze.

"Let's hike, too," I say impulsively to Jim. "We can walk down. There's plenty of time, and it's a lovely day. We can take that "very easy" trail over there. It can't be that difficult if those old people and toddlers are doing it."

Jim looks tempted but wary, and I suspect—though he never says a word—that he's felt regret all those mornings when he didn't join the others.

"It won't be challenging for you," I say, "but it could be fun."

He looks doubtful. "What if you get too pooped? We'd still have to go all the way down?"

"I can do it, Jim. We've been taking little hikes all week. I'm in great shape—for me." I want to do it for myself, but also for him. "Come on, let's try. It's only noon. We have hours before dark."

We watch a family with young children scamper with their dog down the "very easy" trail. Jim paces back and forth. He eyes the sky, which is clear to all horizons. He looks at me, strides back and forth a few more times, then says, "Let's do it"—abruptly, as if committing himself before he can change his mind.

We buy chocolate, water, and oranges at the *refugio,* then set off. I quicken my pace to show off my good will and bravado.

"Take it easy," Jim says. "Budget your energy. It'll be a long day." Being directed that way makes me grit my teeth, but I slow my pace. Jim trudges with the metronome-steady snail's pace he adopts whenever he tries to match my steps. I take a deep, cleansing breath and shed annoyance; I want to relish every footfall, every sense.

The world feels so wide, suddenly. The air is thin and fresh, full of the sharp green scent of pine, clean earth, and wild flowers. It's so quiet we hear the chink of bells on the goats grazing far across the valley. The trail beckons, always sloping down. We find wooden benches, bleached pewter, waiting for us at the most breath-taking overlooks. We rest as much to honor the emerald valleys as for me to catch my breath.

On we walk, side by side, Jim pacing his long, skinny legs to my awkward, four-part strides—crutch-foot, crutch-foot. After an hour or so, we share an orange and a few squares of bittersweet chocolate. We hardly say a word, nearly drowning in pleasure.

The path narrows. Two hours. Three. Now the pitch gets so steep that huge logs have been set into the mud to break the slant. I have to jack-knife my legs over them. My breath becomes hard and harsh. We haven't seen anyone else for hours.

The going gets even rougher as the day moves into late afternoon. Now boulders higher than our heads jut into the path and block our way. I slide on my butt while Jim pulls me over the lower ledges—sometimes by my hands, sometimes by my ankles.

We stop to eat our last oranges and chocolate. My throat is dry from panting; my legs shaking. I wonder how much longer I can go on, but there's no turning back, and I'd never complain. Mercifully, Jim never says or implies "I told you so." I'd crumple if he did—not only for getting myself into this, but for dragging him with me.

It's now just past five. The mountain vaults so high behind us that we're already engulfed in twilight shadows under thick stands of trees. But below us, for the first time, we glimpse golden wheat fields, orderly rows of green crops, the roofs of houses, a gray belt of road. They look very far away. We zip our jackets against the chill and keep going.

More giant boulders. The angle is so steep I move only on my butt, my clothes and crutches filthy with mud and sweat. I'm too tired to speak, wondering if I'll make it.

Suddenly, the trail turns and we see a huge lozenge of sunlight. A few more steps, and the trees thin unexpectedly. The path jigs and jags, dwindles to nothing—and we hear high-pitched squeals. Could that be babies—laughing?

We break into sunlight, onto the lawn of a brightly-painted chalet with window boxes dripping red geraniums. Two young women sit on the brilliant green grass, three fat babies lolling between them on blankets. Two babies are identical blue-eyed blonde twins who look exactly like their mother. She shades her eyes against the sun, spots us, and jumps to her feet. She runs over, speaking rapidly, gesturing to me, my crutches, and the mountain. She shakes her head, amazed, then pounds me solidly on both shoulders.

Though I can't decipher one word of the Ladino language spoken only in that valley, I can feel what she's saying: "You? *You* climbed all the way down this mountain? Hurray for you!"

Yes, I did. Jim and I celebrate with a tight hug and a kiss, then accept the glasses of cool cherry juice her friend brings us from the kitchen.

We look at each other and belly laugh: Yes! We did it.

We climbed all the way down.

PART 4

A Case of Missing Identity

We shall not cease from exploration
And the end of all our exploring
Will be to arrive where we started
And to know the place for the first time.

T.S. Eliot, "Little Gidding"

CHAPTER 18

Home for the First Time

1993

WE'RE LATE, OF COURSE. THE SATURDAY MORNING SERVICE AT B'NAI Jeshurun, an Upper West Side synagogue better known as BJ, starts at 9:30—half an hour ago. Anna, eight, and Alex, eleven, grumble as we wait for the traffic light at 86th and West End. We're usually on a soccer field at this time on Saturdays.

"Why do we have to go to the *whole service?*" Anna moans in italics. "I don't even *know* Hillary. I don't *care* about her bat mitzvah."

I refuse to answer. I've explained a dozen times: This is what you do out of respect for your friends' children. Soon it will be your turn. See what you can learn.

I've never been to this synagogue. In fact, I've rarely gone to any synagogue. But soon our children will enroll in Hebrew school. We're considering BJ and want to check out the service. I didn't tell them that.

"Can I go outside if I can't sit still?" Alex, this time.

"No." "Yes." Jim, then me—in stereo, but not in sync.

The light changes. We cross in steamy silence.

I grind my jaw the way my father did, dreading the next few hours of stage-whispered complaints and hissed retorts. It's a ninety-four degree June morning, the air close-packed as damp cotton. I'm wearing a long black silk jumper to hide my brace; the collar of my gauzy white blouse is already wilting, and so am I. Other latecomers enter the large oak doors just ahead of us. A delicate woman wearing a short white linen suit and white stilettos looks so crisp and stylish that I'm suddenly drenched with shame at my sturdy flats and cane. I watch her disappear into a pew thinking that white linen is totally out of the question given two kids and my relationship with ketchup. But short skirts? High heels? Maybe someday . . .

"Psst, Ellen." Jim beckons, "seats."

We shuffle into seats about seven rows from the bimah, or altar, where Rabbi Marshall Meyer, an energetic, powerfully-built man, towers over Hillary, a tall willow-wand of a girl. They both wear beautiful white prayer shawls.

The four of us rustle around, knocking into each other, trying to find the right page —trying, even, to find the correct book. *The Methodist Hymnal?* The *Tanakh*—the *Torah?* The *Siddur Sim Shalom?* The children roll their eyes and jiggle their feet. A friendly woman gives me her *siddur*—the prayer book, open to the correct page, then smiles at the children. She, too, wears a beautiful *tallit,* embroidered in gold.

The rabbi, Hillary, and the entire congregation begin to sing in Hebrew—to pray in song, I realize from the English translation. The melodies, sweetly dissonant in a minor key, jostle feelings that have been muffled for as long as I can remember. I hear someone playing an electric organ, injecting vivid harmonies that singers weave into a rich tapestry. The music lifts me out of my ordinary self as the voices weave around me like a radiant *tallit*. Something deep in my marrow answers. I've never heard this music before, but it's hauntingly familiar.

As the prayers continue, the center of my chest cracks open, and light pours in. I begin to cry—tears of sweet, unexpected relief. Jim and the children look at me with concern, but—perhaps for the first time—I totally ignore them. I don't want to explain this; it has nothing to do with words. This moment, this awakening, belongs to me. I do not want to justify or share it.

Wide-eyed and weeping, I watch men and women wearing prayer shawls and yarmulkes swaying gently, praying with eyes closed in a kind of ecstasy. Goosebumps trill across my body, and all my little hairs stand up in joy. I see God on their faces, just as I did forty years ago, at Easter Mass with my boy-crazy, twelve-year-old girlfriend, Loretta. But this time, the prayers aren't forbidden fruit; this time, I can own them. A rich, golden grandeur pours down and floods through me. And I feel—can I actually dare to say this, even to myself?—I feel connected to God in a way I haven't felt with such aching readiness since those nights in high school when I knelt by my window and tried to make contact with something—Someone?—way up high. And when my heart blooms open in that same way, I'm shocked that I'm not shocked. All I feel is relief—vast, serene relief.

As if I've come home.

I say to myself, with fierce joy and conviction—a rare, unquestioning certainty that surprises me but feels utterly authentic, "I must have this. I must find a way to have this in my life: This beauty. This sacred time. Somehow, some way, I must have this."

But I can't help wondering: what's all this about? I've lived all my life barely Jewish, so why is this passion awakening in me now, but never before? Why did I grow up a Jew in name only? Why did my parents distance themselves so completely from their Jewish background? Why didn't we attend synagogue or celebrate the holidays?

I can't understand what's happening now until I understand more fully what happened then—to them, and to me.

CHAPTER 19

Barely Jewish

Late 1940s–early 1950s

WE'RE ALWAYS THE ONLY JEWS IN TOWN—SMALL COUNTRY TOWNS slowly turning into suburbs along the border of northeast Philadelphia and Bucks County; towns straight out of movie sets, graced with steepled churches and haunted-Halloween-style Victorian houses. In the early fifties, shops begin to stand elbow-to-elbow in neon strip malls that spread like ugly lichens around the busiest intersections. Narrow country roads wind away from new traffic lights, unrolling over gentle hills to a cider mill, small farms, green meadows where calves moo and kick up their heels, the way they do in my picture books.

Most of our friends and neighbors cheerfully "accept" us. This means people who never knew Jews before proudly tell us, "But we like you," and "But you don't act like Jews"—as if they're doing us a favor to befriend us. It doesn't feel like a compliment.

People who don't like us because we're Jews keep their mouths shut and look away—with one major exception: Robbie Braun, a scrawny, big-mouth bully my age who lives two houses away. He makes my life a walking misery. From the time we're five, Robbie teases me about my freckles, red hair, and skinny legs. He calls me a smart Jew when I get hundreds, and a stupid Jew when I get ninety-fives. He sticks like a tick, though he swears he hates me. He sings, "Her hair comes out of a bottle" and gets the other boys to join in. And he teases me every day about the "Jew food" I eat for lunch.

"Why if it isn't Ellen, Ellen, Watermelon," he yells each morning when we climb onto the yellow school bus driven by Bennie the Beetle, a squat little man in a shiny, ill-fitting black uniform. "Wonder what garbage she'll eat for lunch today?"

Then he grabs my lunch bag and fishes around inside. "Is it smelly salami on pumpernickel with yucky garlic pickles? Liverwurst with mustard on rye?" My lunch was never like his—pale American cheese or tuna on perfectly square, spongy Freihoffer's bread, with a blond Tastycake Krumpet for dessert—everything white and bland. Even when I beg, my mother won't dream of giving me white bread ("No vitamins!") or anything with mayonnaise ("You'll have ptomaine by lunch!")

"Yech." After one final sniff, Robbie makes throw up noises. "Don't you ever eat anything but Jew food?" Then he smooshes the brown bag flat with his foot and charges to the back to the bus chanting, "Redhead, peed the bed, wiped it up with jelly bread." For years, I feel I have to "take it" or make a bad name for all Jews.

"Take the high road," my father always says. "Don't stoop to his stupidity."

Finally, one morning on the school bus, the week before sixth grade graduation, I get sick of being a good girl. I hope pretty soon I'll be wearing a bra, too old to fight with boys anymore. So when Robbie grabs me around the throat in a hammerlock and won't let go, a red rage rises up in me so hot and so wild that I stop caring what anyone thinks.

I don't stop punching and clawing till Bennie the Beetle stops the bus and drags Robbie away. Even then I don't stop till I get Robbie down in the dusty aisle with nice, bright-red blood oozing out of his nose. I kneel on his chest, still swinging. All the kids are cheering, standing on the seats, clapping and stomping their feet. I can taste rusty blood in my mouth after Robbie hits my face, but I still don't care. He's crying and so am I, but my tears are hot and glad, and his are whipped-little-baby-bully tears, so there.

One week later, we all walk down the aisle to the tune of "Pomp and Circumstance" played on a rickety, out-of-tune piano. Robbie's wearing his brand-new two-tone navy-and-cream jacket and skinny knit tie. He has a giant purple shiner in one eye, a smaller blue one under the other, and a scab as long as a pencil down the side of his face. I'm a few steps behind him, trying to act demure and shy.

"What happened to Robbie Braun?" I hear people whisper.

"Ellen Schecter beat him up," the word comes back.

"Well, it's about time."

"He deserves it."

I know he does. And I can't help grinning like the devil in my new pink polished-cotton dress with the white linen collar and black velvet trim. The principal suspended us for three days and made me forfeit the prize for "Best Musician." But boy, was it worth it.

Everything would have been perfect if I only could have worn a bra.

When in Pennypack Woods, Bustleton, or Somerton, PA, do as the Christians do. My mother, father, and I don't actually celebrate Christmas, but we do exchange gifts on Christmas morning with each other and, in the spirit of the season, with friends and neighbors. We have absolutely no decorations that look or smell like Christmas.

Except once, the year I'm five.

"Can we please have a Christmas tree, Mommy? Please? I'm the only one without Christmas in my whole entire school, my whole neighborhood, and my whole entire life." I cry so long and so hard that my mother starts to worry. "I feel so left out, Mommy," I sob. "We don't have any holidays at all, and Christmas is so beautiful."

My parents finally exchange that look that means, all right, we give in.

"Okay," my mother says, "we'll have a tree. But remember"—she shakes her finger—"it's a Hanukkah bush, not a Christmas tree. And don't tell the whole world about it, either." She puts her nose close to mine. "Nana and Poppop must never know."

I jump up and dance around. "Oh, thank you, thank you, I promise, I'll never, ever tell." I run to hug her and she hugs me back, but I can feel that she's still very nervous because she's stiff instead of soft, and her heart's beating fast.

That night, my father brings home a fluffy tree about as tall as my mom. He sets it up in a corner of our living room, in a small bucket of water and sand—"so it won't fall over or dry out too much," he tells us. "It's a Scotch pine."

I'm so happy. But when I dance around it, singing "Oh, Come all Ye Faithful," my father looks as if I've stepped on all his toes. Then he quickly gets to work with a shirt cardboard, scissors, and tin foil. He cuts and cuts, carefully smoothes, then shows me a six-pointed star. "It's a Jewish star," he explains, "and I'm putting it up top to show this is a Hanukkah bush. He climbs on a step stool and fastens the star at the top.

"It's a beautiful Jewish star—a Star of David," he tells me.

I have no idea what he means.

Feeling like we're characters from *The Little House on the Prairie* books we love reading together, my mother and I string popcorn and cranberry chains to trim our tree—uh, bush. I prick my fingers so often they start to bleed, but I don't care: we have a tree—a real tree. Strand-by-strand, we all add spaghetti-streamers of sparkling tinsel. Our tree—bush—is getting prettier and prettier. We stand back to admire it with sheepish satisfaction.

"What about colored lights? Or candles?" I ask. I've studied Christmas trees for many years. I see them in other people's windows, or in magazines or in Coca-Cola ads.

"Never," my mother answers, horrified. "Do you want to burn down the whole house?" Then she shatters the mood by gripping my arm and pushing her face close to mine. "Remember: you must never, ever breathe one word of this to Nana or Poppop," she hisses. "My father will never forgive me if he even suspects we did this for you. Do you understand?"

"I understand. I promise," I whisper back. My brown eyes lock on her surprising light-blue ones. She is so serious, I feel turned to stone.

I try to keep feeling happy about my glittery Chri—uh, Hanukkah bush. Its spiky smell of pine fills our house and climbs all the way up to my bedroom, where I fall asleep dreaming of Santa Claus, even though I know he's just a story. But something feels wrong. I thought our beautiful tree would help us feel like a happy family on a Christmas card. Instead, we're just the way we usually are, a little happy and kind of sad and very worried. And my tree is turning into a magnet for guilt. Every time I walk past, I try to renew my belief in its magical power to create joy and gladness—but it isn't working. It's more like a reminder of my selfishness.

Then, on Sunday afternoon, there's an unexpected knock at our front door. A peek from behind the upstairs curtains reveals Poppop's shiny gray Chrysler parked outside. I spot my short, powerful grandfather pacing on our doorstep, waiting impatiently for someone to answer his loud knocking.

"Oh my God," my mother moans. "George, what'll we do?" She wrings her hands, her face as white as our walls.

"Pearl, go keep them busy by the front door," my father says, "and I'll drag the tree out back. Ellen, help Mommy. No—no, come with me and pick up the scraps of tinsel and pine needles."

We clatter downstairs. My heart bangs as Daddy and I try to get rid of the evidence of our sin, while my mother tries to hold back the enemy with small talk. Daddy quickly drags the tree out to the compost heap where we burn trash. The beautiful tinfoil Jewish star falls crushed and tattered on the ground. I pause to rescue it, trying to smooth the foil back onto the cardboard.

"Ellen, quick! The tinsel, the pine needles, brush them away."

I thrust the star deep inside the belt of my dungarees, hide it with my flannel shirt, then try my best to pick up all the tiny bits of tinsel and dozens, no hundreds, of fragrant pine needles inside the house. But the pathway of tinsel litter that leads outside gives away our secret. And even if the bits and pieces of Christmas didn't point the way, the spicy smell of evergreen would tell our secret even to the blind.

It's hopeless.

My muscular grandfather stalks suspiciously through the living room and into the kitchen, a wet, smoldering cigar clutched in his pink toothless gums. He follows the evidence and puffs up with rage.

"What's all this?" he asks with narrowed eyes, poking at the tinsel with the tip of his work boot. He balls his powerful hands into fists and glares at my mother, who shrinks before him like a child. My plump, beautiful grandmother, Sarah, with her shining silver hair, stands behind her, wringing her hands, whispering who-knows-what in Yiddish, an embarrassing language I don't want to know.

"What did you do?" Poppop rages at my mother. Almost dancing with fury, he looks like one of the fighters he watches on his mahogany TV with the big round screen.

"We did it for Ellen," my mother whispers. "She was jealous of the other children. She wanted—to be like them. I hated to see her suffer, so—"

"It was a Hanukkah bush," I say, trying to protect my mother and my Nana. I hold out the tattered star. "It had a Jewish star on top."

"There's no such thing as a Hanukkah bush," Poppop yells. "Jewish families don't have Christmas trees. Anything else is *meshuggenah*."

He turns to my mother, getting redder with every word. "You—*meshuggenah*! For why do you give in? What are you talking, she's jealous? She's suffering? All you do is confuse the child. She's a Jew and Jews don't have Christmas. Make her Hanukkah like a real Jewish mother, and she won't be jealous."

My father comes into the kitchen without a word, bringing a whiff of smoke. I know our beautiful tree is now burning like any other trash.

"That's why we came today, to bring Hanukkah," Nana says timidly, still behind my mother. I know Poppop will beat her for our mistakes when they get home, just the way he used to beat my mommy with his belt and brass buckle when she was a little girl.

"We brought Hanukkah presents for everybody," says Nana, showing us her bulging carry-all. "Maybe we can have some tea, and the cookies I baked, and—"

"No tea, no cookies, Sarah. We leave now. Get into the machine."

"But—Ben," Nana protests weakly.

My father makes a gesture to stop them. "Ben, how about a little schnapps?" he asks, but Poppop jerks toward the door, pulling Nana by her elbow.

"Puh! We don't eat in no house with no Hanukkah bush." He spits the words at my mother, then walks out the door with Nana waddling behind him, trying to keep up. He turns and points to the carry-all. "And we don't leave no presents, not one." He grabs the bag away from her.

"Doesn't even keep kosher," he mutters, making my mother draw back as he glares at her again. I watch her beautiful blue eyes widen as tears slide down her cheeks, but she's too frightened to say a word. My father puts his arm around her shoulders.

Nana and Poppop slam out the front door. We don't move as we hear the engine of his big gray Chrysler cough and catch. Then the motor turns over and the car glides away into the distance.

My parents and I never celebrate any Jewish holidays; we never go to synagogue or do anything at home to mark their deeper meanings, potential for joy, or extended family connections. There is never a sense of pride in being Jewish, only a vague sense of embarrassment. As a young child, I know only the three major holidays and only by name—"Russia Shunna" (the Jewish New Year), "Young Kipper" (the Day of Atonement), and the first day of Passover (celebrating the Jews' escape from slavery in Egypt). But I know nothing more about them.

The only childhood memory I have of Yom Kippur is of someone playing a lugubrious cello solo on the otherwise upbeat *Ed Sullivan Show*—what felt like an endless and, to me, humiliating moment. Why do the Jews always have to be the ones to spoil all the fun? I remember thinking. Everyone's waiting for the singing and dancing and comedy acts. They must hate the Jews for having to listen to this. I hated listening to it and, in doing so, hated the Jewish part of myself.

My parents make me observe these holidays in the most rudimentary, meaningless ways, forcing me to stay home alone from school "out of respect" while they go to work. With no spiritual observance attached to this enforced solitude, no services to attend, no family celebrations, a Jewish holiday is never a holy day; all it means is being deprived of school and playtime with my friends. And when I go back to school—the only one who stayed at home—I feel awkward and dishonest as I try to explain to my Christian friends why I'd been absent when I wasn't sick and had not observed the day by going to services.

My family also never observes the Sabbath or goes to synagogue. On the few occasions we light the Friday night Sabbath candles—without saying the blessings which bestow meaning upon the ritual—my mother insists that we put them inside the kitchen sink while they burn down so our house won't catch fire, a practice that robs the moment of all beauty and sanctity. We do not keep kosher. In fact, our favorite feasts, usually with friends both gentile and barely Jewish like us, feature forbidden foods: hard-shelled crabs so peppery they burn our lips and tongues; lobsters swimming in butter; clams on the half-shell; charcoal-grilled steaks served with fresh, buttered corn. I vaguely know the Biblical injunction, "Thou shalt not boil a kid in its mother's milk," but have absolutely no notion about what it means.

The one and only Passover Seder I attend as a child is at my Nana and Poppop's house at Tenth and South in Philadelphia. I'm six or seven, and learn from a storybook my mother reads to expect an exciting evening with delicious foods, singing, and a special game of hide-and-seek with a magic matzah, which will bring me a small gift as the only child in attendance.

I am so wrong. While I'm busy admiring the heavy silver Elijah's cup in the center of the table set with gold-rimmed china, hoping the mysterious Prophet Elijah will visit us tonight, tension begins to build around the table before the first blessing.

"Sarah, what kinda matzah you got? Lookit all these crumbs," Pop-pop demands.

"Ben, with matzah you always get crumbs," she answers, "and it's the exact same as every year, I got it by Mr. Levin's."

"Puh! And Sarah! Lookit Elijah's cup. What, no wine? Whatsa matter with you? You can't do nothing right?"

"*Oy, vey es mir.*" Nana jumps up for wine to fill the beautiful silver cup, engraved with bunches of grapes and a Jewish star.

"Ma, sit down," my mother commands. "Let's start the Seder, everybody's hungry."

"Relax, Pearl," my father says, frowning.

"I'm just bringing the wine," Nana says.

"Sarah! Shah. Listen now. Now shah! All of you." Poppop opens his *Haggadah*—Mommy told me it's the book that tells the story of the Exodus of the Jews from Egypt. He begins to read. "*Baruch atah Adonai, Elohaynu, Melekh ha'olam . . .*"

"Daddy," I ask in a stage whisper, 'what's he saying."

"It's Hebrew, Nelle. Just listen quietly," Daddy whispers in my ear.

Poppop scowls at us, then bends his head over the book and reads even faster. Daddy taps my brand-new patent-leather Mary Janes with his dress-up shoes and gives me a secret smile with his eyebrows all crooked.

Poppop reads about four hundred miles an hour. Then he stops and points to the plate that holds all the special seder foods—my father and mother explained about them on our way here. He names them first in Hebrew, then in English: "*Zeroa*, roasted bone. *Maror*, bitter herbs. *Haroset*, apples, nuts, wine, cinnamon. *Hazeret*, Romaine lettuce. *Baytzah*, roasted egg, and *Karpas*, parsley."

Uh-oh. No parsley.

"Sarah!" he bellows. "What's wrong with you? Where's the *Karpas*? There can't be no Seder without *Karpas*." He narrows his eyes and scolds her in a stream of Yiddish I can't understand. Nana puts both hands to her cheeks, which turn scarlet, then white. "Oh, my God, I forgot, well, not really, I just forgot to put it on the plate, Ben, it's right in the kitchen, I'll go get—" Nana struggles up again and turns toward the kitchen.

"Ma! Can't you sit still for one minute?" my mother scolds.

My grandmother ignores my mother and casts a look of terror at my grandfather.

"Relax, Pearl, relax," my father tells my mother, grinding his teeth as she glares back at him, her eyes slick with gathering tears.

Nana quickly returns with a large cluster of parsley, which she arranges hastily on the Seder plate, her worn-out pink hands trembling.

"So, perfect, Ben, no? *Karpas*, just like the doctor ordered. Go, g'won, read," she coaxes. "What page? Tell us what page, Ben."

He glowers at her, his blue eyes hard as marbles. Finally, he bends to read again.

"Baruch atah Adonai, Elohaynu, Melekh ha'olam, boray p'ree ha-ah-damah."

We sit in silence, as if the strange Hebrew words are casting a spell on us. Finally, the time comes to open the door for Elijah. I jump up and run toward the front door. My grandparents live at the corner of Tenth and South Streets in downtown Philadelphia, in what they call "a changing neighborhood." This means that a few scrappy old immigrant Jews still hold on to their homes and stores in an area rapidly turning into a Negro slum.

"Where d'ya think you're going?" Poppop catches my arm and spits at me through his naked gums. He had all his teeth pulled because he waited so long to go to the dentist that they all rotted. Then he refused to go back for dentures. "That shyster pulled all my teeth, then charged me for it," he complains to anyone who listens.

"I'm going to open the front door, Poppop . . . for Elijah," I answer, stung and shaking, trying to wriggle away from his painful grip on my arm. I'm deathly afraid to cross him, even though he always calls me "best girl in the United Stations," and twists my cheeks so hard they hurt, while asking, "Whaddaya want, a mink coat or a college education?"

"Open the front door? Whaddaya, *meshuggenah*?" he says. "Siddown! You want some *schwartzah* to come in, rob all the silver, and kill us in our chairs?"

I don't know exactly what *schwartzah* means, but I think it's a nasty word for Negro, and my father told me never to say it.

"But Poppop," I protest, my throat aching with tears, "how can the Prophet Elijah come to our table if—"

"Forget the goddamned Prophet Elijah! He don't live at Tenth and South in downtown Philly no-how. What does he know?"

Tears climb over the ache and spill out of my eyes and nose. I turn to my father.

"Daddy—"

"Aw, Ben, Ellen just learned about it from a book Pearl read."

"You're the one who insists she get a Jewish education," my mother says. "And now, when I teach her something, you won't even—"

"Ah, shaddup," Poppop snarls. He slams the flat of his hand on the table. Nana's best gold-rimmed dishes jump up and crash back down. We all watch a delicate wine glass lean for a long moment, then fall, spilling wine red as Egyptian blood across Nana's white damask tablecloth. With a choking sound, she springs up again.

"I'll get a dish cloth—"

"Mom, sit down," my mother shrieks.

My father puts his chin on his chest, shuts his eyes, and grinds his teeth again. I'm so frightened my tears stop. Then Daddy speaks calmly through his clenched jaw.

"Ben, Sarah, everybody—let's not spoil the Seder, please. Ben, how about if I open the alley door for Elijah? The gate's locked, the dog's there, nobody can possibly get in that way. Ellen, go to the kitchen and get a dishcloth. Sarah, sit, rest; please don't cry."

When I return, he takes the cloth and dabs at the wine stain.

"Pearl, wipe your tears now. Sarah?" He reaches out and smoothes her hand. "That's better. Ben, why don't you pour some schnapps for us? Ellen, come and look at Elijah's cup: do you think he drank some wine?"

I look, then open my eyes wide: Is it possible? Can it be?

Daddy and I inspect the cup of wine very carefully, and we're sure: before, the wine touched the top of the engraved star; now it barely reaches the bottom of it.

"Elijah came, Daddy, while I was in the kitchen. Did you see him?"

"He must have come when I wasn't watching," Daddy smiles. "I guess we were lucky tonight after all. Now, Sarah: did you say something about macaroons for dessert?

And that was the beginning and the end of my one and only childhood Jewish holiday.

✳   ✳   ✳

When I enter pre-adolescence, my parents suddenly enroll me "over my dead body" in Hebrew school. At age ten I find myself struggling to learn the Hebrew alphabet that everyone else in class mastered years earlier. Usually a dutiful student, I refuse to read the homework in a book whose very title—*When the Jewish People Was Young*—offends me. "How can I learn anything from a book that doesn't even follow American rules of grammar?" I ask my parents defiantly.

They just shrug and turn away.

Early each Sunday morning—never lingering long enough to turn off the engine—my parents drop me at Temple Beth Emeth, a new red brick suburban synagogue that looks like a gas station. I slink inside, trying to be invisible, and slip into a seat at the back of a small classroom with cinder block walls. While the other kids fool around, I hunch over my book and catch up on the reading assignment. Or I stare in panic at the *aleph-bet* chart, trying to decipher bet from vet, worrying about which has the dot inside. No one knows my name, and I pretend not to care. But I'm so nervous my lips tremble.

I pretend to yawn my way through class, trying to avoid answering questions by slouching behind the ungrammatical book. Before we depart with yet another endless assignment, our teacher briskly reminds us, "Attendance is required at Friday or Saturday services each week, preferably both, by all Hebrew school families." Then she smiles a fake smile, looks right at me, and says with an edge to her voice, "I look forward to seeing you and your parents next *Shabbos*, Ellen."

I try to smile back without catching my chapped lips on my braces. Then I creep out after the other kids, feeling alone in the lively chatting crowd. I pray my parents will be right outside, engine running, so I can make a quick getaway. I don't usually pray for favors, but figure my odds are good, since God might hang out around Hebrew schools. But my mom and dad are always late, leaving me to both hope and dread that someone will talk to me.

Finally safe in our car, my rage bubbles up against them as I repeat the teacher's message. I'm met with stony silence. "But, like, you have to. The teacher says. It's, like, a requirement. We're the only family—"

"Watch your overuse of 'like,'" my father says. "It's a very bad habit." When he sees me close to tears, he says kindly, "I'm doing this only for your own good. When your speech is more polished, people will pay you more respect and listen to your ideas."

I slump back in my seat, kicking the door over and over again, but quietly.

"You know I work all week, Ellen," my mother says. "I don't stay home and go to coffee klatches. I need Saturday mornings for food shopping and cleaning, and I'm tired on Friday nights."

"But you could do that stuff Saturday afternoon," I say, remembering the teacher's look.

"I don't need to go to a synagogue anyway," my mother insists. "I can pray anywhere, even in my closet, because God is everywhere."

She's said this ever since I can remember, and I've watched her closely since I was a small child. I've often seen her go into that very closet for dresses and shoes, hats and belts, but I have never seen her do anything remotely resembling prayer. In fact, there isn't enough room in her over-stuffed closet for her to do anything, including pray.

"But, Mom—"

"Stop nagging, Ellen; I don't want to hear one more word." Then she turns up a screamy operatic aria on the car radio to drown me out. My father grinds his jaw and drives.

My dad's response, while my mother is in the bakery, is a bit more complicated, though he, too, categorically refuses to go to services. He tells me his father studied to be a rabbi in Ukraine before he decided to put his faith in politics rather than religion.

"Pop told me he decided labor unions could improve people's lives more than God could," Daddy explains. "He said he grew up watching people praying for protection from the Czar and Cossacks and famine, and it never did a damn bit of good. You know, as a young man he once gave a drink of water from a bucket to Lenin when he spoke near Pop's home in Homel?" He's very proud of that; he's told me at least a thousand times.

"But after Grandpa Abraham fled for his life because he was involved in workers' protests, he gave up religion forever. He agreed with Karl Marx—that religion was the 'opiate of the people'—that it blinded them to what really went on in the world.

"Then, once Pop and Mom came here, they were just too busy working seven days a week in their delicatessen making a living for us four kids to ever go to *shule*."

Then Daddy shrugs. I know he observes *Shabbos* by giving up shaving and smoking. I never quite understood his reasons for this, but at least it was something.

Yet even though I never saw him pray, I know my father believes in God. I still remember the summer evening long ago, when I was four.

While Mommy clatters pots and pans in the kitchen, we walk into our tiny garden outside the Rosebush House. Daddy kneels beside me and prunes all the thorns off some of Jack Scarlet's roses to make me a rich red bouquet. The grass and the rosebushes turn chilly and sweet around us, while the quiet darkness sifts up from the ground like soft blue powder.

"Sniff, Nelle," he says, handing me the roses and inhaling the shadowy scarlet scents with me. "Ah," he exhales, eyes closed. Then he opens them and tilts my chin up so he can talk to me seriously, as if I'm a grown-up.

"You know, I'm a man of science," he says, "a physicist. But the more I learn about the laws of science, the more I believe there must be a God helping all this work." He gestures toward the brightening stars, and the darkening grass and roses, and the sliver of moon rising.

"The world is too beautiful and intricate not to have been created by a God," he whispers, tears in his one good eye. It's the piercing fact of his tears, even more than his words, that beckon me to share his reverence.

One Saturday morning, after I've attended Hebrew school about ten times, my parents finally agree to come to synagogue, but only for the Service of Consecration for my class. The twelve of us are called up in front of the congregation for special prayers and blessings. Though I'm given a formal certificate engraved with a Jewish star and praised along with the rest of my class, I don't understand and cannot read or recite one word of the Hebrew; I don't understand the meaning or significance of the ritual in my life; and still know virtually nothing about my religion.

I hate standing up there in front of everyone, displaying everything wrong about me: my flat chest, my cotton undershirt, my corny clothes and shoes, the braces on my teeth, my red hair that sticks out in all the wrong places. I especially hate my ignorance. I feel more fake, more barely Jewish than ever, now that I know how very ignorant I am. While all the proud Jewish parents smile radiantly at their proud Jewish children, I see mine frowning and uncomfortable, present only under duress, barely able to mouth the prayers and songs I know mean little or nothing to them.

The following day, I refuse to go to Hebrew school even one more time if my parents don't go to synagogue services with me on a regular basis. I don't want to be Jewish all by myself. In fact, I'm not sure if I want to be Jewish at all. I stand my ground and argue my points till my mother and father look at each other in that sidelong way I know means I've prevailed. My days at Hebrew school are over.

And that is the end of my childhood Jewish religious education.

It feels more like a loss than a victory. But I realize: during those weeks at Hebrew school, we never once talked about God, except as an influence on history.

CHAPTER 20
A Case of Missing Identity

1949

MY MOTHER ALWAYS TAKES ME TO SIT AT THE BACK OF THE BUS—WAY back with the Negro housemaids, day laborers, and construction workers, who slump in their seats and refuse to meet my curious gaze. Breaking this de facto Jim Crow law is her way of showing solidarity with the poor and downtrodden. By then, and into in the mid-fifties, while my parents stubbornly avoid any whisper of formal religious worship, it's clear that they have profound beliefs in social justice and racial equality.

These beliefs permeate our household and inform the social conscience they try to instill in me from a very early age by teaching me to respect all people. Closer to home, this takes the form of being scrupulously polite to Diane, the Negro woman who comes every other week for many years to help my mother clean our house.

"Ask Diane about her family," my mother instructs me as she scrubs the kitchen sink and the top of the stove in preparation for Diane's arrival. "And neaten up your room, so it's easier for her to clean. Help her carry things. And when I'm not here, it's your job to serve her a good hot lunch. She deserves a break, and shouldn't have to fix her own meal."

While there's never any thought of my addressing Diane by her last name and an honorific, the way I do all other adults, she's treated with unfailing courtesy. Coming from the deep south, she's initially flabbergasted when we eat together; but over time we enjoy a strange camaraderie, and I love hearing stories about her mischievous twin sons.

I attribute my parents' refusal to worship or seek synagogue affiliation to intense reactions against their families' past and to the Holocaust. They feel the typical first-generation American discomfort with their immigrant parents' old-country ways, flinching when Nana and Poppop lapse into "speaking Jewish"—that is, Yiddish. When Nana bustles to the stove and says, "*Mach der chainik fur un glazele te*"—Put on the kettle for a cup of tea—or when she caresses my cheek and murmurs, "*Ach! Meine schoene maidele, mein kindt*"—My pretty little girl, my child—my mother scolds, "Stop, Ma. Don't speak Jewish—speak English." And my mother constantly criticizes—to me, never to them—what she sees as her parents' slavish but insincere ways of observing *Shabbos*.

"They never light the oven on *Shabbos,* would never when I was a little girl. But they'd pay a *Shabbos* goy to do it."

"What's that, Mommy?" She never notices when she speaks Yiddish.

"Someone in the neighborhood who isn't Jewish—a poor white or Negro adult, sometimes a child, who's paid a penny or a nickel to risk his own soul to light the fire or perform another forbidden task. It's hypocritical. They follow those stupid rules like slaves, just like slaves."

"But why couldn't Nana or Poppop light the oven on Saturday?" I ask, knowing nothing about observing the Sabbath. Nobody of either generation seems to know or care why lighting the oven is forbidden. It would take half a century before I learn the answer: according to the Bible, God created the world in six days and rested on the seventh. On the Sabbath, Jews are not supposed to create anything, including fire or electricity.

Another reason for my parents' rejection of their Jewish identity? I think they are so terrified by the Holocaust that they want to become invisible, not perceived as Jews, just in case. They desperately try to become assimilated into American society as a way of hiding. While there are large Jewish enclaves in those years, even at the far reaches of suburbia where my parents prefer to live, they never choose to buy a home in one of them or to raise me in a strongly Jewish-identified environment. Instead, they try to erase their surface Jewishness and blend into the small-town gentile life of the 1950s.

Sound peculiar? Not in the McCarthy era I remember as a five-year-old, when to be Jewish was almost as dangerous as it was to be a Communist.

***

"Let me listen one last time," my father says. His one real brown eye pleads with my mother's pale blue ones.

"Too dangerous," she snaps. "Walls have ears. If the neighbors—"

"Rose and Bill have heard the Russian Army Chorus hundreds of times." She clicks her teeth closed.

I stand drawn taut between them. What does she mean about walls and ears? What's so bad about the men with red voices? We love those songs.

While Daddy stacks the fat black records on the player, I look at the picture on the album: rows of men standing tall in funny red caps and coats. A red five-pointed star at the top. Everything red, as if I'm seeing it through the red cellophane from one of my lollipops.

My father pushes a lever and the big men's red voices crowd into our small living room, singing important words I can't understand—words that march together in perfect rows. I march along beside them with my arms stiff and my legs strong and long.

"Turn that down," my mother commands. When my father doesn't move, she reaches out. Daddy grabs her wrist.

"Just one more time," he says. A muscle as big as a gumball pops out on his jaw.

"George, don't do this to us," she flashes back.

Do what? I wonder. I'm only five, and I don't understand. I watch her push him aside, skid the needle across the record, and snatch up all four discs.

"Now," she says. "Do it now. Do you want to end up like your colleague, Herb—no job? No income? No nothing? Just for owning books by Karl Marx? Or these records?"

She grabs the album and thrusts it at my father. Still holding the records, she picks up matches and newspapers and walks quickly toward the back door.

"Don't procrastinate," she says, and slams outside.

We follow slowly, and my heart thuds faster than our footsteps.

We catch up with my mother at the large wire bin where we burn rubbish. I watch her crumple the newspapers into tight balls, stuff them into the can, then strike a match. The paper blooms quickly into flames.

"Give me the album," she orders. My father can't move.

"Let's make this very simple," she snaps, bringing her face close to his. "If you are found to be owning records of the Russian Army Chorus while Senator Joseph McCarthy is conducting his vile witch hunt, you could lose your very sensitive federal security clearance. You'll be just like Herb. You'll no longer be able to work for the US Government as a research physicist. You will lose your job."

My father turns aside sharply, as if she'd punched him.

"It will be worse because you are a Jew—a kike. Remember how that kept you from getting a job in private industry?" Little drops of her spit fly onto my father's face and he takes another step back.

"And if you lose this job, you won't find another one, because you'll be branded a Communist or a fellow traveler. Nor will I find a job, because I'm your wife. We'll depend on friends and family for food and clothing." She gestures to our Rosebush House. "We also live here, in a government project. So where will we live? You and I—and Ellen?"

My father turns to look at me with misery in his good eye. His glass eye, as always, stares nowhere at nothing—even though I always hope so hard it will see me.

My mother's voice gets even sharper as tears come to her eyes. "And nobody will give a good goddamn that you gave your right eye to the army, developing one of their lousy guns to help win the war. And for what? So we have the so-called freedom that allows that fascist creep to persecute innocent people?"

My father takes a shaky breath. "I can't believe we're being forced to behave this way," he whispers, all white around his lips. "Here, in the United States. I don't care what those bastards think." He runs both hands over his forehead, drawing it tight as if he's squeezing something inside his skull. "But you're right: I have to care."

He pushes the album into my mother's hands, then picks up a record and strikes it half-heartedly against the bin. It breaks into four pieces. Tears rise into his good eye.

"My parents brought these records with them from Russia. They gave them to me just before they died," he chokes. Tears prick into my eyes, too.

My mother bends over and picks up the four pieces. "Too big," she says. "You can still read the label."

She crashes them into smaller pieces and picks up two more records, quickly shattering them into small, jagged shards. The grooves catch the light in faint rainbows. Those deep red voices are in there somewhere, but we will never hear them again.

Terrible sounds rip out of my father. Tears run down his left cheek. As he smashes the last record, I cry, too.

My mother tears the album apart and tosses the pieces into flames shaped like dragon tongues. As the cardboard catches, bright flames climb the air. Now she tosses big chunks of record onto the fire. The black shards warp as flames curl around the sides and lick the red and gold labels. Then the shards soften, puddling into black tar. Thick, smelly smoke spirals up as we toss the last jags of black into the blaze. The odor is terrible and makes us back away.

We try to go back into our small white row house, but cannot seem to turn away—as if we hope the men's red voices will sing to us once more out of the flames.

❀   ❀   ❀

One afternoon, when I'm five, I creep quietly down the stairs in our Rosebush House after my nap. Mommy and Daddy are sitting on the couch close to each other. They look very sad as they look at the new *LIFE* magazine. I can see the cover—skinny-skinny men in striped pajamas, who look right out of the picture and seem to stare at me. Their eyes are scary, and their hands like claws. They look almost like living dead men. One is taking a cup—of milk?—with his hands. He looks very hungry. Daddy and Mommy are holding each other's hands, like they're very frightened.

"Mommy, what's wrong with those men in the striped pajamas?"

She looks up, sees me, and quickly rolls up the magazine.

"It's nothing, Ellen." She gets up and stuffs the magazine on a high shelf where it's impossible for me to reach it. Daddy is wiping his good eye with his handkerchief.

"Were you crying, Daddy? Why? What's wrong?"

They don't answer.

I ask them again, "What's wrong with those men?" I walk over and lean on my daddy's knees, but he pushes me away gently and gets up. He walks back and forth in our living room with a sad or mad face. Finally he says, "It's something very grown up, Nelle." He turns away. "You shouldn't have to worry about it." Mommy says nothing, then walks to the kitchen. So I realize that something is so wrong, so terrifying, that my parents—who answer all questions—do not want me to know anything about it.

This fear, which strikes so deeply, kills their appetite for being religious Jews. They are so frightened that another Holocaust might kill us, that the very root of the reasons for being Jews—the joy, the celebration, the faith— get buried under all that terror, and they hide.

When I'm thirteen, my parents suddenly try to force me into Jewish social life again. The idea of intermarriage—even inter-dating—becomes as *verboten* as trimming a Hanukkah Bush in front of Poppop. When I'm twelve and "boy crazy," my mother insists that I stop going to dances in churches with my best friend and next door neighbor, Carolyn, and my other Christian girlfriends, and begin solo trips to a dance in a faraway Jewish Community Center where I know no one. At that point, sending me anywhere without my gaggle of girls is tantamount to separating Siamese quintuplets.

Mommy Dearest also insists on dressing me according to her atavistic fantasies of what thirteen-year-old girls wear: a sheer pink nylon blouse with a lacy collar (the better to reveal my cotton undershirt); full black taffeta skirt fluffed out with multiple starched crinolines; tightly buckled black velvet cummerbund to show off my tiny waist (was she thinking Scarlett O'Hara or Marjorie Morningstar?); pumps with bows; and—"Please, God," I beg, "if You're there, please strike me dead before I get to the JCC"—nylon stockings (which squash the thick black hair—not red—that she refuses to let me shave) against my otherwise shapely legs. When she gleefully resurrects someone's antique silver *mezuzah* and tries to fasten it around my neck as the coup de grâce, I threaten to kill myself if God does not show up to rescue me. She relents.

After nearly an hour's drive into Northeast Philly, a foreign zone lined with identical row houses sporting faux Georgian columns and miniature antebellum porticos, we find the JCC. Undaunted by further threats of suicide or double murder, my parents force me out of the car and promise to return in three hours. I'm sure I will die of embarrassment by then, but know they hope I'll be crazy over some nice Jewish boy who's diligently studying for his bar mitzvah while laying plans to study medicine at the University of Pennsylvania, hopefully with cardiology or another snazzy sub-specialty in mind. I know my mom is already imagining barbecues beside the free-form swimming pool in the elegant Jewish suburb of El-kins Park, with Dad grilling steaks while I rest on a chaise, pregnant with the first of many sons who will, in turn, become cardiologists or brain surgeons.

I skulk through the doorway only after Mom insistently flashes the headlights. Inside? Familiar rock 'n roll; disappointingly short, scrawny, pimply boys in nervous clusters; tall, dark, and handsome girls sleekly garbed in pencil-slim long wool skirts and matching sweater sets, bobby socks neatly rolled to show off their closely shaven legs. Many silver and gold *mezuzahs* in evidence—my mother did get that right.

My carefully curled pageboy collapses from suppressed hysteria. I spend most of three horrible hours in a stall of the girls' bathroom pre-tending to be sick—listening to the fashionable Jewish girls whisper and giggle in front of the mirrors. I'm certain their gossip is about my under-shirt and mustachioed ankles. I huddle in my cubicle, wishing I'd been marooned in the Sinai desert. Tears well up whenever I think of Caro-lyn, happily dancing the slow grind at the Maternity of the Blessed Virgin Mary Catholic Church.

Since my girlfriends seem to enjoy an active love-hate relationship with going to church, I want to go with them and see what I can discover. My mother's belief that she can pray alone in her closet embraces a liberal policy about praying in other people's churches, so it's not hard to convince her to let me go. My father remains mum.

I love being in church: it puts me in closer proximity to the Something I seek. Every Christmas, I go to the Redemption Lutheran with Carolyn and her family. We sit close together in a hushed darkness lit by hundreds of flickering candles. We sing soft, loving carols to a real live mother and baby acting out Mary and Jesus as they ride slowly down the aisle on a real donkey, moving to a straw-filled manger in a life-size Christmas crèche, where a real cow and some goats put extra whammy into the haunting Christmas legend. It's so beautiful we clutch hands and cry.

The Easter Sunday we're twelve, I go to Catholic Mass with my pretty dark-eyed, curly-haired Italian friend, Loretta—the Gina Lollobrigida of our neighborhood. She's miraculously sprouting huge breasts and luscious lips way before the rest of us, who are either flat-chested like me or barely-breasted enough for training bras. Not surprisingly, boys are as crazy for Loretta as she is over them.

We go shopping with the babysitting money we've been saving, and buy ultra-chic dresses, stockings, heels, and hats, carefully minding our budgets. I feel ever-so-Audrey-Hepburn in my black pumps and black-and-white windowpane plaid chemise with white linen collar and cuffs, topped off with a black velvet pillbox and veil. Dressing like grown-ups makes the whole enterprise feel very adult, especially since I usually spend Easter Sunday in cut-off jeans and a sweatshirt, digging in the garden with my parents.

The day before, Loretta explains what Mass is and how to behave, though I know I can never bring myself to genuflect or cross myself the way she urges me. For such a giggly, irreverent girl to suddenly become so serious and intent—virtually transformed with religious fervor—seems almost as miraculous as bread and wine turning into the body and blood of Christ. She also mentions what she's learning at school about the Jews killing Christ. I suddenly suspect that I might be her save-the-heathen project for the Easter season, but I don't want to back out of our plan.

On that sunny Easter morning, when we enter the ugly blond-brick church that I pass every day on my way to school, those suspicions disappear. Inside, I'm transfixed by the choir; the majestic, incomprehensible Latin; the light falling in broad shafts through colored glass and blue clouds of incense; the incantatory rise and fall of the priest's prayers, and the low rumble of the murmured responses from the congregation.

With enormous hunger, I see God on people's faces when they kneel, cross themselves with their eyes shut, and murmur prayers with peace on their lips. I get goose bumps from scalp to spine when the gilded bells ring for the transubstantiation. I don't feel qualified to question whether or not I'm witnessing the miracle she described, but perhaps the miracle is all the tiny little hairs standing up all over my body and the inexplicable feeling of expansion inside my chest.

When Loretta and her usually quarrelsome family file meekly up to the rail to kneel with others for Holy Communion, she tugs my white linen cuff and hisses, "Come on, just do what I do."

I shake my head, terrified of my fierce yearning; choking on my sharp regret that this high moment is not for me. I long for some sort of Jewish communion that could be mine—some way to feel tangibly connected to a God who really belongs to me. But as far as I know, nothing with that power and majesty exists in Judaism.

These sips from the well of Christianity only deepen my thirst for a God of my own; for a way to worship that will allow me to pray freely without skipping words or editing forbidden concepts or phrases.

I will not find my spiritual home for nearly forty years.

CHAPTER 21

Singing in Churches

1960

I AM SIXTEEN, A JUNIOR AT FRANKFORD HIGH SCHOOL IN NORTHEAST Philadelphia. I think I'm cool because I wear a pale blue oxford-cloth blouse with a Peter Pan collar, a silver circle pin engraved with my initials, and a Black Watch plaid kilt fastened with an oversized gilt diaper pin. I love to dance the stroll and the grind; sneak and inhale Marlboros; and, above all, I love Teddy Fischer.

I can't help it: his radiant green eyes send out orange sparks, and his teeth are square and white as Chiclets. He has a perfect flattop, propped up with goo that smells like Juicy Fruit gum. He's a sharp dancer, his jokes are funny, and even though he's the shortest guy on the football team, he plays a mean quarterback.

I'm in teenage bliss—when my parents stop bugging me about meeting Jewish boys—because Teddy loves me, too. We're secretly going steady, meaning our friends know we are, but not our parents. It also means I wear his father's heavy gold heirloom ruby ring at school, then hang it on a chain around my neck before I go home. There's a huge wad of ABC (already been chewed) gum behind the ruby, and two or three band-aids wrapped around the gold part to make it fit my skinny fourth finger. That ring is so heavy Teddy teases that my left arm is now longer than my right.

How do I love Teddy? Let me count the ways: I love the smell of starch in his crisp madras shirts and the heat of his body underneath. I love the way he grins at me, and how his eyelids pleat at the corners, and the way something expands inside my chest when he sings a solo in choir that he's secretly dedicated to me. Mostly, I love making out, and so does he. We do this at every imaginable opportunity: in the halls between classes and behind my partially open locker door; before choir practice behind the bass drum or in the music closet; and always, always on Saturday and Sunday nights.

On Fridays, I stay home and take care of my baby brother, Peter, who's only five months old, while my parents go out. I'm not allowed to invite Teddy or anybody else over when I'm babysitting, but I don't mind: I love this little baby so much that I enjoy watching over him, kissing and playing with him, even changing him. I've discovered a brand-new kind of love for Peter that I've never known before—it's complete and sweet, and I would do anything for him. Sometimes I feel that I am his real mother, protecting him from our mother, but I don't have the words to explain it.

After my dates with Teddy, we sit outside my house for a while, making out in his little yellow Nash Rambler, though it's his father's, of course. And that's one reason my mother doesn't love Teddy: because his father is a High Church Episcopal Priest—a Canon, actually, which is something like a Catholic bishop. Teddy and I call him Boom-Boom—behind his back, of course. Reverend Fischer always wears black shirts with white strip collars, even when he washes his car, and even at football games, where he cheers in a very proper, Episcopalian way.

Teddy's not supposed to love me, either, of course. I'm still Jewish, even though I still don't know an *aleph* from a *yud*, which sounds like "yid," which is what some people call me behind my back. So Teddy and I scheme about ways to engender Reverend Fischer's good will. We don't want our families to end up like the Montagues and the Capulets in *Romeo and Juliet*, which I'm reading in English class. I like to imagine Teddy climbing our trellis into my bedroom, except I don't have a balcony and our house is a white stucco split-level.

Sometimes I go to church with Teddy so we can please his father and spite my mother. Teddy is usually the crucifer, which means he wears a white eyelet nightgown over a long red velvet gown. He carries a gold crucifix taller than he is to lead the grand procession—featuring Boom-

Boom—down an aisle about two blocks long in Boom-Boom's church, which is practically a cathedral. A crucifix! Oy, if Nana and Poppop ever knew . . . I wonder which one they'd kill first? Me? My mother? Teddy? His father?

I love Boom-Boom's church. It is high and dark and full of Mystery. I love the language in the *Book of Common Prayer*, which is even more beautiful than Shakespeare.

I especially like the cathedral at Christmas because of the red and green holly, and the five-foot-tall candles blooming through the gloom, and the salty smell of melting wax. Reverend Fischer only mentions the Jews a few times because Jesus is just getting born as King of the Jews, and the Jews aren't supposedly killing Christ yet, so it's pretty safe and I don't feel too squirmy inside.

Teddy and I make out before the service in the vestry hall while he puts on the white nightgown, and after the service at the rectory (in his father's tool closet) before his mom serves very small portions of roast pork or creamed-something-on-toast. She is very polite to me, and laughs a lot, and I help her clear the table and wash the dishes. I think she laughs because I make her nervous just by being there. Teddy and I make out on the way home every time we hit a red light; again under the gray powdery moths that crowd around the yellow light outside my front door; and then down in my basement rec room on the squeaky old studio couch covered with an olive green corduroy slipcover. When we get too loud, we lie on the fake gray marble tiles, which are cold and hard but quiet, until my mother calls out, "It's getting late, Ellen, time for Teddy to leave." So we tuck in our shirts, straighten out our hair, try to breathe naturally, and go upstairs.

Making out with Teddy is an explosive package of pleasure and guilt. When he just looks at me, or strokes my neck, I get orange chills and cream in my white cotton panties. I could kiss him for hours. In fact, I do. His tongue is alive and searching and sweet. I don't always love his hands because he bites his nails to the quick. But when he touches me, I want him to touch me everywhere; I don't care about anything else.

My mother cares. Whenever she walks across the rec room ceiling with a deliberately slow and heavy tread, we push apart. When she opens the basement door, we leap to our feet. Teddy smoothes his madras shirt while I turn on my forty-five-rpm record player and steady my breathing. When she yells, "What's going on down there?" the Platters hit the opening chord

of "Twilight Time" a split-second after I yell back, "Just listening to records."

As soon as the door clicks closed, we're back on the couch while the
Platters sing. We take turns being on top, dancing the grind horizontally,
touching, breathing, and—of course—kissing.

Oh, I love making out with Teddy. It's so cool—and so hot.

The second best thing to kissing Teddy is singing with him in our
high school choir. His strong, clear tenor soars like a snow-white bird high
above us, and something valuable in me rises with it.

Singing with the choir is a central and joyful part of senior high—because of Teddy and the music, and because so many of our best friends sing,
too. It's a major, happy, and substantial part of my social life. But it raises
tricky religious issues: I'm the only Jew in our high school and almost all the
music we sing in churches, or elsewhere, is from the Christian liturgy. I have
to do a lot of fancy inner footwork to make peace with the programs. When
I first join the choir, I mouth the words "Jesus" and "Christ" the way my
Nana begs me. Then I create my ecumenical compromise: God is God, and
holy is holy, regardless of vocabulary. From then on, I sing all the Christian
words and embrace the music without reservation, inviting it to carry me
closer to the hot white heart of the Something I seek so energetically.

When we sing in churches—from the rousing hallelujahs of the black
Baptists who clap and amen in the aisles, to the buttoned-up and battened-
down High Episcopalians, to the quiet, orderly dignity of the Methodists
and the simple elegance of the Lutherans—the prayers lift me somewhere
above myself, and I go willingly. When we sing about God in shimmering
melodies and shifting lines of harmony, something holy blossoms inside
me in ways I know matter. And when we sing, "Holy, holy, holy, the whole
world is full of Your glory," I'm covered with gooseflesh and gripped by an
exultation I can't explain.

I don't know where this strong desire for worship comes from; I certainly didn't learn it at home or through the tiny amount of formal religious
training I endured during my twelve weeks of Hebrew school. That has
nothing to do with the passion I feel. Perhaps it's born in me; or maybe it
grows spontaneously, a need as natural as breathing. The friends I hang out

with in high school have worship and church-going as part of their lives—familial violence and abuse, mental illness and alcoholism notwithstanding—so maybe it's catching, like a cold.

No matter the source of the seed, it grows strong within me.

Most of us in choir also are involved in sports and lots of other activities—meaning, we aren't nerds. My search for some kind of spiritual identity zigzags through weeks crowded with sorority meetings, newspaper deadlines, prom committee, dance and drama rehearsals, stolen moments with Teddy—and yes, homework makes cameo appearances. I try each night, kneeling by the open window in my bedroom, to make contact with . . . Something. But aside from a sense of deep stillness as I reach up and out, there are no responses to my questing. I read poetry for answers I never find, and come away from *The Confessions of St. Augustine*—an ambitious summer project—with a sense of pity (why does religion have to cause such suffering?) and envy (I wish God felt that real to me). But my quest remains alive for something Higher and better than I know.

Perhaps the most challenging piece in the choir's repertoire has only one word—"Alleluia." Randall Thompson's mesmerizing music feels visionary. It requires breath control to make each phrase flow into the next without pauses. The breathing patterns of chant and meditation are known to evoke mystical experiences and altered states of consciousness. The effort of standing through a long concert and singing the melodic lines properly, without breathing in the middle of a phrase—which would be like taking a deep breath in the middle of saying "I love you"—requires enormous stamina.

Perhaps that's why I have an ineffable experience when we sing this "Alleluia" the year I'm sixteen; it's as if all my longing gathers together in one moment of clarity.

Teddy and I often skip eating so we can make out, then dash into a church just in time to don our silvery blue choir robes. Flushed and sweating, we slip into our places for the processional. I rake my short red pixie-cut into place with my fingers, glad I don't wear lipstick so we don't have telltale smudges to scrub away. We're soon singing the opening hymn as we glide sedately down the aisle into the choir stalls, our breathing still ragged.

One Sunday, I must have done everything wrong—or right. By the time we get to the demanding "Alleluia," I'm a bit lightheaded. As we sail through the successive melodic waves of Thompson's piece, I'm amazed to feel the top of my skull gently lift away from the rest of my head. I keep on singing the solid and lovely alto line, my eyes fixed on our director's slender baton and eloquent face. I feel myself let go of my usual reality.

As the music gains volume and mystery, my head seems to expand, to lift up toward the arches of the stained glass windows. Still singing, I feel my whole being open and follow, expanding in a way I've never felt before. My heart, perhaps my soul, opens out, too, as I sing on and on with the rest of the choir through the undulating surges of the music. I feel myself leave my singing body. I leave the church and open up into the universe: starry skies, deep indigo heavens. I encounter the All of everything and understand that everything is connected.

I don't miss a beat or a note, I don't faint, but I am no longer standing on the floor. I'm somewhere way up high that tells me, shows me, that everything is One; that I am an integral part of the Universe, and that there is nothing to fear, anywhere, ever; and that the peace of the Up There can be In Here—in me. I know without question that God and I, and time and space, and everything are somehow One—throughout time.

Or for a moment.

Then, as the choir's voice softens nearly to a whisper, and the key modulates from minor to major, the final notes of the "Alleluia" flow out of my throat. I slowly descend back toward my body. As I enter, my head drifts down to become part of my body; the top of it slowly begins to close, and my feet rest back on the earth. I am once again fully there in the church, still singing the last note. And then it's quiet.

But I am changed—changed forever, because I've had a long look at a unity that I never before imagined. And I know that unity will always be there, above and inside me, no matter what.

It still is.

Singing in churches, in a constant ricochet between the sublime and the sensual, is one of the most deeply gratifying and authentic parts of high school. We don't wear masks all the time, the way most kids do. We are who we are, and we love what we do: making music together. We laugh almost as much as we sing, and we sing almost as much as we make out. The power and joy of singing exquisite and complex music with kindred spirits under the direction of our gifted conductor, Robert Hamilton, put a handprint on my soul, which still feels like a blessing.

Teddy and I agree to break up when I go off to a women's college and he goes into the Marine Corps, but not without tears and regrets as I return his father's ruby ring, shined up, sans wax and ABC gum. A year or two later, he becomes engaged to Judy Leggieri, an adorable cheerleader with shiny black hair and a dazzling smile.

Then he is killed in Vietnam, in 1966.

When a few of us choir members gather to honor him in the grim silence of Boom-Boom's church, we can't meet each other's eyes above his flag-draped casket. We cannot speak, either. But somehow we manage to sing.

The church is high and dark and full of Mystery, and I can hear Teddy's voice, soaring above ours, far up near the arched stone ceiling, like a snow-white bird.

CHAPTER 22

Awakening

I will give you a new heart and put a new spirit in you;
I will take away your heart of stone and give you a heart of flesh.

Ezekiel 36:26–7

1996

MY DISEASE IS CLAIMING MORE OF MY BODY: STILL CRUNCHING ON the myelin covering my nerves, still scratching and digging all the way up and down my arms and legs, now attacking my neck and face, clawing at my torso. I still spend four days a month at the hospital for infusions of IVIG, bringing my laptop, manuscripts, and contracts with me to keep up with my workload at Bank Street.

I now use the crutches and two leg braces to get me where I want to go. Jim is begging me to stop working, but I refuse. Consequently, I never complain about my grueling routine; I don't want to give him any evidence for his arguments. Every weekday, I struggle the six blocks from our apartment on 106th Street to Bank Street College on 112th. On the way, I prop a large container of hot coffee tied in a plastic bag into my brief case. When I arrive on the fifth floor, I have to put everything down, unlock my office door, bring everything in, lock up, and put the coffee on my desk. Then I sprawl out on the floor, sobbing, because the pain is so terrible and just getting to work is so exhausting. Then I get up, drink the coffee and put in a full workday. I try to disguise my deterioration, but probably fool no one. Catch-22? If you say you're fine when you're not, people think you don't want help or comfort. So nobody gives it. Yet I'm desperate to find solace somewhere.

What about B'nai Jeshurun?

One cold, sunny Saturday, three years after I promised to give myself the beauty of Shabbat, the rest of my family sets out for the soccer field and I creep alone into services at the Church of St. Paul and St. Andrew, which is where the B'nai Jeshurun congregation worships on Saturdays ever since the ceiling at the BJ Sanctuary collapsed.

I know nothing and no one, but a great bear of a man with a bushy brown beard wishes me "Shabbat Shalom" at the front door, then escorts me to a seat toward the front of the sanctuary. He's infinitely patient as he helps me stow my crutches, fold my coat, and sit—a laborious process that feels all too public. His energetic kindness is the polar opposite of smarmy, and therefore most welcome. He smiles and touches my shoulder gently before returning to his post by the door. Instead of feeling pointed out as an imposter, he makes me feel welcome.

Now I'm on my own, knowing nothing about the service, which will soon begin. All around me, people are kissing and hugging, saying "Shabbat Shalom." Some even say it to me. As if I belong there.

Music rises from the small electric organ, the rabbi appears and sings, and I feel immediately connected. The service and music are more compelling than I remember, and I return, week after week. No one seems to notice me except that man, who asks my name the second time and never forgets. His name is Lenny Picker, and he greets me as if I'm a valuable person—as if he's genuinely glad to see me. It would be hard to tell him how much this means to me.

Our kids are perplexed. They can't understand why I'd ever choose religion over soccer, especially on the crisp autumn days they know I love, when the blazing leaves sweep down to crackle underfoot. But they don't tease or beg.

They have no idea how much I need to let go and weep. After a dismal week of pushing beyond my physical limits, trying to rise above the pain, I go to BJ and cherish my solitude in the presence of this warm congregation of seekers. No longer protecting anyone, I finally allow myself to cry. People look at me sympathetically and some offer tissues, which I gratefully accept. Sometimes people come closer and ask, "Is there anything I can do to help you?" I shake my head and thank them, sometimes saying, "No, I just need to cry," and they accept that graciously.

Each week, a different phrase or sentence from the prayer book lights up in neon, then sings to me all week as I try to embrace its meaning and remember its haunting melody. I discover that "Holy, holy, holy, the whole world is full of God's glory"—which I'd always thought belonged to Christians, especially Teddy's father Boom-Boom and his Episcopalian Book of Common Prayer—was always mine to claim. I discover that it belonged to me, as a Jew, all along, and was a Jewish contribution to the Christians. There it is, in our prayer book; we sing it several times every Shabbat, in Hebrew: *Kadosh, Kadosh, Kadosh,* literally rising on tiptoes to be closer to God. I rise with the rest of the congregation, holding on to the pew in front of me so I can make it up there. Those moments never fail to be transcendent.

The prayers enable me to honor my losses without being engulfed by them. In fact, the first morning prayer immediately lifts me above my daily defeats: "I am grateful to You, living, enduring God, for restoring my soul to me in compassion." How astonished I feel each time we sing it, as I realize I'm not limited to the prison of my faltering wreck of a body—this body I have to feed one or two hundred milligrams of Demerol, a powerful painkiller, just to get through the service.

Listen: I have a soul. How astonishing.

I focus on it. My soul. I knew I had one, long ago, but it was eclipsed when I had to turn my attention to career, to marriage, to motherhood. But now, as I embrace my soul, my pained body drops away like a tattered shawl, and I'm suddenly flooded with gratitude—a strange notion, standing as I do on the brink of losing so much that I love—my work, the wider world, my name on book jackets and TV screens, awards, and Emmys. It matters to me, that world, largely because the work I devote myself to on behalf of children has genuine value—drawing them to books, asking them important questions, letting them answer for themselves. But now, if I have to let it go, here is this unexpected and valuable ballast to loss: the world dropping away, but encountering my soul.

Gratitude: why haven't I tasted it, drunk so deeply of it before? Perhaps I have to lose so much in order to be profoundly grateful for what I have.

I yearn to enter fully into the service, to join the energetic, joyous flood of prayer, but it's difficult without knowing Hebrew. I have to flip back and forth between the transliteration booklet and the English in the Siddur, the prayer book, trying to connect the meanings of the prayers to the haunting music. I struggle to learn how to pray on my own.

I even ask one of our rabbis, Roly Matalon, how to pray, and he sends me to a book by Abraham Joshua Heschel: *God In Search of Man*. God is searching for us, he tells me; God needs us as much as we need God, so I should reach out to God in my own way.

This is a shocking idea. I live with it for a while, and then find a way to enter into it: I let go of the formal liturgy for part of each service. I imagine that my self, my soul, is a flame. I will that flame to shoot up, out of my heart, through the top of my head, and straight up to God. Sometimes I feel a blazing connection that nearly knocks me over. Sometimes my flame is tall as a torch, hot and high, with that deep indigo at the core that's impossible to squelch. Other times, I have to work to create a smooth fiery bridge to get to a place where I can feel both heat and light. On dry, empty days, I can only construct a little pile of twigs for kindling, and hope something will set them aflame.

And sometimes, when I'm very disheartened, or particularly diminished by disease, my flame is tiny, smaller than the smallest match flame— almost, but never completely, extinguished. But whatever its force on a given day, I reach as high as I can, sending my own true flame into the vast, dim cathedral of the world.

I still do not believe in petitionary prayer—asking God for favors or things. I never did. I don't believe God gives me disease as a punishment or test, an opportunity for growth or strength, or for any other positive or punitive reasons. I don't think God "makes" me ill. I cannot believe God moves that way in the world, meting punishment here, special dispensations there. I don't believe God will "help" me with regard to my illness in any definable way, as in making me a better person, or better able to cope. So I don't keep going back to BJ for any of those reasons.

I go because the beauty of the service turns my heart from stone back into flesh and allows beauty and joy to flood into me. This infusion of rapture rips apart the emotional armor I had to wear on all the weekdays of all the years I've been sick, leaving me vulnerable to my deepest feelings. And after my heart opens for joy, I can't slam it shut against loss. I have to do the work of grieving. Sitting among strangers, my tears will hurt no one, the way I fear my family or friends would be. And so I am reminded of my belief in the amplitude of joy and grief: as far as the pendulum swings for one, that's how far it can sway for the other. I allow both to enter.

And the music—months before I know what the words mean, the music is a powerful Presence knocking on the door of my soul, turning a key in a rusted lock. Once that door opens, questions and ideas that have nothing to do with my workaday life begin to flow: How can I come closer to this palpable sense of Mystery I have no words to describe? How can I take the growing sense of my soul back out into the world? How can I "pray with my feet," as the rabbis require, transform my beliefs into action for social justice, when it's hard to walk? Is it possible to sanctify my illness—to make it mean more than an endless series of obstacles?

I learn the melodies quickly—as if they're waiting inside to be wakened, instead of entering from outside; as if the music is engraved on my mitochondria instead of printed on paper. When I first try to sing after years of silence, my throat feels full of cobwebs and rust, my voice broken into little bits that can't hold together. Here is one more abrading loss: my former strong dark alto is gone. Disease has weakened the strength my diaphragm needs to make smooth, even tones. My vocal range is now only five or six notes. My body shakes, so it's hard to stand, hold the prayer book, and sing at the same time. But—I'm singing with people again, just as I did in high school, and I have a community again. I keep singing, and my voice begins to come back.

Beneath all my trembling, I feel a deep refreshment—an awakening. Lost parts of me—powerful, generative parts—struggle up into the light. I'm no longer passively receiving the energetic blessing of the music from the people singing the prayers during the services. I'm singing, too, and the powerful pleasure of making music makes me feel I'm coming back to life. So even as my body disintegrates, my soul grows stronger. This knowledge lights me each Shabbat like a candle.

Week after week, brushed by the wing of a mystery I choose not to capture with words, my voice flows out of my mouth and soars higher, up into the sanctuary. Singing through several seasons of Shabbat slowly scours away the rust and cobwebs. As I shed my tears and release my rage, there's more room for joy. It's as if the voices around me, and the inner vibrations of my own voice, are waking me into a new life.

Different. Unexpected. But a life.

At BJ, I see the how and why of the Jewish cycle of seasons and holidays. I meet wonderful people and learn about their families and their lives. I even share in the cycles of strangers' lives, as each week there are celebrations for the bar and bat mitzvahs of proud, gangly adolescents; graduations, birthdays, and anniversaries; baby namings for swaddled newborns or wriggly toddlers adopted from across the world; engagements or weddings for blushing couples of all ages and sexual preferences.

Each event prompts the congregation to sing or to jump up and dance in a circle around the happy people. No matter how bleak my own sadness or fear, I rise to these occasions of joy along with the rest, singing along till my cheeks ache from smiling. These exuberant moments speak of all that's hopeful in the world, each week changing my tears of loss into tears of delight. For now that this is my community, my spiritual family, I can share their sweet *simcha*—joy—as my own.

The words of the surgeon on Diagnosis Day finally snap into focus: "Maybe prayer could help." Yes, Dr. Younger. It does.

CHAPTER 23
The Wall Hits Me

*I am lying in my bed . . . and my day, which
nothing interrupts, is like a clock-face without hands.*

Ranier Maria Rilke

1998

I KEEP SWERVING AWAY FROM THE BRICK WALL COVERED WITH BIG
red letters that shout:

"ELLEN'S CAREER: THE END"

Then the wall hits me.

It's February 1998, the end of my treatment week for IVIG in Linda's
Room—the Infusion Therapy Unit at the Hospital for Special Surgery. I'd
been coming for those treatments there for almost three years. Combination
nurse, psychotherapist, and comedian, Linda Leff tucks me and two other
patients under cozy white blankets as we lie in our pink recliners, drugs dripping into our arms. Steve and Jennifer chat softly, but I'm curled up with
my eyes closed, listening through headphones to the jazzy lilt of the *Claude
Bolling Suite for Flute and Jazz Piano Trio.* His music usually makes me want
to get up and dance, but today it barely lifts my spirits. I feel chilly. My head
aches. Perhaps if I stay very still, it won't bloom into a migraine.

When the music ends, I open my eyes. A soft scrim clouds my vision.
Damn. Not again. When I move, that peculiar, agonizing pain I've experienced only twice before stabs across my head and down my neck. The muscles down my back feel coated with shellac and creak when I turn my head.

"Ellen," Linda calls out sharply, "are you all right?"

She notices the tremors in my right hand before I do. I look down. There they are again. My whole body begins to clench around wracking, rhythmic chills I can't control. I gather my blanket tightly around me and realize I'm spiking a fever.

In one smooth move, Linda runs over to shut off the IV and picks up the phone. My head now pounds so hard it feels like construction work is starting inside my skull.

"It's Linda, Joanne. I think Ellen has meningitis again and she may be beginning to seize. I need him stat." Then she grabs another blanket and yanks the privacy curtains closed around me.

I've been through two full-blown bouts of aseptic meningitis before—an unfortunate side effect of IVIG. I know it's serious—an inflammation of the delicate tissues, or meninges, which cover the brain and spinal cord. Because it involves the central nervous system, it can threaten major body functions. Right now I can feel the inflammation grabbing at those fragile tissues with lobster claws, and it hurts like hell.

Dr. Parrish arrives in a blur of action. By now the jackhammers inside my skull are so loud I can hardly hear. I feel safer as soon as he enters the room.

"Let's get her into an exam room," he orders. He and Linda turn the pink chair into a flat stretcher and rush me out of the room. With the help of two nurses, they count to three and lift me, shaking and shivering, onto a gurney. Pilar and Ms. Green, nurses I've known for years, gently tuck more blankets around me, take my temperature and blood pressure, then use pillows to get me more comfortable.

My panic calms under their gentle hands as they settle me down.

"Anything else, Ellen?" Pilar asks softly.

"Could you turn out the lights? They hurt my eyes, my head." Out they go.

Dr. Parrish examines me using the light from the hallway. He manipulates my head—crunch, crunch—and my neck—more crunches. "Does this hurt?" Pain scrapes all the way down my spine, into my legs and arms.

"Ow, yes. Yes!" I feel like I've been dipped into electric starch that shoots painful sparks and shocks whenever my muscles move. "Ouch—do you really have to do all this?"

"Yes." But he continues more gently.

"Dr. Parrish, what's going to happen to me?" I whisper.

"Ellen," he says with an edge in his voice, "let me figure out what's going on first. I'm a doctor, not a prognosticator. I can't predict the future, so don't make me."

"But I'm so frightened about what will happen if I can't take the IVIG anymore. The antibodies will tear the house down without the treatments," I persist.

He finishes his examination and then looks at me, arms folded, stern.

"This is hardly the time to discuss treatment. But you know meningitis is too serious to fool around with. Let's talk about this when you feel better." He sighs, then gives me a few taps on the shoulder as he turns toward the door. "Don't worry, we'll get through this somehow."

We.

He turns back. "Spend the day here, where I can keep a close eye on you. We'll decide when the office closes whether I have to admit you or whether you can go home."

Then he flies back into action, talking to the nurses as he speeds down the hall. I fall into a pained half-sleep. During the next five hours, people give me injections and take my temperature. I hear the brisk staccato of Dr. Parrish's footsteps enter and leave. Once, in my half-sleep, my eyes clenched against the thinnest splinters of light, I feel him lean over and smooth my hair back from my damp face. It reminds me of my father, checking my fever when I was sick as a child, and I fall back to sleep, smiling. He tries to admit me late that afternoon, but there are no beds. Instead of waiting for hours in the ER, we decide I'm well enough to travel, so I go home with Jim, who shows up with half fear, half rage on his face.

It's actually harder for me to go home; I have to look lively for the children, so they don't get too scared.

A few weeks later, finally able to come for an office visit, my hands, legs, and body jerking in the aftermath of the episode, I beg Dr. Parrish to let me continue the IVIG. I'm in the same exam room, sitting on a crackling paper sheet, wearing a hospital gown backwards (I never remember if the gap goes in front or back). Dr. Parrish is riding in restless little circles on the wheeled examining room stool, looking down at the floor.

"Please," I say. I lean forward and the paper tears. "I can stand the side effects because the treatments stop me from sliding downhill. It's the only drug that helps."

Dr. Parrish shakes his head, sighs, then answers wearily, "They're developing new drugs all the time. We have to be patient till they come down the pipeline and—"

I try to keep my voice cool and jocular. "It's hard to be patient when you're the patient. When I feel myself headed for a wheelch—." I stop, swallow, take a breath, and try again, not realizing I would slip into calling him by his first name, as he'd suggested several times.

"Listen, Ed, you know what happened last time we stopped the IVIG. That's when I ended up with these babies." I point to my crutches.

I can see he doesn't want to hear any more, but I can't stop. "Please let me try again." I begin to cry but stop myself. "I'll take total responsibility. I'll even sign a legal paper absolving you completely. And maybe we could change the dose the way we did before—I could get half as much drug over twice as many days. It really worked. Remember? It would mean eight days a month instead of four, but it's worth a try. "When I went from two days to four, the meningitis held off. Remember?"

"That worked only a short while," he says, "remember?" He shakes his head. "I cannot keep giving you a medication with such grave consequences. So far, you've gotten away with no long-term damage. But meningitis can cause visual, mental, and other serious, permanent deficits. I won't put you in that kind of danger. If you insist on getting the medication again, you'll have to be treated by another doctor—if you can find one who'd do it."

"So it's three strikes and you're out?" I ask, my throat aching with unshed tears.

"Yes. I'm sorry."

I'm sorry. I hope he understands the healing in those words. They mean I'm not alone in all this; that he acknowledges my pain and disappointment. And that's when my respect becomes buoyed by love.

❋   ❋   ❋

The meningitis knocks me down for weeks. At first, my vision is foggy, a dark gray scum over everything. I can listen to music, but I can't read through a foggy double vision—a terrifying loss. I can't control my trembling and feel humiliated by the neurological jerks and spasms that make it difficult to eat without the food flying off the fork. I don't want anyone to see me this way. For a few more weeks, it's very hard to sit, stand, or walk. Even getting out of bed is tough, evoking the vocabulary of a drunken sailor and requiring considerable help from a part-time medical aide. Traveling from our bed into a dining room chair, thirty paces away, leaves me panting, wrapped in cold sweat.

I'm forced to take a six-month disability leave from my job at Bank Street.

After four months, I try working a little from home—faxing stories and art for children's picture books back and forth, and conducting meetings in my apartment. My mind works, but my body can no longer rise to the occasion.

One night, near midnight, Jim watches me propped up in bed putting the final touches on the script for a TV pilot after popping a pain pill.

He shakes his head. "Will you please stop trying so hard, Ellen?" he says through gritted teeth. "Rest, for Pete's sake. Let me take care of you. I want you to get better and enjoy yourself, instead of driving yourself deeper into illness." He tears off his necktie. "What do you want, anyway? Ellen Schecter, Writer and Executive Producer, written on your fucking tombstone? Just stop." And he throws both shoes across the room.

Knowing how hard and long he's able to work without the monkey of pain always riding him, I snap back. "It's easy for you to say, Jim. Your career is not in question. Mine is. You know I've worked for decades to get where I am." I throw a pencil at him, all I can manage, screaming, "I don't want to be taken care of like some lacy lady. I love what do, and I won't give it up." Enraged, almost out of energy, I cry, "It'll kill me faster not to do work I care about. Why can't you hear that? You should congratulate me for being strong, instead of criticizing me."

He sighs and shakes his head again, striding out of the bedroom with the heavy, slapping footsteps that express his anger. I know I should try to take his suggestions with more grace, but the thought of giving in is my worst nightmare.

Alex, now in high school, tries a more subtle tack one day after soccer practice, while he's devouring a snack at the dining room table and I'm just sitting after working on a manuscript.

"Mom! Your work makes you so tired and grouchy all the time. Who cares about that job, anyway? Why not stay home and take care of yourself? Then you can write the books you want to write, not the ones you have to."

He walks around the dining room table to massage my shoulders, which are stiff as a saddle. "It makes me so sad to see you so tired out. If you stay home, it doesn't mean the end of your career. You're a writer. You'll always be writing."

Then he leans closer, as if to tell me a secret. "That way, you can be here when we get home from school, and Anna and I can take care of you. You can spend time with us. You'll always be the same old Mom, no matter what you do." He kisses the top of my head. "I've gotta do homework now. Call me for dinner?"

"Will do." What a gift: my son still wants me around when he comes home from school. I never knew.

Another day, Anna, just thirteen, comes to me holding a yellow legal pad and a pen. "Mommy? Let's have tea," she says; "then we'll do pros and cons about your job." We've often done pros and cons for her when she's confused: Should she go to a sleepover with new friends? Is she ready to go to sleep-away camp for a month?

While the kettle comes to a boil, Anna writes LEAVING WORK at the top of the page, draws a scraggly line down the middle, and writes Pros and Cons over opposite columns. As we sip steaming cups of tea—peach for her, Earl Grey for me—Anna questions me and writes down my answers:

Leaving Work

Pros	Cons
More time with family	Will be alone all day
More time to rest	No paycheck
More time to see friends	Alone while friends work
More time for own writing	Might publish less
Can stay home when i want	Nowhere to go, not needed
Closer to my family	No professional title

After we discuss these ideas like two adult colleagues, Anna curves into my arms like a thirteen year old, and I savor her lemony-peach aroma.

"I will never forget this, Annie," I say into her shining hair, "no matter what I decide. This is grown-up love you're giving me—and one of the best kinds: a listening love."

These loving invitations and thoughts would convince a reasonable and prudent person to preserve her health and sanity, and honor her family, by stopping work.

At this point in time, I am neither reasonable nor prudent.

When my six-month disability leave is over, I feel a bit stronger. I go back to Bank Street for one more try. Maybe if I go slowly and steadily, I can work. I think I can, I think I can . . . My friends and family roll their eyes. Eric and Dr. Parrish are furious.

Even with my most heroic efforts and the College's flexibility, I can't do it.

But I finally find a crucial and comforting distinction that allows me to leave: I don't *quit* working; I *stop*. I cannot think of myself as a quitter, just as I cannot think of myself as weak. Finally, trying to turn into an automaton, I guiltily confess—as if I'm a criminal—to Delores Riggins, head of human resources at Bank Street, that I have to *stop* working. She and my colleagues offer every possible accommodation to help me continue, but I know now it must be a clean break. With not one tear, I silently clean out my desk, pack boxes of mementoes and books, sign the papers, and officially descend into permanent disability, a status I still think belongs to old people, goldbrickers, people who have tragic accidents and military vets—never to talented over-achievers and good girls who diligently work their way up the ladder.

It hurts. Terribly.

For the first few weeks of my ruined life, I wake up at the usual time, facing one blank day after another. Jim's busy and so are the kids. The only bright spots are the afternoons I spend with my funny, smart, loving female friends who continue to call me even when I feel too fettered by pain or dissolution to call them. They help me find the ground beneath my feet again. Jane comes with strawberries and stories about her latest feature film production, making me laugh as she acts out all the absurdities of Hollywood with her long beautiful hands and lovely mobile face. Isabel comes late afternoons, small and sweet and soft as a peach, after teaching her museum executives, always bringing an essential sense that the world is still safe, along with flowers or something yummy and brimming with calories—and with a plan for our next outing—"When you're ready." Sarah whisks me off to a movie and we scarf down buttered popcorn while we laugh or cry, spellbound by other people's lives. Mary Ann takes a break from making her art and pops in, nimble and full of laughs, and we lie on my bed chatting, just the way we did as college roommates.

But they're all busy Superwomen with jobs, families, and companies of their own. As much as they love and care for me, my fancy red leather date book is almost blank. No messages blink on my phone. No meetings or screenings, no deadlines, no power lunches. No one expects anything of me and therein lies the anguish: I could stay in bed all day and "rest"—the poisonous prescription which reeks of death before death— and nobody will care. I feel like Rilke, isolated in his illness, when he lay in his bed, "and my day, which nothing interrupts, is like a clock-face without hands."

But I can't stand watching myself cower in bed, the way my mother did. I get up and search for doors in the wall I'm erecting between myself and the rest of the world. At first, I find only narrow slivers of light. The slivers get brighter when I find notes in my daily diary, written in careful cursive, that say, "Anna Loves You." Then I find—rather, create—my first tiny crooked door in that high brick wall: I push one open every day with a promise to myself to create just one thing I can look forward each day: one small pleasure. It could be a short albeit difficult stroll three blocks away to buy a bunch of yellow-and-white daisies; or maybe tulips—deep purple? Or perhaps pure white with black and lemon throats? Or, I'll invite one of my friends to lunch—and if it's impossible for me to get out, they can come here and we'll order from the Mexican or Thai restaurant.

I decide to rent movies I've always wanted to see. Even better, I pick one director and watch her entire oeuvre. I start with Indian director Mira Nair's first film, *Mississippi Masala,* and order every film she's made, in chronological order. Fascinating. I also pile books beside my bed that I can't wait to read.

From one tiny door, I transform a solid wall into a row of windows.

So, I get up every day looking forward to something: make coffee, mm, fresh and hot. The apartment ticks and gurgles inside the walls, and the wind off the river bumps the windows. When it's warm enough, I open them and let the new day wash through. Empty the dishwasher, white dishes that shine like full moons. Sometimes the apartment feels too quiet, so I listen to Brahms, Bach, Mozart, Beethoven. The living room shelves are full of books that call out, each in its own voice, "Read me!" "No, re-read me." Now I have time.

Each room is full of sky, each large window a picture postcard featuring a different vista—the scarlet exclamation mark of the Little Red Lighthouse stands stalwart under the silvery George Washington Bridge. The Hudson River shifts colors hour by hour—pewter, silver, brass, indigo; the tide flashing up-river and back. Hundreds of sparrows raise their broods in nests they build in the narrow, sixteen-story gap between our building and the next. A different kind of music we can hear all day and night—including the one Jim and I name "the Virtuoso"; whenever we wake, we hear him singing; or at dusk or dawn.

Dwelling in the nowhere of my solitude, I study the new, blank pages of my days and begin to realize that the something I want can't come from other people; it has to come from me. I will have to reinvent my life. Perhaps that's why, one morning, when I pluck Theodore Roethke's *Collected Poems* from a shelf, his poem "The Waking" jolts me in an entirely new way. His words shoot straight into the jagged places inside me that are crying out for drastic renovation:

> I wake to sleep, and take my waking slow.
> I feel my fate in what I cannot fear.
> I learn by going where I have to go.

Here is a man worth listening to. Roethke nudges me toward hope and urges me to follow my own fate. Like him, I must go forward, pushing against fear. I have no idea what losses the future will bring me—Will I lose my ability to walk? To take care of myself? Will Jim turn away in disgust if I slide all the way downhill? How can I learn not to fear these things?

Only by living.

But as Jorge Luis Borges tells me later that afternoon, quoting from *All's Well That Ends Well*, "Simply the thing I am shall make me live."

I begin to understand that our apartment is not empty at all. I am there.

PART 5

Wrestling With God

Lech Lecha: Go to yourself.
Genesis 12:1

CHAPTER 24

A Door

You are already everything you need to be.
Entrances are everywhere and all the time.

Lawrence Kushner, **Honey from the Rock**

February 1998

ONE MORNING, OUR DOOR SLAMS CLOSED THREE TIMES—ALEX, ANNA, JIM
on their way out the door.

Then the phone rings.

"This is Rabbi Simkha Weintraub of the New York Jewish Healing Center. Months ago you expressed interest in joining a Jewish Healing Support Group." His voice is gentle, warm, wispy. "I'm about to start a new one. Would you like to join us?"

Another door. I push it open.

I'm the first to arrive at the drab office in an equally drab office building hiding between glittery shops on 57th Street. Inside the New York Jewish Healing Center, someone points me to a big, airless conference room with a dozen chairs waiting expectantly around a large table. I feel heavy as concrete, completely weary, my physical pain an eight out of ten, so I rest my head on the table for a few minutes. Then I swig Diet Coke to churn up some energy and swallow some Demerol (a painkiller) and

Compazine (so I won't vomit from the Demerol). It's the only way I'll be able to sit through a two-hour meeting.

But my curiosity peeks out: Will Rabbi Weintraub match his voice? What will the people be like? What is Jewish healing, anyway? After a few minutes, the Demerol kicks in with an energetic buzz and the welcome sense of being raised softly above my pain.

A slight, ruggedly good-looking man arrives who looks vaguely familiar. Do I know him from children's TV? The Writers' Guild? This could be awkward.

"Hi, I'm Len Belzer," he says affably, shaking my outstretched hand. Fine-boned, sporting five-o'clock shadow, beautifully dressed in linen and tweeds, he gives me a warm smile, then slides into a seat, closes his eyes, and labors to catch his breath.

I forgot; everyone will be sick, majorly sick. I won't be the only one. That will be comforting in a strange way. I won't have to pretend.

Rabbi Weintraub enters, carrying a big bundle of papers. He's so energetic that the hand-crocheted kippah sitting high on his pepper-but-mostly-salt hair looks about to fly around the room. He's tall, almost spindly, probably in his forties despite the boyish nimbus of curls. Three more people quickly follow, as if he drew them like a magnet.

"Hello, everybody," he says. "Welcome. I'm Rabbi Simkha Weintraub. Why don't we begin by taking turns introducing ourselves, our diseases, and our reasons for being here as a way of getting started." He does match his telephone voice—gentle, almost wispy. "I'm expecting one more person, but we should begin anyway.

"First," he continues, "I want you to know that I'm not only a leader, but a participant in this practice of Jewish healing. I had a very terrifying, very brief, and thank God, successful brush with cancer about ten years ago: thyroid cancer. Thank God, it was over after a successful operation. Then I was diagnosed with diabetes type one—the bad kind—that I'll have to struggle with on a daily basis for the rest of my life. So I'm not merely a visitor to the world of illness; I live here, too. I wanted you to know that about myself." There's a pause as we digest this. I welcome his empathy; it reaches much deeper than sympathy.

"And one more thing. I'd like you to call me Simkha. I think it breaks down barriers, makes the conversation flow more freely. Now, who'd like to go next?"

A slender blonde woman with flawless pale skin, her bright blue eyes wreathed with the finest of wrinkles, speaks. "I'm Ursula, age fifty-five," she says, a bit hesitantly. "I've just completed my last round of chemo, for ovarian cancer, and I'm doing great. I used to have a career in banking and finance, but I dropped all that. Now, I'm doing only what I want to do. And what I want to do is paint. Maybe I'll become an art therapist someday. The art therapy in the hospital changed my life, I think." She pauses.

Interesting, I think. She parachuted out of her career and doesn't miss it at all. Why can't I be like that? Would art therapy change my life, too?

"That's all," Ursula continues, "except—I'm not very good in groups, so don't expect anything from me." Her eyes dance as her voice drops to a mock whisper. "And I'm really a WASP. I converted to Judaism about ten years ago, so I'm still pretty new at this touchy-feely stuff."

Rabbi Weintraub asks gently, "And why are you here?"

After another pause till Ursula answers, "I guess . . . I was curious. I wanted to know more about healing now that my treatments are over."

Simkha nods and thanks her.

"And Rabbi?"

"Simkha."

"I don't know if I can ever call a rabbi by his first name. Anyway, I don't know if I'll stay the course here. I am quite the skeptic."

"Your choice, Ursula. I hope you will, but no pressure."

"I hope you'll stay, too," the man across the table says. He smiles at her. "I'll go next. I'm Len Belzer. I am not my brother, Richard Belzer, the TV star. Everybody mistakes me for him and I hate it."

I've never heard of Richard Belzer, but don't feel bold enough to say it.

"I used to be a celebrity, too," Len Belzer continues. "I had my own radio show, comedy and guests, and I loved it, just loved it. I could not believe my work was so much fun. And now . . . I have nothing."

My eyes well up; I taste the bitterness—his and mine.

"About four years ago, I became very sick with cardiomyopathy. Nobody knows what caused it, but it means I have heart failure, even though I'm only forty-five, because my heart muscle is so weak. There's no cure, and it could kill me at any moment"—he snaps his fingers—"like that." His face gets redder and redder as he speaks.

"It means I can't work, can't run, can't walk very far—can't do any of the things I love to do, or hate. Can't walk up stairs, carry groceries, weed the garden. I hate it. I'm angry all the time. I just cannot seem to get a handle on it. I thought maybe this group would help. Because most of my friends—and my wife, Emily Squires, a producer for *Sesame Street*—are still running around having their careers and flying all over the world, and they don't want to hear about illness."

Pop! It's Emily—that's how I know Len. Emily and I worked together on *Allegra's Window*, a children's TV show for Nick, Jr. and that's how I met Len. Emily called me after Len got sick, to ask what I could tell her about how to help him, how to encourage him, how to be there for him in the best way. I tried to help, based on my own experience with Jim.

But that's not important for either of us . . . not now, so I decide not to mention it.

Len pauses and puts his hand on his chest. "I can't talk any more," he says. "Even talking puts a strain on my heart."

Even talking? We all nod in sympathy.

"Losing your career, Len," I say, "I can taste your bitterness in my mouth." He looks at me and nods. "I'm sorry," I tell him.

But I feel more than sympathy. Or empathy. I think, uh-oh, danger. Angry all the time? Every session? Anger makes my stomach knot. Can I handle this?

Len turns to the older woman beside him. "What's your story?" he says.

Hmm. Interesting. Len might be angry, but he says he had a comedy show. Can this guy make illness funny? Or is he too angry?

"Hi, I'm Roz. I'm in my early sixties." She looks at each of us in turn as she speaks. She's a small, softly rounded, brown-eyed woman, with a light dusting of freckles and a warm, open smile. Laugh lines around her eyes and mouth suggest the history of her character, but her eyes are full of fear, her forehead deeply creased with concern.

"I've just been diagnosed with breast cancer and I'm looking at a mastectomy. For the second time. I've done it before, I know what's involved, and I need some support to get through it, some spiritual guidance. I guess . . . that's it." She doesn't cry or whine, her voice doesn't even shake. Yet she admits her vulnerability. My kind of woman. When she looks at me, I smile and she smiles right back.

"Do you have family to help you?" I ask.

"I have two daughters who live in the city, and they couldn't be more supportive. My other daughter lives in Israel and calls me every day." She looks down at her clenched hands. "My husband died thirty years ago—when I was thirty-one. I never married again."

It feels like a punch in the stomach. My eyes flood with tears.

"When is your surgery?" Simkha asks gently.

"In about three weeks."

"We can find many ways to support you, I'm sure," he says softly, "and if you know others, please tell us."

"I will." Roz looks up and smiles. "I won't be shy." She turns to the woman on her left; tall, pretty, in her mid-to-late thirties, with long, very shiny dark hair, almond eyes, long tapered fingers. She looks down and strokes her own hair like a pet for a while before she speaks.

"I don't know what to say," she says, taking a few deep breaths. "Everything is so hard; so hard. I don't know where to begin." She takes a few more deep breaths and fiddles with her hair some more. There's a very long pause as everyone's eyes rest on her.

What's she waiting for? I wonder. Get on with it. Please.

"Just begin somewhere," Simkha says. "You don't have to say everything at once."

"I—I've been suffering for many years," she says, "and most people don't even believe me." More deep breaths. Something stiffens inside me.

"It's even hard for me to speak. Just like you, Len." More sighs, more fiddling. I try to tamp down my growing irritation and replace it with curiosity.

She sighs again.

Oh, dear, I think, a whiner? I can empathize with pain and difficulty, but I don't know if I can deal with whining.

She sighs again and speaks. "I have fibromyalgia, and it has taken my life away. I used to be a social worker. I used to write—poetry—but now I'm very depressed, and I can't do…everything. I guess that's it. Oh, and my name is Seena." More breaths. "I also have epilepsy and clinical depression. I stay in my apartment almost all the time. It was a major effort just to get here today. And—I don't even know why I'm here. I'm not sure about God myself. But I do know my days are like blank pages I never get to write on."

What a beautiful way to say that. She knows that degrading feeling of empty days. If only she didn't use that needy tone, I could get curious instead of judgmental. But her neediness reminds me so much of my mother that I will have to be very careful not to elide the two. It would be extremely unfair.

"Well, we're glad you came," Simkha says. Everyone else murmurs yes. I murmur. . . something, but I'm not sure what.

Suddenly the door flings open, and I can't believe it. There's my dear friend, Marcia—one of the first people I ever met who had CIDP, my rare one-in-one-hundred-thousand neurological disease. Marcia and I also have lupus in common, and she is featured in *Voices of Lupus,* the video I produced. Whenever we screen it, there are no dry eyes when she describes how her love story with her husband of forty years became stronger than ever despite the trauma of illness. Marcia and I also share social workers, neurologists, drinks, movies, plays, and—no matter how bad things get—flash floods of giggles. She's the best comedian I know, and I'm her best audience; no matter how many times she tells a joke, I forget the punch line and we laugh as if it's brand new.

Now she sweeps over and we hug and she shrieks, "What are you doing here?"

"No, what are *you* doing here?"

"Sorry I'm so late, Rabbi," Marcia says.

She's always late, rushing from one fascinating activity to another. She tries to take her seat quietly but drops several things along the way. She and I keep shaking our heads and laughing in amazement while everyone else watches our strange performance open-mouthed. Now that she's here, I know it won't be all *Sturm und Drang.* I'll stay if she does. I know there will be valuable exchanges of ideas—and, of course, jokes.

"Will you go next, Marcia?" I ask her. "I'm supposed to introduce my disease and why I'm here, but have no idea what to say. I want to know what brings you here when I thought you were doing so well."

Her huge green-brown eyes immediately overflow with tears—Marcia has the most beautiful tears I've ever seen. I imagine that they have a much higher atomic weight than everyone else's. "I've had lupus, or some kind of autoimmune disease, for many years. It's. . . eaten away at my life. But . . . Ellen, do you see how short I am?"

She stands up to show us. "I'm shrinking. I'm . . . getting a hunchback." The last thing I notice about this incandescent woman—tall, slender, with honey hair and eyes that could melt prison bars—is her height.

"I disguise it with clothes, but I've lost almost five inches of height. My waist is nearly gone because I have very bad scoliosis and my spine is turning around me like a corkscrew. I've been told to have radical surgery soon, before it's too late to straighten me up." She giggles. "My body, at least. And

. . . I thought I could use some spiritual support in making the decision. I can't seem to decide. Maybe God can."

Everyone is silent. It isn't unusual to kick off a disease-related support group by introducing ourselves by name, disease, and intention. But Marcia immediately clarifies why this group is different: there's a Presence in the room that changes, and charges, everything. It's certainly one reason I'm here; though I probably won't say so, I am interested in the spiritual part of the support. That's why I'm not at a CIDP group; I want to learn more about healing; about God.

"We'll do what we can to aid your decision, Marcia," Simkha says softly, "including calling on God's presence. But in the end, the decision will have to be yours."

"I know that," Marcia whispers, her words almost lost in more tears. She turns and looks at me. "And you?"

"Like Marcia—and Seena—I have a double whammy. Two incurable, painful, potentially fatal autoimmune diseases: systemic lupus and CIDP—chronic inflammatory demyelinating polyneuropathy. I don't expect you to remember the names. What it means is that cockamamie antibodies are chewing away the myelin coating that's supposed to protect my peripheral nerves." I can see the question marks on their faces. "Think of it this way: eroding the coating on all the nerves in my body that are not in my brain or spinal cord. It causes pain, muscular weakness, and progressive disability." I point to "Exhibit A" (crutches) and "Exhibit B" (braces).

"I'm here because my neurological disease forced me to end the career I loved—and I'm—falling apart." I look at Len and he nods. "Except for loving my family and friends, I'm afraid my life will become meaningless."

Len leans toward me and says, "I know exactly what you mean. That's how I feel, totally at a loss. I don't know what to do with myself. I don't know what matters anymore. It sucks, really sucks." He turns to Simkha. "Sorry, Rabbi."

Simkha just waves his hand.

Seena reaches out and touches my hand. "I think I understand, too. I haven't written one poem in six years. It's like losing a leg." Her rush of understanding takes me by surprise, and we look straight into each others' eyes.

"Why are you here, exactly?" Simkha asks. He radiates kindness.

"I want to explore the possibility of healing, since cure is out of the question. I don't know what 'Jewish healing' means but it sounds. . . promising.

I also thought that learning more about Judaism, and God, might help me understand how I can reinvent myself. I don't believe God made me sick or can make me well. But what does God do?"

I begin to cry. "I never cry," I say, as tears run down my face and out of my nose. "I'm proud of the fact that I don't cry over things I can't change." I put my hands over my face, but the tears dribble through my fingers and down my chin.

"I hate that I'm doing this," I say, "please forgive me. But I just signed my final disability papers before I came here, and I feel I don't have a place in the world anymore." I sit up and blow my nose on the tissues Simkha hands me. "But—I will always be a writer. And I just started writing a book about my adventures in the World of Illness. I'm trying to make sense of what's happening to me."

I cannot believe I'm saying this. I've just started to shape the journals I'd kept since the beginning of my illness into a coherent narrative. "Even if nobody ever sees what I write, I think it'll help me find some meaning in what's happening to me. I think maybe my writing could be like spinning straw into gold—a way of taking what's so painful and using it in a positive, creative way."

There's a long silence. I wipe my face and blow my nose as quietly as I can, then take the last swig of my tepid Diet Coke, trying to hide my vibrating hand.

"Sometimes," Simkha says sadly, "all the straw can't be spun into gold, no matter how hard you try. It's just . . . straw." He stares at me with his pale blue eyes. "Maybe you don't have to try so hard, Ellen. Trying to turn all the straw into gold may be too big a burden." I feel my pupils dilate, as if to let in this idea. And I am amazed that he would know this truth about me the very first time we meet: I do try so hard; too hard, perhaps.

Simkha clears his throat and everyone turns to him. "Let me give you a sense of what our sessions will be like. I'll check in with each of you in the beginning to find out how your week went. Then we'll study a bit of Jewish text—from Psalms, Talmud, midrash, the weekly Torah portion—or something you suggest. We'll discuss it through the prism of your ideas and feelings."

"When does the healing part come in?" Ursula asks.

"The whole time," says Simkha. "When you're sick, illness is always the elephant in the room, but most people won't talk about it. We will. And I'd like you to take this away with you: When you're ill and Jewish, you're not supposed to suffer alone."

"Is that why we bring each other so much chicken soup?" asks Marcia.

We laugh, but I am deeply moved by what Simkha just said. Perhaps I'm wrong, then, to cry at BJ alone? It would be such a relief to move beyond that.

Simkha begins to hum a melody, then stops. "Each week," he says, "I'd like to begin and end with a *niggun*—a wordless ancient melody that will help us leave behind the chaos of our lives and become present, here, together in this room. Listen, and join in when it feels comfortable."

He closes his eyes and begins to hum. One by one, we pick up the melody and make it stronger. It's as if the music not only rises out of our throats but out of some shared memory—of women singing under willows in some primeval wadi, or men humming as they descend the sun-warmed, golden steps toward Solomon's Temple in Jerusalem. After several cycles, as if planned, our voices drift into silence.

"In the Jewish tradition," Simkha says softly into the silence, "you are not to be sick alone; you are not expected to heal alone. Even a *niggun* is not supposed to be sung alone. There is no healing without community. So—welcome."

CHAPTER 25

An Invitation

*You must sanctify the deed with the spirit
and embody the spirit with the deed.*

Lawrence Kushner, Honey from the Rock

1998

IN EARLY SPRING, INSTEAD OF THE IVIG THAT GAVE ME ASEPTIC MENINGITIS, I begin monthly infusions of Cytoxan, a chemotherapeutic drug also used to treat breast and other cancers. Both cancer and antibodies are fast-growing cells, and Dr. Parrish hopes this drug—which Dr. Lewis warned would make me puke my brains out—is designed to suppress my body's production of the destructive antibodies that are damaging my peripheral nerves.

It turns out not to be the scourge she described. I have to drink a liter of a liquid with electrolytes, not just water, the night and morning before the infusion, then another one and a half liters plus an IV of saline solution before and after the drug is administered. Linda Leff, the infusion nurse, gives me Kytril, an anti-nausea drug, before the Cytoxan is infused, which does a pretty good job of quelling vomiting. And in her inimitable fashion, Linda—The Empress of Infusion—turns the whole process into a mantra: "Drink, drink, drink, pee, pee, pee," making the whole procedure more fun. But even though I drink another liter the next day, there are always a few days of low-level nausea and fatigue. Not so bad after all.

One sticky Shabbat morning at BJ later that spring, I perk up at this announcement from our rabbinic fellow, Shoshanah Dworsky: "This fall, I'm offering a weekly class for any adult woman who wants to become a *bat torah*: a daughter of Torah. You'll learn Hebrew and Torah cantillation—the ancient way of chanting the Torah. We'll begin in late August and by next spring, you will come up here to the bimah and read from the Torah scroll. It could be the bat mitzvah you never had, shared with up to ten other women."

I'd watched groups of women perform these rites and thought I might like to be one of them. Is this another door? Maybe. Then I remember a dream that still haunts me.

The dream begins in gray and white. It's early winter, on a chilly Shabbat morning. I hurry to synagogue, the music of the morning prayers rising in my bones.

I run up the steps, push open the huge old oak door, and find— an empty, shattered space. No rabbis. No congregation. No prayer books, no roof, no music. Only a charred, broken bimah, and white sky above a blasted roof.

But the ark is there, the curtains are open, and I can see one Torah scroll wrapped in crimson velvet, vibrant against all the gray.

Slowly, soundlessly, a handful of people gather behind me.

Behind me, and slightly above my head, I hear a voice I never knew.

"Now it is your turn. Now it is up to you."

Slowly, uncertainly, one by one, we gather closer—first closer to each other, then closer to the blasted front of the sanctuary—closer to the Torah.

In a broken, tentative voice, I begin to sing the morning prayer I love, alone into the silence: "Moda Ani lefanecha, Melech chai v'chayam. . . I am grateful to you, Adonai, for restoring my soul to me in compassion." Another voice joins me, then another. Another. Our voices grow stronger.

We sing the prayers. We hallow the Sabbath.

I dreamed this nearly a year ago and puzzled over it many times. Now I think I see: perhaps the dream is telling me that it's my turn to step forward. Except—in dreams I can do anything. I can run, I can fly, I can sing alone, I can even lead the Shabbat service without terror. But in reality, can I risk going up to the bimah alone? Before hundreds of people? Using crutches? Weighing twenty-five extra pounds? Can I possibly chant the words of the

Torah alone, flawlessly?

The commitment to study means I'll finally become a real Jew, no longer ignorant, no longer a Jew in name only—much less a nasty name like "kike" or "yid," flung as a curse that makes me cringe. I'll no longer be the know-nothing, fake Jew I'd been for all those years since I quit Hebrew school after twelve awkward weeks.

When Alex, then Anna, had their bar and bat mitzvot, I remember how proud Jim and I were to give them a Jewish education. I was particularly proud of breaking several generations of ignorance in my family, who knew virtually nothing about Jewish traditions. I remember standing beside each of our children at the bimah as they sang the *Shema*, then sitting to listen to them chant their Torah portions and *Haftorah* perfectly. Each time, I felt they were becoming the Jewish adults and I was now the only child, as Jim also had become a bar mitzvah at the proper time.

Now, it could be my turn: I'd finally take my place as a Jewish adult.

After attending services for about two years, I understand the surface meanings of the text by singing the Hebrew as I read the English translation. But despite my growing store of sight words, I know I'm merely singing along, mispronouncing the Hebrew the way I once sang "Jingle Bells," thinking it was about "a one-horse soap-and-slay." If I really learn Hebrew, I can stop parroting the prayers and sing them as they're meant to be pronounced—a giant step closer to unlocking their meanings.

"I'm thinking of joining a class at BJ so I can become a bat torah with a group of women," I tell Jim and the kids a few nights later at the dinner table.

Dead silence.

Then a half-hearted "Great," from Jim. "But why?" from both kids.

"After all my years of total ignorance about Judaism, I want to give myself what I never had. What Daddy and I gave both of you."

My throat is getting tight. Do.Not.Cry, I tell myself.

"We've talked about this before," Anna says softly as she slides her chair closer to mine, "how you give us what you didn't have, and sort of get it for yourself that way." Our chairs bump together softly. It's our ritual when one of us is upset and needs to talk. Or listen. "This time you'd really get it, just for you. But—"

"Don't do it, Mom," says Alex, leaning closer to make his point. "It's really hard, and it isn't worth it."

"When would all this happen?" Anna asks.

"Next May."

"No way," says Anna, shaking her head. "Too soon."

"Much too soon," Alex agrees. "It took us years of Hebrew school, and tutoring for six months just on cantillation. It has to be perfect. One teeny mistake and the rabbis make you do it over."

Anna puts her head on my shoulder. "No, Mom. Too much pressure on you."

"Whoa," says Jim, "wait a second here." We watch him scrape up the last drops of his coffee ice cream, vigorously chiming his spoon against the porcelain.

"Don't close the case too soon," he says. "Let Mom tell us why. And— why this and not a PhD? Rabbinical school? Or finishing your book?" Jim probes, always ready to put us on the witness stand.

I open my mouth and close it. "Too many questions. I'm not even sure I want to do it, much less why. Case adjourned."

I wake up in the hot black predawn and try to answer their questions: Why do I want to do this? Without work I love, a mission I cherish, a snazzy job title, an office with my name on the door, a salary, even just a job, there are no objective external markers to prove my success, to validate my being. Performing a difficult task now will help prove my value, if only to myself. I'm so aware of what I can't do; this may be something I can. I'm challenged by the intellectual and spiritual dimensions of the task. And I'd be in the company of like-minded women; I might make some valuable new friends along the way.

Now that I've lost so many of my professional affiliations, my connection to Judaism and to BJ is one of the most significant parts of my life. I want to braid myself into it even more tightly. Above all, I want to learn the language of prayer, which still holds a deep sense of mystery because I can't fully grasp its meanings. Mystics describe the words of the Torah scroll as black fire written upon white fire, and of seeking to grasp the meanings of the white spaces between the words and the lines of words.

I've never seen an open Torah scroll up close, but the bold, elegant, Hebrew letters printed in the prayer book seem to hold back their meanings from me, as if they're ornate iron gates waiting to be unlocked. Study is the key that will unlock them, so I can finally go inside and genuinely understand what they mean.

My internal debate about whether to join the Bat Torah class isn't taking place in a vacuum. My disease is rampaging through my body. My strength and walking are noticeably weaker, and all the markers—electric shocks, burning patches, clawing pain—are more brutal despite months of Cytoxan. Treatment with this drug usually stops after six months, but Dr. Parrish is now projecting several more, hoping for some flicker of improvement. So far? Nothing.

I try never to think of living with chronic illness in military terms—of "battling the enemy"—but it is, nevertheless, essential to push back, to fight it. I'm growing weary of living in that constant state of siege. I'm trying harder than ever to make a truce with illness, to gently push it further and further to one side of my awareness so I can concentrate on more interesting and important things. The deeper the disease intrudes on me and my body, the more determined I become not to succumb, spiritually and psychologically. When Simkha asks us to grapple with the deeper meanings of the story of Jacob, who becomes Israel after wrestling with the angel-messenger, I can't help claiming the story for myself.

Even though I try not to confront my illness head-on, I still feel it cutting me out of the herd, as Len Belzer says, making me more and more invisible in the outside world. And the more people, especially Jim and the kids, try to convince me to just-rest, just-read, just-lunch-with-friends, the more I know that's not enough. I know how much I need to engage with something meaningful. That's why mastering a challenge like this is so alluring. I cannot exist alone all the time. I need to reach out. Or is it up?

And there's something else, something I don't completely understand. I not only want to make peace with my illness; I want to sanctify it. I want to discover—or create—a deeper, even sacred meaning for—from?—my illness. And I want these new meanings not to be merely transformational, but transcendent. I want to transform grief and loss into something beyond—and above—themselves.

Sanctify.

As I am learning how to be a Jew, I'm being taught how we can sanctify time by honoring the Sabbath; sanctify space by honoring God with prayer—even an ugly gray conference room can be sanctified by what happens there. And food—we can bless not just bread and wine but any food, by acknowledging it comes from God. Jews even sanctify death by acknowledging the Creator as we stand, anguished, at the gravesite yet say kaddish, a prayer to acknowledge the Giver of Life.

If I can participate in those transformations, is it also possible to sanctify my illness by taking it beyond the physical? By bringing it into the realm of the sacred? I think so.

And there's this: There's a passage in the *Mahzor for Rosh Hashanah and Yom Kippur: A Prayer Book for the Days of Awe*, compiled by the Rabbinical Assembly, which we use at BJ, that haunts me. It may be the spark that lit this idea of sanctifying my illness. It says:

> "[S]he who loves brings God and the world together. The meaning of this teaching is: You yourself must begin. Existence will remain meaningless . . . if you do not penetrate into it with active love . . . and discover its meaning for yourself. *Everything is waiting to be hallowed by you; is waiting to be disclosed and to be realized by you*" [italics mine].

Everything? Mosquitoes? The blustery cross-town bus? Spiders or spinal taps, which never fail to terrify me? But then: what about my illness? I think it is possible to elevate it into something greater than itself, and thereby transform it. I look up "hallow" to grasp its full meaning: "to make sacred, to bless, to sanctify."

And there's this: *Moda Ani* . . . When I say my very first, often only, morning prayer, as I wake, I bless God for giving my soul back to me for another day. It's a sanctification of the day, of my soul, and maybe of me. That moment, that sanctification, reminds me every day that I am more than flesh and bone; that the sacred actually resides in me. Even in me.

So if my soul, my *neshama*, is returned to me daily by God, and is a small manifestation of the Breath of Life, then perhaps learning to read and chant the Torah can be a way I can sanctify my illness with actions, not only by thought or prayer. I don't have to explain it to anybody, just do it.

Another door? I push it open. I pick up the phone to call Shoshanah Dworsky.

CHAPTER 26

Beginning Again

If I am not for myself, who will be for me?

Rabbi Hillel, Pirke Avot [Ethics of the Sages], 1:14

August 1998

OUR BAT TORAH CLASS MEETS FOR THE FIRST TIME ON A SULTRY AUGUST night at the Jewish Theological Seminary, where Rabbi Shoshanah Dworsky greets us in her tiny stifling living room. When I look at her from afar, she strikes me as a tall, slightly hesitant woman who offers interesting insights in her teachings and brings an ardent radiance to the bimah. Her singing voice has an elegant lilt that moves me. Now, up close, she has the ripe beauty of a fully opened rose. Ordained just months before, she's in her mid-thirties.

There's a ragged silence as about eighteen of us, ranging from our late twenties to early sixties, smile nervously. Rabbi Dworsky waves her arms for attention. "First, let's see if everyone's here." She quickly calls out names, then sets our date for May 15, 1999. I begin to smell various notes of body odor and hope my deodorant holds up.

"Don't panic yet," she says over the rising din, "you'll have plenty of time later." The hum of conversation rises. "Now I'd like to find out a little about you," she says, moving her hands like a schoolteacher trying to bring down the noise level, "and give you an opportunity to meet each other." The volume decreases. "So please, tell us your name, and why you're here." The murmur swells again. "I'll go first." She blushes.

"I'm Shosh—please drop the 'rabbi'—and I'm . . . in transition. I'm trying to incorporate being a rabbi into my deepest self."

She's honest. Quiet descends.

"I'm Robin," says the slim attractive brunette sitting near me. "I remember the men in the center of my synagogue, with the women and girls pushed to the side, out of the conversation with God. I want to enter that conversation."

"My name is Micki," says a small woman with shining dark hair. "I want to become a model mother for my three-year-old son. I remember all the beautiful hats the women wore in my Orthodox *shule*. But they were never allowed near the bimah. I want to make up for all I missed."

"I'm Sheila," says a stylishly dressed woman as tears fill her eyes. "I remember looking way, way up at my father, enveloped in his *tallis*. He's dead now. I want to wrap myself in that *tallis* and chant from the Torah—a privilege unthinkable for women when I was growing up."

Jen, at twenty-something, is the youngest, blond and radiant. "I'm Jen. I had no bat mitzvah, no opportunity to learn Hebrew or chant Torah. May 15th is exactly a week before my wedding. Two of the most important things in my life."

"Will it be too much for you?" Shosh asks.

Jen flushes, becoming even lovelier. "It's a lot, but I'll study well in advance to be sure I'm ready. And, yes, I can do it. I want to do it."

"Hi, I'm Suzanne," says a tall, attractive blond. "I want to learn so I can help my two kids." Then, my turn.

"My name is Ellen. I'm here to be educated. I want to explore my Jewish heritage in depth for the first time."

Other women introduce themselves and then Shosh brings us back together.

"Excellent, thanks," says Shush. "Now here's an overview of our course of study."

I scribble notes:

Master Hebrew alphabet/aleph-bet: 22 consonants, 5 final consonants

Vowel sounds: marked over and under words—changes meaning: like cat/cot

Marks appear only in books, NEVER on Torah scrolls—

must memorize

Before recite from scroll use Tikkun—printed book, no vowels or tropes

Our Torah portion or parsha: First Ch. of Numbers—Bamidbar in Hebrew.

How does anyone ever do this?, I wonder. Yet . . . Alex and Anna did. So can I.

"Read the *Haftorah* before we meet, then we'll read it together," says Shosh.

We collect our things, chatting, expressing panic and/or encouragement. Fear is gnawing at my belly, a sense of excitement bubbling at the same time. Isn't this what I wanted? A major challenge? A chance to become a real Jew? I'm overwhelmed, but also glad to get started. I say good night, wondering which of these interesting women will become friends.

❋   ❋   ❋

Our next class is in Suzanne's sleek, modern, and—ah, air-conditioned—living room. She, too, is sleek and attractive, warm and welcoming. Shosh hands out copies of the story of Jonathan and David, our *Haftorah*.

"I'll set the stage for this beloved story," Shosh says. "David, the shepherd boy, just shamed King Saul and his warriors, who were too frightened to fight the giant, Goliath. As they watch, quaking, *whomp!* David kills Goliath with one smooth stone from his slingshot. David hacks off the dead giant's head and carries it, dripping blood, to King Saul, whose son Jonathan stands beside him. At that moment, 'the soul of Jonathan was bound to the soul of David, and Jonathan loved him as his own soul.' This is in *Samuel, Book One*.

All my little hairs spring to attention. What bound Jonathan's soul to David's? It must be passion: inchoate, wordless passion. I imagine it, there in the golden hour of late afternoon, when even the dust in the air is gilded. David stands in the honeyed light, holding the giant's head out to the King as Jonathan watches. The young men's eyes meet and—soul comes to soul. I know it can happen: my soul cracked open and light poured in when I first came to BJ. Against all reason, I knew I'd come home. I promised to give my soul that radiance, that passion. And here I am, still keeping my promise.

Shosh keeps reading from *Samuel*: "So the men made a pact based on Jonathan's great love for David. Jonathan removed his cloak, his armor, even his sword and bow? Remember, this is a prince, the next king, giving all his symbolic garments to David. His passion leaves him completely unprotected."

It strikes me: like Jonathan, I lost my armor when I first came to BJ. Words are my armor. Now I sing prayers in words I can't understand. I rely on that flame flaring up to God, completely unmediated by language. My soul, which I ignored for so many years, is now flaming back to life. My passions have transformed from my passion for work I loved into ardor for the numinous world of the spirit, where words are much less important than they used to be. I no longer feel quite so crushed that I have no place in the world of work; I've discovered a new world of Torah that I can spend my life, ten lifetimes, seeking to comprehend. Like Jonathan, my soul is now passionately bound up in something besides my self—and I am no longer alone. That commitment leads me right into this living room, into this quest for learning.

"Would you like to read first, Ellen?" Shosh is saying. Then she sing-songs, "Oh, Ellen, come back to us." Everyone is staring at me. Apparently, they've been waiting patiently for my response.

"Oh, sorry," I manage. "It's just—so beautiful."

Then I read, "'And Jonathan said to him, 'Tomorrow is the new moon . . .'"

CHAPTER 27
Inside the Volcano

If I am only for myself, what am I for?

Rabbi Hillel, Pirke Avot [Ethics of the Sages], 1:14

1998–2000

EVERYONE COMES RIGHT ON TIME FOR THE SECOND SESSION OF OUR Jewish Healing Support Group. Everyone but Seena. Simkha sits at the head of the table, arranging his papers in neat stacks. I wash away the bitter taste of Demerol and Compazine with Diet Coke. C'mon, let's go, I think; I need this so much . . .

"Welcome again," says Simkha. "Seena said she might not be well enough to come today, but we'll give her a few more minutes." He checks his watch. "Let's begin with a *niggun*, check in, then study a bit of Talmud." He glances at his watch again, then says, "Shall we get started?" He closes his eyes and begins to hum. We pick up the strand of melody. The room fills with peace.

Then the door bangs open and Seena collapses into the nearest chair, breathing heavily. The mood shatters. "I didn't think I could make it," she pants. "I'm in so much pain I can hardly walk down the street."

I clench my fists and tamp down my irritation. Stop it, I scold myself; be good.

"Have you tried pain medication, Seena?" I say softly. "It could help so much. You can experiment till you find just the right dosage—"

"Thanks, but no thanks. I have terrible reactions to all drugs, and I don't want to take any medication I don't have to, not even aspirin."

I grit my teeth, thinking of all the work I did with Eric, and how much it helped. It could be different for her if she just tries. My rage takes over. Take something, or shut up, I want to spit at her.

But Seena is on a riff, eyes closed, her long, graceful fingers making staccato motions. "I feel five thousand bees buzzing inside me," she says, "I know it's rage, but I don't know what to do about it."

"Do you know what you're angry about?" Simkha asks.

"Everything—my body, my life, my pain. All of it."

I'm pissed at my body, too, I think, but I could never erupt like Seena, who's spewing her fury all over us with no thought of restraint, or how it makes us feel. It seems so selfish to me.

"I know exactly what you mean," Len says, leaning toward Seena. "I'm so angry I could chew glass. I know it's destructive, but I can't let go of it."

"Sometimes I have to shake my mental fists at the Temporarily Well and say—'Just you wait. No one gets out of this life alive," says Marcia, shaking both fists. We all laugh, even me, and nod in agreement.

"I feel radical rage at this damned illness that keeps taking away my manhood," Len says.

"I think there's always rage when we're stuck with illness," Roz adds. "It makes me want to break things. But I don't think rage brings healing, or solace." She looks down at her open palms, as if she'll find words there. "I'm praying a lot, trying to calm and center myself for the breast surgery. And sometimes I accomplish . . . peace. Find that peaceful, wonderful place inside. Other times . . . ." She shrugs.

We nod again: we know what she means, too. And she's able to put into words what I feel: that rage makes things worse, not better.

When it's my turn to check in, they all look at me, but I sit with my mouth locked. By now my rage could fill the whole room. I'm furious at Seena, furious at my diseases, furious at my losses. But I can't talk about it. And that makes me furious, too.

Is that why I'm so angry with Seena? I envy her and the others when they erupt, yet I hate them for it, too. Probably because my mother let her rage splatter all over me every day and never thought of editing her complaints. I might feel better if I express my own rage, but I'm too afraid of hurting other people the way my mother hurt me. Too afraid of beating up on Seena. Too afraid of retaliation. Too afraid that once I get going, I'll never stop. I have bottled up my rage for years, decades, and am afraid to let it out.

I look at Simkha, hold out my empty hands, and shrug.

"Perhaps another time," he says gently.

❀   ❀   ❀

It isn't as if I never feel rage. All my life, illness has attracted anger like a magnet. I remember it in the Rosebush House, when Daddy went to the hospital.

Dinnertime. Mommy and I sit at the white porcelain table in our kitchen. I want the blue plate but she gives me orange, so I don't want to eat.

"Eat your string beans, Ellen," Mommy says.

She can't make me.

"Stop pouting and eat."

I push them back and forth. I put them in a box shape. I don't like string-beans from a can. They have stiff little sticks that scratch my throat. I tell her, but Mommy likes stringbeans. Even from a can.

I bang my high brown shoe against the table leg. Bang, bang, bang. I like that sound. Banging makes my feet feel better in the hot high shoes the doctor makes me wear for my pigeons toes.

"Stop banging," says Mommy.

I wonder how it sounds to bang both feet. I try. Bang-bang, bang-a-bang.

Sounds nice. Now I bump both brown shoes against her leg just a little bit. That feels even better. It makes me feel close to her, and safe. She's so soft and warm.

She pulls her leg away. Her face gets dark, and her forehead wrinkles. Something warm in her turns ice. But I want to be near her softness, so I kick out further to be near.

"Stop kicking me," Mommy says. Her voice is spiky.

I stop.

Then I start again. I don't mean to, but I forget. I want to be close again. Bang-bang, ba—

"Stop! STOP BANGING," Mommy yells. Her voice is even more spiky.

I stop. I know she's mad and my throat gets tight. But I just want to be closer.

"I'm sorry, Mommy," I say. She's too stiff to look at me. "I miss Daddy."

"I miss him, too. Now eat your dinner."

She won't look at me. I get a big lump at the back of my tongue.

I try to eat mashed potatoes but I want Daddy, and they won't go past the lump.
I forget, and my foot starts to bang, and suddenly Mommy kicks me hard
under the table. Then, quick as switching off the light, she swats me fast on my
face. I half-fall off my chair, then scrabble back. I'm crying too hard to breathe.

❄   ❄   ❄

Simkha speaks to us one day about the *Shekhinah*—the female, nurturing Presence of God, who is thought to take Her place above the head of a sick person's bed. "She is usually described as a radiant female Being made of light," he says, "who was present to Moses and the Israelites while they wandered in the wilderness for forty years." I sit bolt upright. Could this be the same bright Being I met years ago during my meditation?

"She is also said to be present where ten gather for prayer, or one learns Torah, but She is especially present to watch over the sick. Those under Her protection are said to be 'under the wings of the *Shekhinah.*'"

Wings. Light. I don't say a word, but perhaps my Woman with Wings can now have a name, even if I won't use it. I don't want to discuss Her with anyone, including Simkha. She's too sacred.

I ask if anyone else would be interested in learning more, as I'm burning to know a lot more. There's mild enthusiasm, so Simkha promises to bring something to read next time.

"I'll bring you an article from the *Encyclopedia Judaica*, Ellen, that's much more detailed." He senses that there's something very important about this for me.

After I leave the meeting, I keep thinking about Her. She doesn't come to me often, but I know She's always there. Whenever I sense Her Presence, or concentrate on Her, my consciousness suddenly snaps UP! to the top of the sky and beyond. And if I think very carefully about Her, even if I am not specifically graced by Her Presence, as now, a sense of spaciousness fills me, expanding the world I inhabit.

CHAPTER 28
Trying to Crack the Code

If not now, when?

Rabbi Hillel, Pirke Avot [Ethics of the Sages], 1:14

Fall 1998–Spring 1999

I SIT BEFORE MY PAGES OF HEBREW LIKE A CHILD—EVEN MORE HUMBLY than a child, because I learned my ABCs almost as easily as I learned to speak. My parents taught me, like a game, the sounds of each letter, then how to sound out words. Then, one day I broke the code. I remember it as clearly as this morning.

I was about four, riding on a trolley car in Philadelphia with my mother. I was kneeling on a shiny yellow wicker seat that made woven red patterns on my knees. I looked out the grimy window and saw blue and purple sparks splash down from the pole that rode the wires overhead. I watched stores and buildings go by and then—I saw. Just then. The letters made words and I could read and understand them.

I said, my voice more like a trumpet than a flute, "Look, Mommy, that sign says P-AA-RR-KK– PARK." My mother hugged and kissed me and called me a clever girl, and the ladies sitting near us wearing hats and white gloves smiled and clapped lightly and—that was it. I could read. The world suddenly teemed with words. And with each new word, I felt I owned whatever I named.

Now, at fifty-four, when I stare at a page of Hebrew, I can't understand the words or even the names or sounds of the letters. Shame washes over me like a painful full-body blush. I promise myself: someday I'll take this humility to a child who is trying to read.

One afternoon in October, I sit at our dining room table staring at my list of Hebrew letters, using the mnemonic devices I've invented to help me remember the twenty-two consonants and their special forms when they appear as final letters in a word. I've been doing this for days, and think I know all of them. I test myself by reading a sight word I know—S-H-A-L-O-M, peace—which is written in gold on the spine of my new prayer book. Simple, right?

Wrong. Somewhere between the first letter *sin* (or is it *shim*?) I'm stymied by *ayn*—a silent letter. And I don't recognize *mem* because I forget about final *mem*, which looks different. Moron. I rest my forehead on the table, examining the oak grain in an extreme close-up, when Anna sails in from school.

"Mommy, what's wrong?" she asks.

"Everything," I tell her. "*Vet. Bet. Shim. Sin.* I'll never get them right."

"Yes, you will," she says. She checks my list, her fingernails sporting dark blue nail polish with starry sprinkles. They go well with the dark blueberry highlights in her shiny dark hair—the result of a new fad: coloring her hair with Jell-O. It's quite striking.

"You can't learn it alone," Anna says. "Neither could I. Wait a sec. I'll be right back." She runs to answer her phone, which always rings the instant she comes home.

That's the end of that, I sigh. I won't see her till she's hungry. I go back to my *aleph-bet* and try—again—to link sound to letter to word.

Then Anna lopes back into the kitchen with a stack of dog-eared three-by-five cards, some fresh ones, a pen, and a handful of colored pencils. "See these?" She fans her *aleph-bet* flash cards across the table. They're adorned with grape jelly fingerprints, peanut butter, and splats of blue-black-crimson-silver nail polish. "First, make yourself a set of cards like mine—left over from my bat mitzvah last year."

"Can't I use yours?"

"No. Making them helps you learn. Write down each letter, and then put its name on the back—see? The writing makes the letter go from your eyes to your brain to your hand and back again. Use plain ball-point pen for the letters." She smacks one into my hand like an OR nurse. "Then call me and we'll do the vowels. There's a trick to the vowels."

"Uh-oh," I say.

"Just wait," she says. "Wait, and remain calm, Mommy."

I turn to the task, hopeful, grateful for something positive to do.

"Take your time," she warns. "Don't make mistakes and learn the wrong thing. Call me, and we'll check them before you start memorizing."

She starts out of the room then doubles back. She leans over and kisses me on both eyelids. Familiar: she loves it when I do that to her. And here is my lovely thirteen-year-old-daughter teaching me to be a brave woman. "Don't worry, Mom. You can do this, I promise. And I'll keep helping you." Then her phone rings and she runs to answer it.

I bend to my work.

When Anna glides back on her socks, I'm finished. "Let's go through them," she says and finds a few errors. I start to cross them out, but she tears up the cards. "Do them again. Make them perfect. It will only confuse you if you have to look at the scratch-outs every time."

I follow her instructions. Then we start on vowels: each one written in pen, then covered with colored pencil with the specific color that indicates how it should be pronounced: ee as in green, ay as in gray, etc., each with its own symbol, sometimes two.

The antique clock above our heads chimes.

"Damn, it's seven, and I haven't even started dinner."

"I'll start dinner," Anna says. "Tortellini?"

"Perfect."

The Tuesday before Roz's surgery, Simkha asks her how we can help.

"I don't want visitors at the hospital," she tells us. "My daughters will make sure I'm never alone." She pauses to think, worry pinching her eyebrows. "So, what do I want from you? Your prayers, of course."

'What time is the surgery?" I ask.

"Eleven a.m. tomorrow."

"We'll be with you," Len says.

"All of us," says Marcia.

Roz frowns. "What I'd really like is if you could help me figure out how to make those few minutes I'm awake in the OR into a more . . . human time with my surgeon. I know his system. He has a script he follows. It sets up an atmosphere that helps him, but not me," she sighs.

"I'm peripheral. The whole routine takes away my will and turns me into a sterile lump instead of a person. This time, I want him to be there for me, not just for my breast. I want a one-on-one connection."

She looks at us with a peculiar look on her face. Is it fear? "Is this crazy? Is this a selfish-old-lady-weak-female thing to want? Am I expecting too much?"

"Not at all."

"It's your right."

"Absolutely."

"But how?" Seena says. "How do we turn doctors back into human beings?"

"I think they turn back into human beings when we treat them like human beings," I say. "When we refuse to let the white coats or scrub suits turn them into gods or automatons. It's especially hard in the operating room, when they have to armor themselves against their humanity—and ours—in order to cut us open."

"So true," says Marcia. "I know, because I see my husband do it in the morning: he's a surgeon."

"Some people ask their surgeons to pray with them." says Simkha, "and most often, they will. I've found in my work with doctors, when I help them in almost the same ways I help you, that they need the compassionate human contact as much as we do—they're really not automatons."

"Not this guy," Roz says. "I think he'd rather swallow a scalpel."

"I know someone, a pert young thing, who wrote a note and taped it to her abdomen," I say. "It said, 'Please picture me in my teeny bikini and make a very good scar.' When the doctor saw it, they both had a great laugh that broke the ice."

"I've looked at the surgeon and said, 'I trust you completely, and I'll pray for the best outcome for both of us,'" Simkha says. "It's amazing how the doctor softened and thanked me."

"It helps to be a rabbi," Len points out.

"As we talk about this, I think I understand why the surgeon follows his script," Roz says, "because it prevents the patient from getting too emotional. I wish he knew I can have emotions and stay calm."

"Roz, I think if you look for a way to connect with your particular doctor, he'll probably respond," Simkha says. "And don't be afraid to try: it's your right."

Roz sighs and nods. "Now that you've helped me feel it's legitimate, I know I'll find a way. He's not a monster, just a surgeon."

I impulsively grasp Marcia's hand on my right and Seena's on my left. The handhold goes all around the table till we're a tightly connected circle.

"Let's do an *aliyah*," Len says. He pauses. "Exactly what does *aliyah* mean, Rabbi?"

"It means to raise up," Simkha says, smiling. "And you're using it in the right sense, even if it isn't the traditional one. In a synagogue, it means going up to the bimah, near the Torah scroll."

"Okay," says Len, and closes his eyes. "Dear God, I wish Roz the least painful, most blessed surgery possible."

Roz grins. I can't help peeking.

Simkha picks up the impulse and carries it on. "I pray Roz has the best biopsy reports possible." Roz nods.

"And the best, most painless reconstruction in the world." Marcia.

"That tomorrow she finds out that 'kind surgeon' isn't an oxymoron." Me.

Seena pauses and takes a deep breath. We wait. And wait. "Roz, I pray for you years, decades...of healthy, happy life... with no more biopsies or surgeries ever again."

"Amen," we chorus.

Performing our *aliyah*—offering up prayers or hopes for each other in the week ahead—becomes our way of ending each session.

At the next session, Simkha reports that Roz's surgery went well, and that she was pleased about the rapport she created with her surgeon. Using the most slender thread of connection, she's asked him how he chose the music for his operating room. While they chatted, he held her hand until the anesthesia carried her to sleep. We all cheer.

Months pass, and my life feels richer with the help of my healing group. Through the studies for my bat torah, I'm also finding new friends: I meet Robin for lunch, and we discuss the work on her *d'var* for our Torah portion. I spend more time working on mastering my Hebrew and cantillation, and less worrying about what I look like, which is pretty bad. I feel as busy as a college freshman, trying to conquer these new languages.

Our healing group keeps wrestling with the many-layered personal meanings of ancient texts. The Jewish New Year brings us back to Genesis, the first book of the Torah. When God orders Abram, later Abraham, to leave everything he knows and travel to an unknown place, we explode with empathy.

"Abraham's just like us," Seena says. "Being taken over by a chronic illness with no way to get back to my healthy self is like being ordered to go on a never-ending journey to an unknown place . . .with unknown people."

"Yes, and there's no place stranger or more hostile than a hospital . . ."

"With all its strange rituals . . ."

"Ruled by stern, masked witches and wizards . . ."

"And, like it or not, we get transformed, body and soul . . ."

"And where the hell is God?" Len finishes the riff.

"But listen to this," says Simkha, jumping into the fray. "The Hebrew words God uses to send Abram on his journey—'Lech lecha'—also can be translated as 'Go to yourself.' I find that very thought-provoking."

I do, too, but I'm not sure what the meaning is. Yet.

CHAPTER 29
Two Pockets

You do not have to go anywhere to raise yourself...
You are already there.
You are already everything you need to be.

Lawrence Kushner, Honey from the Rock

Fall 1998–Spring 1999

HADASSAH WEINER IS TEACHING OUR GROUP TORAH CANTILLATION. SHE'S a small, tidy woman who says little yet evinces enormous personal power and intelligence. When she reads Torah on Shabbat, she never repeats a word or stumbles, never blushes or trembles. She stands erect in her handwoven *tallit* and chants musically and perfectly. I hope her polish and confidence will shine me up a bit.

The night of her first class, Robin, Suzanne, and I enter Hadassah's apartment together. It's elegant, pristine, with a few fine pieces of Judaica: silver Shabbat candle holders, a graceful menorah, some richly bound leather books with Hebrew titles stamped in gold. Our hostess/teacher directs us to seats at a long table, where neatly stapled pages and cassette tapes wait before each chair. She sits at the head of the table. "Tonight, we'll look at your course of study, which is elaborated in the pages before you. The tape accompanies what's on the pages and will aid your practice. And you must practice. This work is demanding. It must be perfect."

"Why perfect?" Suzanne asks. "We keep hearing that."

"Because the words of the Torah must flow through you to the congregation with no mistakes, no hesitations, in order for people to grasp the meaning as clearly as possible. Reading Torah is a high honor and a deep responsibility. Many in our congregation read and speak Hebrew. Because English translations often do not fully represent the complexities of meaning in the text, they rely on hearing the Hebrew for full understanding."

"Before we start, I will read to you from Deuteronomy to help bring us very pointedly to the reason I hope you are all here." She recites first in Hebrew, then in English. Not needing to read the texts, she searches our faces one by one as she speaks: "Surely this instruction which I enjoin upon you this day is not too baffling for you, nor is it beyond reach. It is not in the heavens . . . Neither is it beyond the sea . . . No, the thing is very close to you—in your mouth and in your heart, to observe it."

As she completes her recitation in English, her eyes finally come to rest on me. The tears in my eyes spill over and run down my face. By putting her finger on the deepest meaning of our study, she also puts it on my heart.

Hadassah now turns to the pages of phrases or tropes—different combinations of dots, squiggles, diamonds, and what look like fallen eyelashes—that appear above or below the Hebrew words in the printed Torah. "There are forty-eight," she says. "Each designates a series of musical notes or tones, which link with the words of the Torah so we can chant them and be understood, just as they have for over 2500 years."

I look at the tropes and shudder. Will I be able to add this complex new layer?

Hadassah sings the trope, and then we take turns singing it alone. Oh, I realize with relief—it's music. I can do music. It sounds terribly complicated, but—I look at it closely—I think I can figure out how to learn this because I read music so easily. I hope.

A few days later, I go to my closet to get dressed for Simkha's group, scraping hangers back and forth, trying to find something that will help me feel attractive despite my extra dress sizes and the need to accommodate the cuffs of the crutches. As I root disconsolately through my fat clothes, my fat-fat clothes, and my really-fat clothes, I feel desolate when I see the dust that sits like a broken promise on the shoulders of the lovely silk blouses I once wore to work.

They hang in a morose row in colors I love: lustrous emerald green, delicate rose, ivory, larkspur, even my scarlet Superwoman blouse, all unworn for so long that a soft sift of neglect has settled on their shoulders. Where in my new life will I wear these beautiful shirts that feel so sensuous against my skin? To Linda's Room? They'd come away blood-stained or with holes from the toxic chemo. To synagogue? I'd freeze, even in the summer, chilled by the air-conditioning. To our healing group? Overstated.

I let them hang quietly in the dark. But the dust reminds me of something Simkha taught us: "Put in one pocket the certainty that we are dust and will return to dust. Put in your other pocket the certainty that God created the universe for you. Each of you."

I take the five lines of my Torah portion to the copy shop on Broadway. I ask Manassa, the Egyptian man there, to enlarge it until the five lines fill an 8 1/2 x 11 inch page. Now I can easily see the differences between a cantillation mark and a fly speck, eyelash, or ink splotch.

At home, I mark the vowels with different colors and then draw rectangles around each phrase so it matches my color-coded cantillation sheets. Now the page looks like an elaborate secret code, except—I actually understand it.

From then on, I carry my coded paper and tape player everywhere, listening to Hadassah while I stir pasta; go to the hospital for my monthly chemo, where Linda protects me from idle chit-chat while I study; and on the crosstown bus, where elderly Jewish men pat me on the shoulder, sometimes with tears in their eyes; and bar- and bat-mitzvah-age kids look surprised, then grin sympathetically.

My goal: achieve perfection by May 15 or leave town.

Slowly, I engrave those five lines into my brain. Then I practice out loud, taping myself so I can hear how I sound. And—it sounds good: soft, tentative, but . . . good.

I feel hopeful—I really can do this, even in my present state.

I feel so confident that I volunteer, along with Jen, to lead the Torah service. This means we'll go up to the bimah like replacement rabbis, or bar and bat mitzvah kids, and sing together as we lead the congregation in prayer. Since we're both musical and familiar with the service, we assume we can do this without problems.

We're wrong.

It's another case of "Jose, can you see?" When we start to practice, we realize that the words we were singing by heart were—the wrong words. That would be fine if we were buried in the congregation, but not with mikes an inch from our lips.

Allison Rosenblith, Anna's bat mitzvah tutor, a rabbinical student with a merry heart and a flair for teaching, comes to our rescue. It means another two evenings a week, but we only check in occasionally with Hadassah now. It's fun working with Jen, and after we color-code the relevant vowels in our siddurs, we soon master our parts.

I begin to breathe again—and sleep at night. We'll be fine, maybe even better than fine. Now I can go shopping for the perfect camouflage.

Then I do something incredibly stupid.

CHAPTER 30
The "Thing"

Spring 1999

IN MID-MARCH, SHOSH ASKS, "OH, BY THE WAY—WHO'S WRITING THE *Haftorah d'var?*"

Silence.

"You have to write it, Ellen," Robin says. My heart begins to hammer. "You're clearly obsessed by the Jonathan and David story."

"You'll do a great job," says Suzanne.

I shake my head. No speech, not for me. Though it is true: the story still gives me chills.

"I'll help you," says Shosh. And Robin. And Jen.

"You'll be our perfect spokeswoman," says Sheila.

My Before voice says, *Why not?* But After says, *No! Do not do this!*

Their confidence fans a dead place in me back to life. Afloat on their encouragement, I rashly agree.

On the way home, questions pour over my excitement like an icy waterfall: Can I research and write something significant in only six weeks, when Robin began writing last November? What if I fail and write something puerile? And can I count on my body? I have two more chemo treatments before May 15—that means two days at the hospital, and two or three days after each treatment when I'm knocked out. That brings me down to five weeks . . . The teaching has to offer wisdom about an iconic and beloved story in less than five minutes, and do it with elegance. And there's that word "perfect" again . . .

I immediately plunge in, deciding to explore the themes of commitment and passionate transformation, to explore what draws me so powerfully to the story and relate that to my own commitment to Judaism, Torah study, and BJ. I begin looking into the major texts, but Shosh insists I do no research. "You have only five minutes, so share what the story means to you. That's what'll interest them." I'm not so sure. My knowledge of the treasures of Judaism is thinner than gold leaf; how do I deserve to stand where the scholars do, "teaching" about one of the most haunting episodes in Biblical literature? One that's so precious to the gay community?

I try a new approach and interview each woman in our group about why she made a commitment to become at bat torah, hoping to incorporate the spirit of their words into my text. But that doesn't work and wastes time. Thirteen drafts later, too frightented to ask anyone for help, I'm still not satisfied, sickeningly closer to writer's block than I have ever been, ready to commit myself to the Jewish Asylum for Overkillers.

When our class meets one final time at Sheila's apartment, May 15 is a week away. Everyone is gabbing about their normal jitters, clothes and shoes, and the menu for the Kiddush after the service. I'm so panicky I hardly say a word. As we leave, Micki drops back to walk beside me. "Is something wrong, Ellen? You're so quiet tonight."

"I've lost all perspective on my *d'var*, Micki. I can't even tell if it makes sense any more." I have to clench myself tight not to break into tears.

"I used to coach speakers for a living, so maybe I can give you some pointers. If you like, I'll take a look at it tomorrow afternoon and see if I can help you," she says.

As soon as Micki reads the Thing the next afternoon, she looks up. "What are you so worried about?" she asks. "This is more than fine. It's interesting and well-written. So you can relax about the content. Now let's work on delivery. You can use Teddy's high chair as your bimah."

I take a deep, welcome breath, then get up to read. Micki suggests pauses, places for emphasis, and tells me to slow down and speak up. Her comments are so simple and easy that the spider of dread stops crawling all over me. I go home buoyed and, back at my computer, incorporate her few suggestions.

Anna comes to my desk. "Listen, Mom, stop obsessing. Do the best you can, then stop. I did this when I was twelve, and you're a grown-up." Then she hugs me and says, "I'm proud of you for doing this. I love you no matter what, but I know you'll be fine."

Now two people believe in me.

When Jim comes home late from work, he kisses me at my desk, and says, "Why don't you give yourself a break, Ellen? I sneaked a peek and it's really fine. Come to bed with me now, and get some rest." I kiss him. "Just a few more minutes, sweetheart, I promise." Now three believe.

"Mom." Alex comes in a few minutes later, "I don't understand why you're so worried. You're an excellent writer, you present yourself well—you'll be fine. Please don't do this to yourself anymore." Then he gives me one of his iron hugs. Four.

I turn out the light and join Jim in bed.

I swing into action first thing the next morning. I close myself in the living room and begin to rehearse out loud into a tape recorder. I mark the speech with accents, pauses, and volume changes. Then I record it over and over, listening objectively, as if I were someone else. After about ten or twelve repetitions, it doesn't sound half bad.

CHAPTER 31

Bake a Cake

Something sacred is at stake in every event.

Abraham Joshua Heschel

1999

LEN ARRIVES AT OUR GROUP UNCHARACTERISTICALLY LATE AND LOOKING particularly done-in—face red and blotchy, white around the eyes and mouth, trembling. "Does anybody have trouble asking for help?" he pants, his voice thin and hard to hear. "I do. Unfortunately, I need it." He struggles for breath. "But . . ."

"Slow down and catch your breath, Len," Simkha says gently. "We're not in a rush."

"I don't know how to ask," Len continues, breathing a bit easier. "Maybe because I'm a man and I carry around all that machismo shit—whoops, sorry, Simkha."

Simkha just waves it away.

"It's not just a guy thing," I say. "I know people who love you like to help, but I still can't say the H word."

Len nods, takes a deeper breath, then continues. "I'm in bad shape because I decided to take the subway today. Big mistake, especially when I'm carrying snacks in my book bag. I could hardly make it up the stairs. I had to rest every other step, and people pushed past me. I needed a boost, but I couldn't ask." He steadies himself. "When I was only halfway up the steps, this very sleek, fashionable black woman stopped. She took my bundles and helped me to the top, then to a nearby bench.

"She was so gracious," Len continues. "She told me her mother often needed help on stairs, and that's how she knew. She smiled and shook my hand, saying, 'Get better,' then went on her way."

I realize I'd have done what Len did. Yet when someone else needs help, it seems so matter-of-fact. "Why are we so hard-headed?" I ask. "Stupid, really. No offense, Len."

Len puts out his flavorless macrobiotic snacks: cardboard bread, pretzels without salt, dried apricots. I adore Len, but not his food. As I chew on an apricot that might have been rescued from King Tut's tomb, I watch Simkha put aside the text he'd prepared, and give us copies from another folder. He asks us to take turns reading it aloud.

ONE RECIPE FOR SOLACE: A Hassidic Tale

Once there was a woman who was very ill, beset with doubts and fears: Where could she turn? How could she care for her family? How could she feel less alone?

In despair, she went to the rabbi. "I'm so sick and worried," she cried, "and I'm ashamed to ask for help."

The rabbi thought for a long time. Then he said, "I want you to bake a cake."

"Bake a cake?" Was the rabbi losing his mind?

"Yes," he said, "and you must get all the ingredients from your friends and neighbors—but only from homes where there is no illness, pain, or suffering."

The woman was astonished, but did as the rabbi said. All day, she went from door to door trying to get the ingredients. By nightfall, she was weary and empty-handed. She got not one egg or drop of milk, not one dot of flour or grain of sugar. She discovered that her neighbors would have been very happy to give her what she needed, except that their homes, like hers, knew loss.

"Perhaps my neighbors would share their compassion as willingly as their eggs, milk, flour, and sugar," she thought. "Perhaps I only need to ask."

When we finish reading, there's a singing silence.

A few weeks later, I enter our session furious and humiliated. Some do-good dodo just gave me the "oh, you-poor-thing basset hound look, and nearly knocked me down rushing to open the lobby door for me. Then she actually said, "Oh, you poor thing. What happened to you? What's your name, sweetheart? I want to pray for you, dear."

Damn! Why don't people realize that a) I'm not a poor thing, I'm doing quite well, thank you very much; b) I'm not obligated to tell every dimwitted stranger my medical history; and c) you are not entitled to know my name, you fuck face. Why don't you just go look for Tiny Tim and leave me the hell alone? I don't want or need any of your pious, smarmy, piss-pot prayers or help.

But by the time I got to our fifth floor meeting room, my rage mysteriously morphed into shame. "Does anybody else ever feel this greasy green feeling that makes you want to become a recluse or pound people over the head with hard, heavy objects?"

"Why is shame a part of illness?"

"No kidding."

"As if it's our fault."

"Yeah, why?"

"And we get cut from the herd because we're not good enough."

"I think the shame may be related to the punishment idea," I say. "I think maybe a tiny part of us secretly thinks what most of the temporarily-well think—that we're being punished by having illness. Even if it's only because we don't jog four times a day or eat macrobiotic fodder—sorry, Len." He waves it away.

Now I can't contain my rage. "They hate us because we're the living antithesis of the American Dream—that everyone and everything is getting better and better every day in every single, imaginable way—like the General fucking Electric ad."

I feel safe letting the anger out because it isn't aimed at a person, but a mythology that does much more damage than good. "Chronic illness and disability smash that dream, and show it's a lie. So Pollyanna people who don't want to lose their comfortable security blankies, reassuring them that they'll always be well, turn around and punish us for being sick. In retaliation for threatening their nice, comfy little illusions."

"They want to blame the victim," says Seena.

"Yup," I say.

"They're afraid someday they'll be like us," adds Marcia, "so they want us to be gone. They disempower us by patting us on the head and treating us as if we're feeble-minded public property." There's much under-breath cursing, out of respect for Simkha.

"I've studied this terribly difficult issue of illness and shame from a psychological point of view when I'm wearing my social worker hat," Simkha says, "and many psychologists trace these concepts of shame and illness back to"—he puts his hand on his heart—"I swear it, and I know you won't like this"—to toilet training."

Everybody goes ballistic.

"No!"

"Not really!"

"You've got to be kidding!"

"They blame it all on Mommy?"

"Yes, really," Simkha says. He makes a peace sign with his fingers. "Try to listen? When children who are supposed to be potty-trained soil themselves, they're made to feel inordinately guilty in this pathologically clean society of ours. They're made to feel there's something shameful and wrong with them because they cannot do what they're supposed to do.

"So when sick people don't do or act the way they're supposed to, or control their bodies as they should," Simkha continues, "those feelings of shame come rushing back. We feel soiled, weak—and shamed."

"Listen, I don't want to accept this shame business no matter where it comes from," says Roz. "I want to let my spirit fly free from the prison of my body and of destructive accusations like this."

"Maybe this helps," suggests Simkha. "When Nelson Mandela was sentenced to prison for twenty-seven years, he said, 'They can lock me up, but I am not going to let them have my heart and mind.'"

Now there is a man to emulate, I think; he offers a deeper spiritual and moral translation of "stay within yourself," something to aspire to.

One bitter winter day, I try to be a good mother even if I can't be a healthy one. I cook in the kitchen in total defiance of my body, forced to sit down frequently just to finish the simple tasks of boiling, stirring, and mixing a casserole of baked ziti. It's the only thing I accomplish that day other than struggling out of bed, showering, and dressing, but I know it'll feel good to gather around the table and enjoy a meal, hearing about everybody's adventures after my long, lonely day.

There's a flurry of setting the table and bringing bread, butter, and beverages for everyone, then Jim and the kids sit down. I proudly lift the fragrant meal in a brand-new blue casserole out of the oven and carry it toward the table when it slips from my hands and smashes to the floor. Even my strong desire to do the Betty Crocker thing can't defy gravity: the casserole is too heavy. I stand in the middle of our kitchen wearing hot-mitts, with red sauce, ziti, and cobalt shards all over the wooden floor, the oak and glass cabinets, even the ceiling.

Jim and the kids glance surreptitiously at each other, then down at their empty plates. I retreat beneath my skin, locked in rage and shame. Trying not to get blown around the room by humiliation, I reach for paper towels and Fantastic.

It would be a perfect time for a tantrum if I were Len, or maybe Seena. It would feel terrific—no, glancing at the bottle I'm holding, fantastic—to spew anger all over the exploded ziti and my family, as they sit there in their healthy, hungry bodies. But rage would only temporarily trump shame, and it would fan everyone else's rage. If I were Marcia, I'd help us laugh this off. But I won't think of something funny till next week.

"Let's order pizza from Domino's," I say. "Or Japanese. It could be here in—"

Jim, trying to contain his billowing fury, gets up and elbows me aside, snapping, "Stop. I'll do it," with that bossy tone that makes my skin crackle. "Alex, order a pizza," he commands. "Let's eat our salads till it comes," he commands, as if only he can resolve this.

I know he's spinning between despair, hunger, and the fatigue of a ten-hour workday, and wants to help. In truth, I can't bend down far enough to clean up. On a much deeper level, we're both horrified and enraged at this new evidence of encroaching disease: Now she can't carry a casserole. I know that's erupting in the air between us.

But something shifts inside me because of our discussions with Simkha. Instead of being whisked into a tornado of self-loathing by my shame and Jim's rage, I decide: I won't let this mishap push me deeper into humiliation and shame.

We eat pizza. And at nine the next morning, I order an identical casserole from Williams-Sonoma sent overnight express. As soon as it comes, I make another batch of baked ziti. This time, Annie helps me put it into the oven, and Jim carries it to the table.

It's delicious.

The group applauds when I tell them about the casserole incident and my refusal to apologize. But Len has mortality on his mind, so we switch gears, do a 180 degree turn, and jump into a discussion about death and dying.

"I'm looking at the possibility of sudden death every hour of every day," Len sighs. "My heart muscle—that's all it is, just a muscle—some days is weaker, some days stronger. I can judge by what I can or can't do. And someday—snap!—that could be it. So I suck as much as I can out of each day. But that doesn't mean I'm not scared to death. So to speak." The joke doesn't hide the look in his eyes. "But even though death is standing right there in our living room, nobody wants to talk about it."

"They're afraid to talk about it. It upsets them too much," says Roz.

"Or they think it'll upset us too much—when not discussing it makes us feel lonelier and more forlorn," Len adds, "more stranded with our fears and feelings because they refuse to admit it's even a subject."

We quickly find that none of us can explore these issues with our families and friends, even though we're all giving them serious thought.

"I can't talk about it with anybody either," I say, "but it's weird—I'm not afraid of death anymore. I see it as a distinct advantage in the right, rather, wrong, circumstances. It could release me from a bad physical meltdown—if all the myelin on all my nerves is destroyed, I won't be able to breathe. I'm nowhere near that and may never be, but I'm worried about what will happen to my body and my life before that—how bad, how widespread, the neuropathy might get. So I've written one of those—what are they called, Simkha?—explaining when I want them to turn off the machines."

"I think it's important to consider Advance Directives," says Simkha, "a written document of how you'd like your families to deal with end-of-life issues when you are too ill to make your wishes known. It's ultimately very kind to the people who love you. Is anyone opposed to exploring that?"

No opposition.

"What does yours say?" Simkha asks me.

"I want all necessary measures to give me relief from pain. But I don't want to live when I'm permanently unable to express my love in reasonable ways, not just eye-blinks, unless it's a temporary situation. But if it is permanent, and there's no hope of real communication, or if I'm no longer really 'there'—then that's it, turn out the lights, the party's over. It will help Jim or the children make decisions based on what I want, so it's there in writing. It also states that I hope someone will put me out of my misery if I want to end my life and am no longer able do it myself. It says I'd consider that an act of love. And I'd like to donate all my organs."

"Deciding how to die is such an individual decision," Len says, shaking his head. "One I'm not ready to make yet."

"What are the Jewish laws about donating organs??" Marcia asks.

"The ultra-Orthodox are against it," Simkha says, "but most Jews believe that donating your organs to a stranger is lovingkindness of the highest level. But you must write it down so your family will know your wishes."

"I wouldn't wish my heart on anybody," Len quips.

"I'll give away any organs they'll take, but I don't know if anybody will want them," I laugh. " I can't even donate blood because of my overzealous antibodies. But I've signed my driver's license and organ donation cards."

"I don't think they accept organs from people with cancer," Roz says.

"It gives me the heebie-jeebies," says Seena. "But I'll try to think about it."

Ursula says nothing.

Throughout this discussion, we've been munching pistachios from the big bag Marcia brought, idly pushing our empty brown shells toward the center of the table. I watch curiously as Roz slides little bunches of the empty shells in front of her and shapes them into an ever-changing pattern. She joins in the discussion with her usual mix of gravitas and humor, her delicate fingers all the while following some alternate inner vision.

After we hold hands and pray our *aliyah* and get ready to leave, Roz cups one hand on the edge of table, ready to sweep the intricate shell pattern into the trash can.

"Stop, Roz, please don't destroy it," I call out. "Let us see it first."

We all lean forward. Roz has taken our empty, discarded pistachio shells and arranged them in a graceful, orderly collage. She turned some shells down to show their smooth beige backs, and their unique markings add texture to the symmetry of the arrangement. Others, she turned belly up to show their brown and beige insides—some still with the smooth brown casings that hold the nuts in place, others with the palest green remnants of the vanished pistachios.

We stare. It's ornate and compelling.

"It's so lovely, Roz," Seena breathes; "look what you've made out of . . . scraps."

"You make beauty wherever you go," says Len.

Roz looks skeptically at her design. "It's just a bunch of pistachio shells."

"No, it's not," I say. "You have a gift, Roz; you always say what you feel without drums and trumpets. And now you've said something important without one word

"You think so?" she says, looking up at me. Then her eyes go bright with tears. "My life is in chaos," she says. "I have no idea how long I'll live. I don't want to walk around without breasts. I guess—no, know—that this urge to not waste a moment—to create order and beauty—is my way of celebrating life. No matter what."

"Is there any way we could preserve this for you?" Len asks softly.

Roz smiles. "I don't have to have it," she says. "I did it. I'll remember. And, next week, maybe I'll find myself doing another—whatever-it-is."

We continue our discussion about death and dying the next week. Why does Jewish custom demand burial by sundown the next day, wrapping the corpse in a simple white linen shroud with no pockets, burial in a plain pine coffin, unadorned grave sites, no flowers, no gold or silver decorations, and sitting shiva for seven days? We live these traditions without understanding them.

"These customs arose as Jewish reactions to the elaborate cult of death they witnessed as slaves in Egypt," Simkha explains. "These very simple rituals kept them separate and apart from their Egyptian captors' lavish funeral rites—mummification, splendid golden sarcophagi, elaborate gold and silver ornamentation of the dead, entombment with all their possessions for use in the land of the dead, and, of course, the magnificent pyramids for royalty and the wealthy."

"The Egyptians needed extravagant burial ornaments to pay the gods of death so the Egyptian soul could travel into the next life able to use all the comforts and riches of this world. In contrast," Simkha continues, "Jewish ritual and burial were utterly simple and unadorned. Good deeds are the only treasures Jews can take into death."

"So what about it, Simkha? Can I hope for immortality?" asks Len, more than half-serious. "Emily and I don't have children like Roz, Marcia, and Ellen—so we can't count on genetic immortality."

With a gleam in his eyes, Simkha pulled another article out of his carefully stacked piles. "I thought you'd never ask," he says. "You can take this home and read the details. But by the Middle Ages, Judaism held that there are two worlds: this world and the world to come. So even though your body dies, Len, your soul continues to exist. There is that kind of life of the soul after the death of this body. Does that make you feel any better?"

Len raises his wonderfully bushy eyebrows and shrugs. "I'm not sure yet."

I'm changing, and it shows up at odd times and places—like the New York City sidewalks. When I first used crutches, I didn't care if people brushed me aside on the sidewalk or claimed the right of way when it should have been mine. My slow lane was very slow and wide because I needed space for my angled crutches. So people in a hurry—almost everyone—often pushed past me from behind or barreled toward me, expecting me to step aside.

Oh, well. I didn't care. I wanted to be as unnoticed as the trees. I stepped aside.

But after a year or two, I begin to care—care big time. I decide: I want to claim my right to the sidewalk, no matter how slowly I use it. I'll stay in the snail's lane. But when somebody heads straight toward me and tries to push me aside, I will not yield.

One day, I glance up and see a pinstriped man with burnished face and briefcase march straight at me. His rapid pace, burly body, and shiny pink cheeks broadcast self-importance and contempt. They signal that he is important and I—I am irrelevant. I do not change my course. Nor does he. We both must stop in our tracks but—I.do.not.yield.

He steps aside.

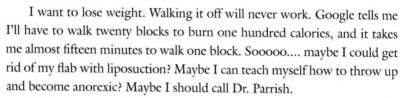

I want to lose weight. Walking it off will never work. Google tells me I'll have to walk twenty blocks to burn one hundred calories, and it takes me almost fifteen minutes to walk one block. Sooooo.... maybe I could get rid of my flab with liposuction? Maybe I can teach myself how to throw up and become anorexic? Maybe I should call Dr. Parrish.

He's often cheerful in inverse proportion to my despair. It makes me cranky but inestimably grateful. He immediately sends me to a physiatrist: a rehab specialist, who quickly pronounces me, "One of the worst cases I've ever seen, in terms of pain and related disability."

Thanks, doc. "So what next?"

He sends me to a physical therapist, who tells me my nerves are so inflamed that PT is impossible. She tries a little massage and heat therapy. I can't walk for days.

Back to the rehab doctor, who does something wonderful: he sends me to special aqua-exercise classes in a heated pool for disabled people. Another door.

I leave his office and immediately sign up at Asphalt Green, which has an easy access pool. It's one of the most refreshing and pleasurable things I've ever done to take charge of my illness and help heal myself. The water frees my body to exercise and play like an able-bodied child. I take an extra dose of pain-killer before class and then my body feels alive and graceful, even for an hour. I can walk and jog because the water holds me up, and its buoyancy—which offers twelve times the resistance of air— makes movement both easier and more challenging. I luxuriate in water as beautiful as a liquid aquamarine, enjoying its flares and frills of bubbles, its sensual slither across my body. Over the years since then, I've exercised two to three times a week, and gone beyond my size six goal to the size two I was before my pregnancies. Water exercise makes me feel like a child again and wakens my body to the pleasure of pure play.

CHAPTER 32

If Not Now, When?

May 1999

ONCE MY *D'VAR* IS UNDER CONTROL, IT'S TIME TO SHOP FOR THE PERFECT camouflage. And it strikes me: part of my fear over this public ritual must be rooted in my memory of how I looked at my one other Jewish ceremony, not counting my wedding to Jim—that service of consecration for my Hebrew school class when I was twelve. The other girls wore grown-up slim wool skirt and sweater sets. I wore that same sheer white nylon blouse and undershirt my mother insisted on, which revealed the faint swellings she called my budding breasts; the gray, once-pleated skirt that hung from my hips; the braces on my teeth; and my raggedy red hair I thought looked cut by a lawn mower.

This time, I'm wearing another kind of braces and my hair is brittle, thinned by months of chemo. I want to look stylish and sophisticated, but face strict limitations set by the braces and crutches. I toy with skipping the braces, but why mar the ceremony with a tooth-splitting stumble? I find what I want at Eileen Fisher: a sleek black silk jacket, shell, and long skirt that conceal my unwanted weight and braces, but won't hide the rest of me.

As I leave with my purchases, I ponder how my mother, now dead for seven years, might have felt about my becoming a bat torah. Proud?

Uncomfortable? Would she understand why it was so important to me? Unlikely. I start to imagine explaining it to her, and then to my father, also dead these five years, then remember how my parents always arrived late to bar mitzvahs, just in time to hear the boy's speech, so they could comment on it at the party. I decide to pull myself away from regret.

❋   ❋   ❋

On Thursday morning, we gather before seven a.m. at the B'nai Jeshurun sanctuary to read from "our" Torah scroll at morning minyan—the daily service for those who begin their day with formal prayer and/or to recite Kaddish, a special prayer to mourn the death of a close relative. It's our "dress rehearsal," a last chance to practice reading our portions from the actual Sefer Torah scroll we will read on Shabbat. I'm startled at how the sunlight through the stained glass windows illuminates the inner dusk. The high rose window opposite the bimah blazes in indigo and gold, picking out details in the elaborately painted designs around the Ark, and making the crimson and deep green, the touches of gold and silver, sing out into the dark.

We stand silently at the bimah as Freddy Goldstein, the *gabbi* or sexton, opens the sheer golden curtains of the ark and takes out one of the largest Sefer Torahs. It's fitted with a dark blue velvet cover decorated with silver hand-embroidery. Jingling silver ornaments decorate the two wooden handles—the *etz chaim*—around which the scroll is wrapped. A silver *yad*—used to point to each word as it's read—and a *hoshen*—a rectangular silver ornament incised with the Ten Commandments—hang on silver chains across the slightly worn velvet cover.

Freddy lays the large scroll on the bimah as gently as if it were a newborn child, then carefully unrolls it to find the first verses of *Bamidbar,* speed-reading the Hebrew calligraphy as easily as I scan the phonebook. He finds our place, then carefully covers the scroll with the velvet until we read it, placing the *yad* close at hand.

I wonder what kind of woman I'd be now if I'd grown up in an observant family like Freddy's. I often watch the twelve-year-old girls speak their ideas, thoughts, and dreams so confidently during their bat mitzvot. What might I have done with my life, if I'd started way back then; if being and becoming had not been such a terribly lonely struggle? My answer comes quickly: Look how far you've come without that. And today, I'm giving myself what I never had. Go forward, don't look back.

When it's my turn to read, I step before the Torah, and my breath stops in my throat. I've never been so close to a Sefer Torah. In the gold and indigo light burning from the window, I seem to see black fire written upon white fire in the Torah scroll, just as the sages say. The parchment shimmers before me. How stately the letters are—matte black ink that appears engraved upon pale parchment with the soft nap of suede, each section carefully glued and stitched to the next, the words standing in dignified panels about seven inches wide, with less than an inch between each block of calligraphy.

Now, the words no longer hold back their meaning: they are welcoming, waiting for me to breathe life into them. In that sustained moment, I see time gather in radiant layers above the parchment, above each letter, each word. How many times, over how many years, has a *yad* mindfully pointed from this word to the next, to reveal, *pasuk* by *pasuk,* the wisdom of this book and the people who study it? Who has read the black fire, and who the white? What flames of recognition have leaped from the words into the air? What meanings still remain clasped within the words, waiting to be freed? Am I now worthy to be a messenger who carries the words to the congregation, to let the words flow through me?

"This is not a performance. The congregation needs you. It must be perfect." I hear Hadassah Weiner's words as if she is speaking them aloud this very moment. Yet she stands silently at my side, one of the two always standing guard on either side of the scroll, ready to read the Torah with me word by word to catch and correct any mistake. It's reassuring now, rather than frightening.

The blazing black and white suddenly blur before my eyes, and I instinctively reach out in time to catch a warm tear in mid-air, before it falls on the scroll. The parchment is sacred, not to be touched by human hands—or tears. I quickly wipe my eyes, kiss my *tallit,* touch it to the scroll, say the blessing, and set my yad upon the first two words of my portion: "*Vayakah Moshe:* So Moses said . . ." I never let my chanting get ahead of the silver forefinger of the *yad* until I reach " . . . *bamidbar Sinai* – in the wilderness of Sinai."

I finish, finding utter clarity for one single moment in my own wilderness. I touch the final word with my *tallit,* kiss it, and say the closing blessing. Hadassah gives me the slightest nod, now concentrating on Pene's reading, but I know she's pleased.

Please celebrate with us

as

Ellen Schecter

together with her Bat Torah class

is called to the Torah

Saturday, May 15, 1999

Congregation B'Nai Jeshurun

located at

The Church of

St. Paul and St. Andrew

West End Avenue

at 86 Street

Shabbat, May 15th, 1999. I think it's a beautiful day, but I don't notice the weather. I leave home in plenty of time to meet Hadassah, Shosh, and the rest of my class before services. I want to feel the power of us seven women and our teachers.

At the church, we gather in a close circle around Shosh, who prays a *Shehecheyanu*—the prayer for important sacred occasions: "Thank you, *Adonai*, for giving us life, for keeping us in life, and for bringing us to this day."

Being alive for one more celebration always gives me shivers.

Pene and Micki each wear her grandfather's *tallit*—frayed, yellowed or grayed, soaked in prayers and memories. "I don't think my father ever could have imagined us anywhere near the Torah," Sheila says. "I wish he could see me today." She reminds me that women reading Torah is still an act of defiance. I love that.

As the first notes of the morning service ring out, Jim, Alex, and Anna quietly come up to me, all beautiful in their own prayer shawls. They kiss and hug me, then take seats in the pew behind us. I feel drenched in joy: I know they shine with love and pride for me, just as Jim and I once sat shining for Alex and for Anna. Every seat is taken, up to the very highest in the balcony. Almost everyone I love is somewhere in that crowd.

When the congregation stands for the *Barchu* and I bow, full of gratitude, Jim's hand rests lightly on my back, his heat pouring through me. How can I be afraid of anything when I'm buoyed with such love?

My heart feels as if it rocks my body with each beat when it's time for Jen and me to go to the bimah to lead the Torah Service. We stand before the microphones with our color-coded prayer books, just as Alex and Anna once did. Then, Jen, Pene, and I mount the steps to stand before the ark. Now comes the moment I've dreamed about for years, and worked for over many months: the honor of singing the sacred prayer that lies at the heart of Judaism. Jen and Pene move in close enough for me to feel their bodies supporting mine, Pene holding our Torah. I close my eyes, and sing alone with all the dignity I can muster:

She'ma yisrael Adonai Eloheinu Adonai ehad.

Hear, O Israel: The Lord our God, The Lord is One.

My voice isn't strong, but my intention is granite.

Our individual pride is magnified by our joy for each other. Robin's *d'var* is brilliant. She choreographs her voice, pacing, and movements to underline the meanings of her text, and all her deep thought shows.

Now it's my turn. Again to the bimah. I've passed through nervousness into complete determination that looks and feels like poise. I take a deep breath: "The *Haftorah* can be found on page 1216." I wait for the rustling to quiet.

"The story of Jonathan and David is a story of passionate love and hate, political intrigue, and unswerving devotion. It is also a story about the soul. It reveals how a force as ineffable as the soul can become a fulcrum to move the world."

People lean in a bit closer to listen. I lean into the mike, remembering what works in auditoriums full of antsy kids on rainy day school visits: the softer the delivery, the harder they listen. "Jonathan and David should be bitter rivals for the throne of Israel. Instead, they share a passionate love: a love strong as death. In 'loving his fellow as himself,' Jonathan embodies one of the major principles of the Torah. This is human love in one of its highest forms."

Just as I'd hoped, a gay couple seated right up front are nodding with a sense of recognition.

"Once Jonathan's soul becomes bound up with David's, their lives change forever. The two men immediately create a covenant, which propels Jonathan into a cascade of concrete actions that demonstrate his deepening devotion to David. His soul dictates his devotion and his deeds.

"These aspects of the love between Jonathan and David help explain why I stand before you today as a bat torah. Like Jonathan, something shifted in my soul the first time I came to BJ. That experience led me to create a very private covenant with God, and bound up my soul with the soul of this community.

"This sacred commitment leads me deeper into study and prayer. It is no longer enough to be a passive witness at BJ. It is time to be an active participant. And because I grew up with virtually no Jewish education, this means I have a lot of work to do."

I can see Margaret, one of my cherished BJ friends, smiling in the second row. Just looking at her always gives me a jolt of courage.

"I found it baffling to learn to chant Torah. I felt like a child again as I worked to master my *aleph-bet*. I studied my flashcards and tapes of Torah trope everywhere—on the bus, in the hospital, in our kitchen while I stirred pasta." A few chuckles.

"Like Jonathan, I took off my armor—words are my armor—and followed my soul into a world where I was wordless. For a long time, the Hebrew letters looked like ornate iron gates, locked against me. I struggled to make those gates swing open and reveal the meanings behind them."

I spot Sarah, a fair and foul-weather friend, slender as willow, who's crying, of course, but this time with joy. She knows how much this means to me.

"Each of the seven women called to the Torah for the first time today experienced her own moment of commitment that propelled her to more fully embrace learning as a Jewish adult. We somehow made room in our

overcrowded lives to take specific steps on a journey to this moment. Today, like Jonathan, we make the private public; we confirm our covenant."

I find Hadassah in the crowd and will myself to achieve her dignity.

"Hadassah Weiner blessed the moment she began to teach our class
Torah cantillation by reading to us from Deuteronomy. I share these words
with you now, with the hope that you will continue—or begin—your own
journey of commitment:

> *Surely this instruction which I enjoin upon you this day is not too*
> *baffling for you, nor is it beyond reach. It is not in the heavens. . . Nei-*
> *ther is it beyond the sea. . . . No, the thing is very close to you, in your*
> *mouth and in your heart, to observe it.*

"Shabbat shalom."

I stand still, and the moment stretches the way time can, perfectly clear
and sharp. There's Mary Ann, lighting up the space between us. And there's
Jane, David to my Jonathan—with Peter, her husband, three friends knit
into each other's hearts.

As I float back to my seat, people smile and nod, calling out the traditional *"Yasher koach*—more strength to you," reaching out to touch my
arms, my shoulders, my *tallit*. Jim, the children, and my classmates greet
me with hugs and kisses. I sit, my hammering heart slows. Quiet now,
and peaceful, I know I've kept my pledge to my community. I've proved I
could take on a challenge and come shining through—confirmed that even
though my body is damaged, my brain and soul are fully alive.

Most important, I've fulfilled my sacred, secret covenant with God and
sanctified my illness.

CHAPTER 33

Embracing the Wolf

2011

I DREAM I HAVE A STARRING ROLE IN AN IMPORTANT DRAMA, AND THE whole cast is rehearsing outdoors on a perfect summer day. When we set off through the sunny meadows toward our theater, the others leave me far behind because I am a slow walker, but I know my way so I'm not alarmed. I sit down to rest and rehearse my lines in a small valley beside a bubbling brook. On the other side of the water, a red-clay cliff, perhaps thirty feet high, rises to meet the cobalt sky.

Suddenly, a silver wolf appears at the top of the cliff, brilliant against the blue. He is strong, stunning, fearsome. He has snow-white and black markings on his face, and black lines, drawn as if with kohl, around his eyes and along his brows.

The wolf gazes down at me, panting. I can see his sharp teeth. He gathers his muscles to leap for my throat.

"No," I think; "don't harm me. We are no longer enemies."

But his muscles uncoil, and he leaps at me in terrifying slow motion. I feel his enormous power as he pins me to the ground. His muzzle finds my throat; his body stretches full-length against mine; his tail trails between my legs.

My breath is stapled to my chest.

Then all fear drains out of my body as the wolf relaxes into me. He is soft and warm, light as silver snowfall nestling over me. His breath is warm and sweet in my ear. We are not one and the same, but we are as one.

We rest in a feathery-warm embrace of peace.

These days, when I walk from West End Avenue to Riverside Drive, I don't always need to rest beneath every tree. Because of the bio-engineered drugs I inject into myself, I can walk with a cane—no more crutches—only sometimes needing the braces. Yet I still walk slowly, to acknowledge the tulips, the shuddering iridescent pigeons, and my young pear tree at the corner, which has now grown three times taller than I am.

I've learned that trees show less than half of themselves above ground: their other half reaches deep underground, which in New York City means far beneath concrete and asphalt. Otherwise, no tree could stand upright, or live, or grow.

So I look at each tree and imagine its shadow-tree of roots stretching out underneath it, wide and deep and even more intricate than the tree I see that reaches skyward. The tree needs what's hidden as much as what's seen.

I'm like that, too.

And now, as I walk home under these trees, rooted in my life, aware of my shadows, I find that sometimes—when I see the old moon in the new moon's arms, or when the pear tree blooms through the night, or for no discernible reason at all—I burst into bloom.

BIBLIOGRAPHY

There were few books that met my needs when I was first diagnosed and in the years after. Many on bookstore shelves were saccharine and simplistic, or stayed on the how-to level. I found these challenging and thought-provoking in a variety of ways—not to mention well-written—and still turn to them from time to time. Asterisks flag those I found particularly helpful because they went far beyond surface details and delved into the changed meanings of life lived with illness.

Bauby, Jean-Dominique. *The Diving Bell and the Butterfly: A Memoir of Life in Death.* New York: Vintage Books, 1997.

*Brill, Alida and Michael D. Lockshin, M.D. *Dancing at the River's Edge: A Patient and Her Doctor Negotiate Life With Chronic Illness.* Tucson, Schaffer Press, 2009.

Brody, Howard. *Stories of Sickness.* New Haven: Yale University Press, 1987.

Cassell, Eric J., M.D. *The Healer's Art.* Boston: MIT Press, 1985.

*_____. *The Nature of Suffering.* New York: Oxford University Press, 1991.

Frank, Arthur W. *The Wounded Storyteller: Body, Illness, and Ethics.* Chicago: University
* of Chicago Press, 1995.
_____. *At The Will of The Body: Reflections on Illness.* Boston: Houghton Mifflin, 1991.

*Groopman, Jerome, M.D. *The Anatomy of Hope: How People Prevail In the Face of Illness*. New York: Random House, 2004.

*_____. *The Measure of Our Days: A Spiritual Exploration of Illness*. New York: Penguin Books, 1997.

*Kleinman, Arthur, M.D. *The Illness Narratives: Suffering, Healing, and the Human Condition*. New York: Basic Books, 1988.

*Mairs, Nancy. *Carnal Acts: Essays*. New York: Harper Perennial, 1990.

*_____. *Plain Text: Essays*. Tucson: University of Arizona Press, 1986.

_____. *Waist-High in the World*, Boston: Beacon Press, 1996.

Price, Reynolds. *A Whole New Life*. New York: Penguin Book, 1982.

Radner, Gilda. *It's Always Something*. New York: Simon and Schuster, 1989.

**Remen, Rachel Naomi M.D. *Kitchen Table Wisdom: Stories That Heal*. New York: Riverhead Books, 1996.

_____. *My Grandfather's Blessings*. New York: Riverhead Books, 2000.

Sayantani, DasGupta and Marsha Hurst, eds. *Stories of Illness and Healing: Women Write Their Bodies*. Kent: Kent State University Press, 2007.

*Webster, Barbara D. *All of a Piece*. Baltimore: Johns Hopkins University Press, 1989.

Stone, John, M.D. *In the Country of Hearts: Journeys in the Art of Medicine*. New York: Dell Publishing, 1990.

ACKNOWLEDGEMENTS

Charles Salzberg merits special thanks as my teacher, publisher and friend. This book was born over years in your classes; how fitting that your publishing company, Greenpoint Press, is ushering it into the world.

Bettina Drew, my first adult writing teacher, acknowledged me as a "real writer" after reading Chapter One so long ago. You gave me courage to continue, and I'll never forget it.

Thanks to Jonathan Kravitz for publishing the first two chapters on ducts.org-the book's maiden voyage into the world.

My writing must be accomplished in-spite-of so much illness, so there are more than literary mentors behind this book:

Deepest gratitude to you, Eric Cassell, M.D. for helping me learn that tears can speak of strength; that pain medication doesn't make me a coward; and that it's possible to be sick without suffering.

Dr. Ed Parrish—You keep me alive and functioning with warmth, respect, and mutual compassion. How can I ever thank you enough?

Dr. Gary Saff, Dr. Ronnie Hertz, Nurse Carol St. Pierre, and the Fellows at the Manhattan Center for Pain Management: you take away my pain and give me a body I can live in. Deep thanks.

And Empress-Comedian-Cheerleader—and most important Nurse— Linda Leff, Queen of Infusion—how you ever manage to make us laugh, surrounded by calamity and terror as we are, is simply miraculous. I applaud and love you.

Patricia Booth: You helped me discover myself and my strength. Thank you.

A special thank you to Rabbi Simkha Y. Weintraub, LCSW, Rabbinic Director of the Jewish Board of Family and Children's Services and its New York Jewish Healing Center: Your kind wisdom and gentle spirit graciously sustained our spirits in your Jewish Healing Support Group. Deep thanks for the courage you gave all of us. And my gratitude to Marcia, Roz, Len, Seena, and Ursula for your loving support at such difficult times in our lives. Thanks, too, to the Jewish Board of Family and Children's Services for its financial support.

Thank you to Rabbi Marcelo Bronstein for affirming my Midrash.

I am grateful beyond measure to all my foul-weather friends, who shared the secret handshake of illness and taught me pride in my new status of disability: Carmen Hylton, who showed me how to feel beautiful in spite of her profound disabilities—"Just go from A to B, Girlfriend; it doesn't matter how you get there;" to Stephen Mantell, who taught me how to laugh no matter what; to Marcia Miller, who soul reaches sky high and has the most delicious giggle I've ever heard.

And, of course, deep appreciation always to my many writing friends, who taught me by example and commentary what worked and what didn't as this book was growing. Special thanks to our very talented West Side Writers Group: Hilda Meltzer, Diana Kash, David Peréz, Tom Pryor, Millie Ehrlich—and especially to Maura Mulligan and Dan Rous: I could not have done this without all of you.

And, of course, I'm grateful to those of you who helped with feedback in the writing workshops at the 63 Street Y and at the JCC Writers' Workshop. Thank you for your thoughtful, insightful suggestions. You helped me grow into a real writer.

Thanks to my Readers, whose insights and careful eyes helped shape the final-final draft of the book you're reading now: Peter Barton, Isabel Byron, Sarah Lang, Roz Meyer, Virginia Morris, Allison Rossett, and Jane Startz.

And particular thanks to Vivian Conan for her bionic eyes and discernment as copy editor, and to Anna Altman as proof reader: what a blessing to learn from my daughter.

I will always be profoundly grateful to my husband, Jim Altman, who loved me when I felt fat and ugly, yellow and scrawny, and forgotten by the world. He has supported my hunger to write ever since we met. And thanks to our children, Alex and Anna, excellent and professional writers themselves now, who have always supported my writing even when it didn't make their lives easy. Gratitude also to my mother-in-law, Doris Altman, who is always eager to find out what's going on inside my head and flowing out on paper. And not least, I want to thank Esperanza Montes, whose gracious presence and hard work in our home make it possible for me to write.

First seen and last thanked: the perfect book cover created by David Wander, a gifted, generous artist and dear friend. You dug deep to find the right equivalents for fierce joy because you know what that means.

Thanks, also to Noah Arlow: your design and finishing touches brought the interior and cover of the book to life in ways I'd never dreamed, and I will always be grateful.

And one last thanks to the Hospital for Special Surgery and to Phyllis Fisher for cooperation in allowing us to shoot the necessary photographs used on the cover.

Ellen Schecter's first novel, *The Big Idea* (Hyperion), won the 1996 Americas Award for Children's and Young Adult Literature. Her *Family Haggadah* (Viking, 1999) was a Book of The Month and Jewish Book Club selection. She has written or collaborated on many award-winning TV series for children and families, including *Reading Rainbow*, *The Magic School Bus*, and *Allegra's Window*. She was Executive Producer of the award-winning *Voices of Lupus*, produced by FM Productions and The Hospital for Special Surgery, and distributed free to every English–speaking Lupus Foundation in the world through a grant by Winthrop Pharmaceuticals. Ellen lives in New York City with her husband, James Altman. They have two children, Alex and Anna.

www.FierceJoythebook.com

CPSIA information can be obtained at www.ICGtesting.com
Printed in the USA
LVOW040901080612

285096LV00003B/15/P